GAMBLING

WHAT'S AT STAKE?

ISSN 1534-4915

GAMBLING
WHAT'S AT STAKE?

Kim Masters Evans

INFORMATION PLUS® REFERENCE SERIES
Formerly published by Information Plus, Wylie, Texas

THOMSON

GALE

Detroit • New York • San Francisco • San Diego • New Haven, Conn. • Waterville, Maine • London • Munich

Gambling: What's at Stake?

Kim Masters Evans

Paula Kepos, Series Editor

Project Editor
John McCoy

Permissions
Margaret Abendroth, Edna Hedblad, Emma Hull

Composition and Electronic Prepress
Evi Seoud

Manufacturing
Drew Kalasky

LIBRARY OF CONGRESS CATALOGING-IN-PUBLICATION DATA

ISBN 0-7876-5103-6 (set)
ISBN 0-7876-9073-2
ISSN 1543-4915

Printed in the United States of America
10 9 8 7 6 5 4 3 2 1

TABLE OF CONTENTS

bling; how nonpayment of outstanding credit card charges incurred through online gambling affects some financial institutions; certain economic and social effects of Internet casinos; and estimates for growth in the industry.

PREFACE

Gambling: What's at Stake? is part of the *Information Plus Reference Series.* The purpose of each volume of the series is to present the latest facts on a topic of pressing concern in modern American life. These topics include today's most controversial and most studied social issues: abortion, capital punishment, care for the elderly, crime, gambling, health care, the environment, immigration, minorities, social welfare, women, youth, and many more. Although written especially for the high school and undergraduate student, this series is an excellent resource for anyone in need of factual information on current affairs.

By presenting the facts, it is Thomson Gale's intention to provide its readers with everything they need to reach an informed opinion on current issues. To that end, there is a particular emphasis in this series on the presentation of scientific studies, surveys, and statistics. These data are generally presented in the form of tables, charts, and other graphics placed within the text of each book. Every graphic is directly referred to and carefully explained in the text. The source of each graphic is presented within the graphic itself. The data used in these graphics are drawn from the most reputable and reliable sources, in particular from the various branches of the U.S. government and from major independent polling organizations. Every effort has been made to secure the most recent information available. The reader should bear in mind that many major studies take years to conduct, and that additional years often pass before the data from these studies are made available to the public. Therefore, in many cases the most recent information available in 2005 dated from 2002 or 2003. Older statistics are sometimes presented as well, if they are of particular interest and no more-recent information exists.

Although statistics are a major focus of the *Information Plus Reference Series,* they are by no means its only content. Each book also presents the widely held positions and important ideas that shape how the book's subject is discussed in the United States. These positions are explained in detail and, where possible, in the words of their proponents. Some of the other material to be found in these books includes: historical background; descriptions of major events related to the subject; relevant laws and court cases; and examples of how these issues play out in American life. Some books also feature primary documents, or have pro and con debate sections giving the words and opinions of prominent Americans on both sides of a controversial topic. All material is presented in an even-handed and unbiased manner; the reader will never be encouraged to accept one view of an issue over another.

HOW TO USE THIS BOOK

Gambling has long been a favorite pastime worldwide, and its history in the United States dates back to the founding of the nation. It has been estimated that Americans spend more than $1 trillion per year on charitable gambling, betting on horse and greyhound races, lottery purchases, casino wagering, and other legal and illegal gambling activities. Despite this economic incentive, though, much controversy surrounds the industry. While pro-gambling elements argue that the economic benefits of gambling far outweigh any potential risks, some individuals oppose gambling on moral grounds or argue that it can cause an increase in various types of social problems. This book presents in-depth information on how casino gambling, sports gambling, lotteries, and Internet gambling work, provides up-to-date financial data for each, and discusses the effects of these and other gambling activities on the communities in which they take place. Also discussed are American attitudes toward gambling.

Gambling: What's at Stake? consists of nine chapters and three appendices. Each of the chapters is devoted to a particular aspect of gambling in the United States. For a summary of the information covered in each chapter, please see the synopses provided in the Table of Contents at the front of the book. Chapters generally begin with an overview of the basic facts and background information on the chapter's topic, then proceed to examine subtopics of particular interest. For example, Chapter 8: Sports Gambling begins with a historical survey of wagering on sporting events and a summary of American attitudes about sports gambling. A substantial section on pari-mutuel gambling defines and explains the term and then goes on to discuss horse racing, greyhound racing, jai alai, and the future of pari-mutuel gambling in general. Next, legal sports gambling (which mainly takes place in Nevada) is covered. Finally, sections illuminate the prevalence and effects of illegal sports gambling in the United States. Readers can find their way through a chapter by looking for the section and subsection headings, which are clearly set off from the text. Or, they can refer to the book's extensive index, if they already know what they are looking for.

Statistical Information

The tables and figures featured throughout *Gambling: What's at Stake?* will be of particular use to the reader in learning about this topic. These tables and figures represent an extensive collection of the most recent and important statistics on gambling, as well as related issues—for example, graphics in the book cover gambling participation by adolescents; how much consumers spend on casino gambling as compared with other recreational pursuits; public opinion on the economic benefits of casinos; types of modern lottery games; horse-racing purses paid out by state; and estimated revenues from Internet gambling during a five-year period. Thomson Gale believes that making this information available to the reader is the most important way in which we fulfill the goal of this book: to help readers understand the issues and controversies surrounding gambling in the United States and reach their own conclusions.

Each table or figure has a unique identifier appearing above it, for ease of identification and reference. Titles for the tables and figures explain their purpose. At the end of each table or figure, the original source of the data is provided.

In order to help readers understand these often complicated statistics, all tables and figures are explained in the text. References in the text direct the reader to the relevant statistics. Furthermore, the contents of all tables and figures are fully indexed. Please see the opening section of the index at the back of this volume for a description of how to find tables and figures within it.

Appendices

In addition to the main body text and images, *Gambling: What's at Stake?* has three appendices. The first is the Important Names and Addresses directory. Here the reader will find contact information for a number of government and private organizations that can provide further information on aspects of gambling. The second appendix is the Resources section, which can also assist the reader in conducting his or her own research. In this section, the author and editors of *Gambling: What's at Stake?* describe some of the sources that were most useful during the compilation of this book. The final appendix is the index. It has been greatly expanded from previous editions, and should make it even easier to find specific topics in this book.

ADVISORY BOARD CONTRIBUTIONS

The staff of Information Plus would like to extend their heartfelt appreciation to the Information Plus Advisory Board. This dedicated group of media professionals provides feedback on the series on an ongoing basis. Their comments allow the editorial staff who work on the project to continually make the series better and more user-friendly. Our top priorities are to produce the highest-quality and most useful books possible, and the Advisory Board's contributions to this process are invaluable.

The members of the Information Plus Advisory Board are:

- Kathleen R. Bonn, Librarian, Newbury Park High School, Newbury Park, California

- Madelyn Garner, Librarian, San Jacinto College—North Campus, Houston, Texas

- Anne Oxenrider, Media Specialist, Dundee High School, Dundee, Michigan

- Charles R. Rodgers, Director of Libraries, Pasco-Hernando Community College, Dade City, Florida

- James N. Zitzelsberger, Library Media Department Chairman, Oshkosh West High School, Oshkosh, Wisconsin

COMMENTS AND SUGGESTIONS

The editors of the *Information Plus Reference Series* welcome your feedback on *Gambling: What's at Stake?* Please direct all correspondence to:

Editors
Information Plus Reference Series
27500 Drake Rd.
Farmington Hills, MI 48331-3535

CHAPTER 1
GAMBLING IN AMERICA—AN OVERVIEW

What is gambling? Merriam-Webster's dictionary gives half a dozen definitions, including playing a game of chance for money and making a bet on an uncertain outcome. One definition says that gambling is staking something on a contingency. Another says that gambling is taking an action with an element of risk. Combining various terms together provides the following overall definition: Gambling is an activity in which something of value is risked on the chance that something of greater value might be obtained, based on the uncertain outcome of a particular event.

Organized gambling has become an industry because so many people are willing and even eager to risk their money in exchange for a chance at something bigger and better. The elements of risk and uncertainty actually add to gambling's appeal—and to its danger. Throughout history, various cultures have considered gambling harmless, sinful, respectable, corrupt, legal, illegal, and tolerable. Some people love it, some people hate it, and some people just ignore it. Societal attitudes are dependent on cultural issues such as customs, traditions, religion, morals, and the context in which gambling occurs.

In 1999 the Gallup Organization quizzed 1,523 adults on whether they considered the following activities to be gambling: buying lottery tickets, playing poker with friends for money, participating in office pools, playing church-sponsored bingo, and investing in the stock market. The largest majority (78%) considered buying lottery tickets to be gambling. Only 59% considered playing church-sponsored bingo to be gambling, and just over half (52%) believed that investing in the stock market is gambling.

Lawmakers have struggled to define gambling and determine which activities should be legal and which should not. For example, betting activities with an element of skill involved (such as picking a horse in a race or playing a card game) might be more acceptable than those based entirely on chance (such as spinning a roulette wheel or playing slot machines). Acceptability also depends on who profits from the gambling. Bingo games held for charity and lotteries that fund state programs are more commonly legal than casinos run for corporate profit.

In the article "In Defense of Gambling" (*Forbes,* June 23, 2003), Dan Seligman estimated that Americans legally gamble approximately $900 billion a year. According to findings reported in the National Gambling Impact Study Commission Report (1999), illegal gambling levels could be as high as $380 billion per year. This means Americans gamble more than $1 trillion per year. But why do people gamble at all? Common sense suggests that risking something of value on an event with an uncertain outcome is irrational. Scientists who study gambling give a variety of reasons why people gamble, including the lure of money, the excitement and fun of the activity, and influence from peers. At its deepest level, gambling may represent a human desire to control the randomness that seems to permeate life. Whatever the drive may be, it must be strong. An entire gambling culture has developed in America in which entrepreneurs (legal and otherwise) offer people opportunities to gamble, and business is booming.

HISTORICAL REVIEW

Ancient Times

Archeologists have discovered evidence that people in Egypt, China, Japan, and Greece played games of chance with dice and other devices as far back as 2000 B.C. According to *Encyclopedia Britannica,* loaded dice have been found in ancient tombs in Egypt, the Far East, and even North and South America. (Loaded dice are weighted or shaped to make a particular number come up more often than others.)

Dice are probably the oldest gambling implements known. They were often carved from sheep bones and known as knucklebones. They are mentioned in several historical documents, including the *Mahabharata* of India, which is approximately 2,500 years old. A story in the New Testament of the Bible describes Roman soldiers throwing dice to determine who would get the robe of Jesus. Roman bone dice have been found dating from the first to third centuries A.D. The Romans also gambled on chariot races, animal fights, and contests between gladiators.

The Medieval Period

During medieval times (approximately 500–1500 A.D.), gambling was legalized by some governments, particularly in what is now Spain, Italy, Germany, and the Netherlands. England and France were much less permissive, at times outlawing all forms of gambling. French king Louis IX (1214–70) prohibited gambling during his reign for religious reasons. Still, illegal gambling continued to thrive.

During the eleventh, twelfth, and thirteenth centuries, Christian powers in Europe launched the Crusades—military expeditions against Muslim powers that held control of areas Christians considered holy lands. Gambling was permitted, but only for knights and those with higher titles. Violators were subject to severe whippings. Even among the titled gamblers, there was a legal limit on how much money could be lost, a concept that later would come to be known as limited-stakes gambling.

English knights returning from the Crusades brought long-legged Arabian stallions with them that were bred with sturdy English mares to produce fine racehorses. Betting on private horse races became a popular pastime among the nobility. Card games also became popular in Europe around the end of the fourteenth century. According to the International Playing-Card Society, one of the earliest known references to playing cards in Europe dates from 1377. During the late 1400s and early 1500s, lotteries began to be used in Europe to raise money for public projects. Queen Elizabeth I (1533–1603) established the first English state lottery in 1567.

Precolonial and Colonial America, and Seventeenth- and Eighteenth-Century Europe

Native Americans played games of chance as part of tribal ceremonies and celebrations hundreds of years before America was colonized. One of the most common was a dice-and-bowl game in which five plum stones or bones carved with different markings were tossed into a bowl or basket. Wagers were placed before the game began, and scoring was based on the combination of markings that appeared after a throw. The Cheyenne people called the game *monshimout*. A similar game was called *ta-u-seta-tina* by the Arapaho and *hubbub* by New England tribes.

Colonists from Europe brought gambling traditions with them to the New World. Historical accounts report that people in parts of New England gambled on horse racing, cockfighting, and bullbaiting. Bullbaiting was a "blood sport" in which a bull was tethered in a ring or pit into which dogs were thrown. The dogs were trained to torment the bull, which responded by goring the dogs. Spectators gambled on how many of the dogs the bull would kill.

In 1612 England's King James I created a lottery to provide funds for the settlement of Jamestown, Virginia, the first permanent British settlement in America. Lotteries were later held throughout the colonies to finance the building of towns, roads, hospitals, and schools and to provide other public services.

Many colonists, though, disapproved of gambling. The Pilgrims and Puritans fled to America during the 1620s and 1630s to escape persecution in Europe for their religious beliefs. They believed in a strong work ethic that considered labor morally redeeming and viewed gambling as sinful because it wasted time that might have been spent in productive endeavors.

Cockfighting, bear- and bullbaiting, wrestling matches, and footraces were popular gambling sports throughout Europe during the sixteenth and seventeenth centuries. The predecessors of many modern casino games were also developed and popularized during this time. For example, the roulette wheel is often attributed to French mathematician Blaise Pascal (1623–62). He is also famous for the *Pensées* in which he presents "Pascal's wager": "If God does not exist, one will lose nothing by believing in him, while if he does exist, one will lose everything by not believing." Pascal concludes: "We are compelled to gamble."

Gambling among British aristocrats became so customary during the early years of the eighteenth century that it presented a financial problem for the country and led the reigning monarch, Queen Anne, to take legal action in an attempt to control it. Gentlemen gambled away their belongings, their country estates, and even their titles. Large transfers of land and titles were disruptive to the nation's economy and stability. The queen, who reigned from 1702 to 1714, responded in 1710 with the Statute of Anne, which made large gambling debts "utterly void, frustrate, and of none effect, to all intents and purposes whatsoever" (9 Anne, ch. 14, § 1). In other words, large gambling debts could not be legally enforced. This prohibition has prevailed in common law for centuries and is still cited in U.S. court cases. Queen Anne is also known for her love of horse racing, which became a popular betting sport (along with boxing) during her reign.

A surge of evangelical Christianity swept through England, Scotland, Germany, and the American colonies during the mid- to late 1700s. Many historians refer to this as the first "Great Awakening." It was a time when conservative moral values became more prevalent and widespread. Evangelical Christians considered gambling to be a sin and dangerous to society, and religion became a powerful tool for bringing about social change.

In October 1774 the Continental Congress of the American colonies issued an order stating that the colonists "will discountenance and discourage every species of extravagance and dissipation, especially all horse racing, and all kinds of gaming, cockfighting, exhibitions of shows, plays, and other expensive diversions and entertainments." The purpose of the directive was to "encourage frugality, economy, and industry."

Into the Nineteenth Century

In general, gambling was tolerated as long as it did not upset the social order. According to "Gambling in the South: Implications for Physicians" (*Southern Medical Journal,* September 2000), Georgia, Virginia, and South Carolina passed versions of the Statute of Anne during the colonial period to prevent gambling from getting out of hand. New Orleans became a gambling mecca during the 1700s and 1800s, even though gambling was outlawed during much of this time. In the 1830s almost all southern states outlawed gambling in public places, although there were some exceptions allowed for "respectable gentlemen."

In 1823, eleven years after becoming a state, Louisiana legalized several forms of gambling and licensed several gambling halls in New Orleans. Even though the licensing act was repealed in 1835, casino-type gambling continued to prosper and spread to riverboats traveling the Mississippi River. Professional riverboat gamblers soon developed an unsavory reputation as cheats and scoundrels. Several historians trace the popularization of poker and craps in America to Louisiana gamblers of this period. Riverboat gambling continued to thrive until the outbreak of the Civil War in 1861.

From 1829 to 1837, America's president was Andrew Jackson (1767–1845). The Jacksonian era was associated with a new attention to social problems and focus on morality. A second "Great Awakening" of evangelical Christianity swept the country. According to I. Nelson Rose of Whittier Law School, gambling scandals and the spread of conservative morals led to an end to most legal gambling in the United States by the mid-1800s.

Frontier gambling, both legal and illegal, in the Old West peaked during the mid- to late nineteenth century. Saloons and other gambling houses were common in towns catering to cowboys, traders, and miners. Infamous gamblers of the time included Bat Masterson, Doc Holliday, Poker Alice, and Wild Bill Hickok. Reportedly shot in the back while playing poker in 1876, Hickok held a hand of two black aces and two black eights, which came to be known as the "Deadman's hand."

Across the country, private and public lotteries were plagued by fraud and scandal and fell into disfavor. By 1862 only two states, Missouri and Kentucky, had legal lotteries. Lotteries, which were objectionable to many southern legislators on moral grounds, had been banned in most southern states by the 1840s, but then reinstated after the Civil War to raise badly needed funds. In 1868 Louisiana implemented a lottery known as "the Great Serpent." Although it was extremely popular, the lottery was ridden with fraud and eventually outlawed by the state in 1895. Casino gambling, which had been legalized again in Louisiana in 1869, was also outlawed at the same time.

Gambling in general fell into disfavor as the nineteenth century ended. In England, Queen Victoria (1819–1901) ruled, and the Victorian era was characterized by concern for morality and the spread of conservative values. These attitudes spread through American society as well. Gambling fell out of favor as a pastime for respectable people. In the United States, many eastern racetracks and western casinos were pressured to close for moral and ethical reasons. As new states entered the Union, many included provisions against gambling in their constitutions. For example, in 1896 Utah forbade all games of chance in its constitution. By federal law, all state lotteries were shut down by 1900.

The Twentieth Century

THROUGH THE 1920s. As the twentieth century began, there were forty-five states in the Union. The territories of Oklahoma, New Mexico, and Arizona gained statehood between 1907 and 1912. According to Rose, the closure of casinos in New Mexico and Arizona was a precondition for statehood. In 1910 Nevada outlawed casino gambling. That same year, horse racing was outlawed in New York, and almost all gambling was prohibited in the United States. The only legal gambling options at the time were horse races in Maryland and Kentucky and a few isolated card clubs.

GROWTH IN NEVADA IN THE 1930s AND 1940s. The 1930s were a time of reawakening for legal gambling interests. Many states legalized horse racing and charitable gambling again. Nevada went even further. In 1931 its legislature passed Assembly Bill 98, which relegalized casino gambling in the state. The bill came to be known as the "Wide Open Gambling Bill." Historians point to several reasons for the legalization. Frontier gambling was widely tolerated in the state, even though gambling was officially illegal. Also, Nevada, like the rest of the country, was suffering from a deep economic recession, and the state was sparsely populated and poor in natural resources. Nevada's divorce laws were also changed in the early 1930s to allow the granting of a divorce after only six weeks of residency. People from other states temporarily moved into small motels and inns in Nevada to satisfy the residency requirement. At the same time, construction began on the massive Hoover Dam project in Boulder City, Nevada, only thirty miles from Las Vegas. These two events brought thousands of construction workers and visitors, all potential gamblers, into the area.

Although small legal gambling halls opened in Reno (in the northern part of the state), they catered for the most part to cowboys and local residents and had a reputation for being raunchy and wild. In April 1931, however, the first gambling licenses were issued in Las Vegas. The first big casino in Las Vegas, El Rancho Vegas, was opened in 1941 on what would later be known as "the Strip."

Many in the business world doubted that casino gambling in Nevada would be successful. The casino hotels were mostly small, sometimes converted dude ranches, operated by local families or small private companies. They were located in hot and dusty desert towns far from major cities, had no air-conditioning, and offered few amenities to travelers. There was virtually no state or local oversight of gambling activities.

Prohibition was enacted under the 18th Amendment and went into effect in 1920. It became illegal to import or sell alcoholic beverages in the United States. Prohibition remained on the books, but was widely violated, until 1933. During the Prohibition Era, organized crime syndicates operated massive bootlegging rings and became very powerful and wealthy. When Prohibition ended in 1933, organized crime families switched their focus to gambling. Mobsters in New York and Chicago were among the first to see the potential of Nevada. Gangsters Meyer Lansky and Frank Costello sent fellow gangster Bugsy Siegel to the West Coast to develop new criminal enterprises. Siegel invested millions of dollars of the mob's money in a big and lavish casino in Las Vegas that he was convinced would attract top-name entertainers and big-spending gamblers. The Flamingo hotel/casino opened on December 26, 1946. It was a failure at first, and Siegel was soon killed by his fellow mobsters.

POST–WORLD WAR II: THE 1950s. Nevada's casinos grew slowly until after World War II (1939–45). Postwar Americans were full of optimism and had spending money. Tourism began to grow in Nevada. Las Vegas casino/resorts attracted Hollywood celebrities and famous entertainers. The state began collecting gaming taxes during the 1940s. The growing casinos in Las Vegas provided good-paying jobs to workers who brought their families with them, building a middle-class presence. In 1955 the state legislature created the Nevada Gaming Control Board within the Nevada Tax Commission. Four years later, the Nevada Gaming Commission was established.

It was also during the 1950s that one of the most important organizations dedicated to problem gambling was founded. In January 1957 two men with gambling problems decided to start meeting together regularly to discuss their gambling obsession, the problems it had caused them, and the changes they needed to make in their lives to overcome it. After meeting for several months, each realized that the moral support offered by the other was allowing them to control their desire to gamble. They decided to start an organization based on the spiritual principles used by Alcoholics Anonymous and similar groups to control addictions. The first group meeting of Gamblers Anonymous was held on September 13, 1957, in Los Angeles.

CORPORATE GROWTH: THE 1960s. During the 1960s, the casinos of Las Vegas continued to grow. By this time, organized crime syndicates used respectable "front men" in top management positions while they manipulated the businesses from behind the scenes. Publicly held corporations had been largely kept out of the casino business by a provision in Nevada law that required every individual stockholder to be licensed to operate a casino.

One corporation that was able to get into the casino business was the Summa Corporation, a spin-off of the Hughes Tool Company, with only one stockholder— Howard Hughes. Hughes was an extremely wealthy and eccentric businessman who owned the very profitable Hughes Aircraft Company. He spent lots of time in Las Vegas during the 1940s and 1950s and later moved there. In 1966 he bought the Desert Inn along the Strip in Las Vegas. Later, he bought the nearby Sands, Frontier, Castaways, and Silver Slipper casinos.

Legend has it that mobsters threatened Hughes to get out of the casino business in Las Vegas, but he refused. He invested hundreds of millions of dollars in Las Vegas properties and predicted that the city would be an entertainment center by the end of the century. In 1967 the Nevada legislature changed the law to make it easier for corporations to own casinos.

In the early 1960s New Hampshire was the first state to relegalize the lottery. It was called the New Hampshire Sweepstakes and was tied to horse racing results to avoid laws prohibiting lotteries. New York established a lottery in 1967. During the 1970s twelve other states followed suit, and most were located in the northeast.

GOVERNMENT REVIEW IN THE 1970s. In 1970 the U.S. Congress created the Commission on the Review of the National Policy toward Gambling to study Americans' attitudes about gambling and their gambling behaviors, and to make policy recommendations to state governments considering legalizing gambling activities. The results were published in *Gambling in America: Final Report of the Commission on the Review of the National Policy toward Gambling* (October 15, 1976). The commission found that 80% of Americans approved of gambling and 67% engaged in gambling activities. It was concluded that states should set gambling policy without interference from the federal government, unless problems developed from organized crime infiltration or conflicts between states.

Federal statutes against racketeering were enacted at the federal level in 1971 to combat organized crime. Nevada officials overhauled the casino regulatory system, making it more difficult for organized crime figures to be involved. Corporations and legitimate financiers began to invest heavily in casino hotels in Las Vegas and other parts of the state.

Also during the 1970s, the National Council on Problem Gambling, the first treatment program for pathological gambling, was established by Dr. Robert Custer, and Maryland established the first state-funded treatment program. In 1978 the first legal casino outside of Nevada opened in Atlantic City, New Jersey.

During this decade, Native American tribes began operating bingo halls to raise funds for tribal operations. As the stakes were raised, the tribes faced legal opposition from state governments. The tribes argued that their status as sovereign (independent) nations made them exempt from state laws against gambling. Tribes in various states sued, and the issue was debated in court for years.

NEW FORMS OF GAMBLING AND GROWING POPULARITY IN THE 1980s AND 1990s. In 1980 the American Psychiatric Association recognized pathological gambling as a mental health disorder and listed it in its official publication, *Diagnostic and Statistical Manual of Mental Disorders* (DSM; the 1980 version of the DSM is known as DSM-III). Pathological gambling was listed under disorders of impulse control and described as a "chronic and progressive failure to resist impulses to gamble." During the 1980s many states began setting up programs to deal with problem gamblers. In 1989 Harrah's Entertainment became the first commercial casino company to officially address problem gambling with Project 21, an educational project aimed at the company's employees and minors, and Operation Bet Smart, a training program to help frontline casino employees learn about and recognize potential problem gamblers.

Lotteries were legalized in twenty-three states and the District of Columbia during the 1980s and 1990s. It was during 1988 that the first multistate lottery game was begun. Lotto America went through several revisions before becoming the Powerball game in 1992.

In February 1987 the Supreme Court's landmark ruling in *California v. Cabazon Band of Mission Indians* (480 U.S. 202) opened the door to tribal gambling. The Indian Gaming Regulatory Act was passed by Congress in 1988. It allows federally recognized Native American tribes to open gambling establishments on their reservations if the state in which they are located already permits legalized gambling.

Between 1989 and 1996, nine more states legalized casino gambling: South Dakota, Iowa, Mississippi, Illinois, Colorado, Louisiana, Missouri, Indiana, and Michigan.

In 1995 the American Gaming Association (AGA) was formed. The AGA is a trade organization that represents the commercial casino industry. Within the industry, casino gambling is universally called "gaming." Some critics claim that this represents an attempt by the industry to give gambling a more wholesome and respectable image. The AGA defends the use of the term, saying that it has come to be used interchangeably with the word *gambling*.

The AGA collects and publishes data about the industry and is an advocate for the industry regarding regulatory and legal issues. It founded the National Center for Responsible Gaming (NCRG) in 1996 to fund research on gambling problems among adults and youth. The first grant was given to Harvard Medical School for *Estimating the Prevalence of Disordered Gambling Behavior in the U.S. and Canada: A Meta-Analysis.*

During the mid-1990s Internet gambling sites began operating. By 1997, fifty to sixty Internet casinos were in operation, most based in the Caribbean. By the end of the decade, there were approximately six hundred to seven hundred Internet gambling sites.

In 1996 Congress authorized the National Gambling Impact Study Commission (NGISC), a federally funded group, to study the social and economic impacts of gambling in the country. The NGISC, which held its first meeting in 1997, included nine commissioners representing pro- and antigambling attitudes. Existing literature was reviewed, and new studies were ordered. The commission held hearings around the country at which a variety of people involved in and affected by the gambling industry testified. The NGISC's final report in 1999 concluded that with the exception of Internet gambling, gambling policy decisions are best left up to state, tribal, and local governments. The commission also recommended that legalized gambling not be expanded further until all related costs and benefits were identified and reviewed.

Also during 1999, *Pathological Gambling: A Critical Review,* published by National Academies Press, identified and analyzed all available scientific research studies dealing with pathological and problem gambling. The studies were reviewed by dozens of researchers on behalf of the National Research Council, an organization administered by the National Academy of Sciences, the National Academy of Engineering, and the Institute of Medicine. The effort was supported by the NGISC. Although the researchers were able to draw some general conclusions about the prevalence of pathological gambling in the United States, they cited the

FIGURE 1.1

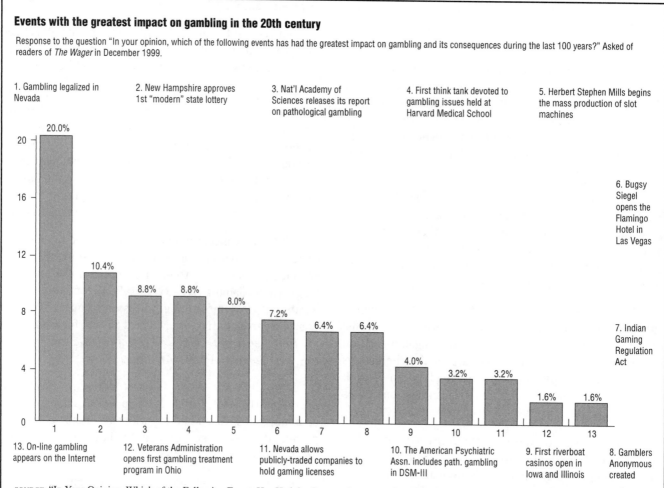

Events with the greatest impact on gambling in the 20th century

Response to the question "In your opinion, which of the following events has had the greatest impact on gambling and its consequences during the last 100 years?" Asked of readers of *The Wager* in December 1999.

1. Gambling legalized in Nevada

2. New Hampshire approves 1st "modern" state lottery

3. Nat'l Academy of Sciences releases its report on pathological gambling

4. First think tank devoted to gambling issues held at Harvard Medical School

5. Herbert Stephen Mills begins the mass production of slot machines

6. Bugsy Siegel opens the Flamingo Hotel in Las Vegas

7. Indian Gaming Regulation Act

13. On-line gambling appears on the Internet

12. Veterans Administration opens first gambling treatment program in Ohio

11. Nevada allows publicly-traded companies to hold gaming licenses

10. The American Psychiatric Assn. includes path. gambling in DSM-III

9. First riverboat casinos open in Iowa and Illinois

8. Gamblers Anonymous created

SOURCE: "In Your Opinion, Which of the Following Events Has Had the Greatest Impact on Gambling and Its Consequences during the Last 100 Years?" in "Talking Back: Readers Choose the Gambling-Related Event of the Century," in *The Wager*, vol. 5, no. 5, Harvard Medical School, February 1, 2000

lack of scientific evidence as a limiting factor in their ability to draw more specific conclusions.

MILESTONES OF THE TWENTIETH CENTURY. One well-respected journal on gambling issues is *The WAGER*, short for *The Weekly Addiction Gambling Education Report. The WAGER* is published as a public education project by the Division on Addictions at the Harvard Medical School. In December 1999 the journal asked its readers to rank thirteen gambling events of the twentieth century in order of their importance. The results are shown in Figure 1.1. The legalization of gambling in Nevada in 1931 was voted the most important gambling event of the century. The introduction of the first modern state lottery in New Hampshire in 1964 was ranked second. Publication of *Pathological Gambling: A Critical Review* in 1999 was ranked third.

The Twenty-First Century

In 2000 California voters passed Proposition 1A, amending the state constitution to permit Native American tribes to operate lottery games, slot machines, and banking and percentage card games on tribal lands. Previ-ously, the tribes were largely restricted to operating bingo halls. According to the National Indian Gaming Association (NIGA), more than two hundred tribes were engaged in Class II or III gaming in twenty-eight states in 2003. Class II and III gaming includes bingo, lotto, card and table games, slot machines, and pari-mutuel gambling.

South Carolina began operating a lottery in January 2002, following voter approval in a 2000 referendum. In November 2002 voters in Tennessee and North Dakota approved referendums allowing lotteries in their states. Both began operating in early 2004.

Table 1.1 shows the legal gambling options offered in each state as of August 2004. Charitable gambling was the most common type of legalized gambling, operating in forty-seven states and the District of Columbia. Gambling on horse races was also very prevalent, both at live venues and via offtrack betting. Lotteries operated in forty states and the District of Columbia during 2004. Although tribal casinos were less common, they were operating in more than half of the states. Gambling at greyhound races, racinos (horse and dog racetracks with

TABLE 1.1

Gambling operations by state, 2004

State	Charitable gambling	Horse racing	Lottery	Tribal casinos	Greyhound racing	Card rooms/ mini casinos	Commercial casinos	Racinos	Slot machines at other businesses	Jai Alai
Alabama	Yes*	Yes		Yes***	Yes					
Alaska	Yes			Yes***						
Arizona	Yes	Yes	Yes	Yes	Yes					
Arkansas		Yes			Yes					
California	Yes	Yes	Yes	Yes		Yes				
Colorado	Yes	Yes	Yes	Yes	Yes	Yes	Yes			
Connecticut	Yes	Yes	Yes	Yes	Yes					
Delaware	Yes	Yes	Yes					Yes		
D.C.	Yes		Yes							
Florida	Yes	Yes	Yes	Yes	Yes	Yes				Yes
Georgia	Yes		Yes							
Hawaii										
Idaho	Yes	Yes	Yes	Yes						
Illinois	Yes	Yes	Yes				Yes			
Indiana	Yes	Yes	Yes			Yes	Yes			
Iowa	Yes	Yes	Yes	Yes	Yes		Yes	Yes		
Kansas	Yes	Yes	Yes	Yes	Yes					
Kentucky	Yes	Yes	Yes							
Louisiana	Yes	Yes	Yes	Yes			Yes	Yes	Yes	
Maine	Yes	Yes	Yes					Yes		
Maryland	Yes	Yes	Yes			Yes				
Massachusetts	Yes	Yes	Yes		Yes					
Michigan	Yes	Yes	Yes	Yes			Yes			
Minnesota	Yes	Yes	Yes	Yes		Yes				
Mississippi	Yes			Yes			Yes			
Missouri	Yes	Yes	Yes				Yes			
Montana	Yes	Yes	Yes	Yes		Yes			Yes	
Nebraska	Yes	Yes	Yes	Yes						
Nevada	Yes	Yes		Yes		Yes	Yes		Yes	
New Hampshire	Yes	Yes	Yes		Yes					
New Jersey	Yes	Yes	Yes			Yes	Yes			
New Mexico	Yes	Yes	Yes	Yes				Yes		
New York	Yes	Yes	Yes	Yes				Yes		
North Carolina	Yes			Yes						
North Dakota	Yes	Yes	Yes	Yes		Yes				
Ohio	Yes	Yes	Yes							
Oklahoma	Yes	Yes		Yes				**		
Oregon	Yes	Yes	Yes	Yes	Yes	Yes			Yes	
Pennsylvania	Yes	Yes	Yes							
Rhode Island	Yes	Yes	Yes		Yes			Yes		Yes
South Carolina	Yes		Yes	Yes***						
South Dakota	Yes	Yes	Yes	Yes		Yes	Yes			
Tennessee	**		Yes							
Texas	Yes	Yes	Yes	Yes	Yes					
Utah										
Vermont	Yes	Yes	Yes							
Virginia	Yes	Yes	Yes							
Washington	Yes	Yes	Yes	Yes		Yes				
West Virginia	Yes	Yes	Yes		Yes			Yes		
Wisconsin	Yes	Yes	Yes	Yes	Yes					
Wyoming	Yes	Yes		Yes***						

*Certain counties only
**Approved in 2004
***Bingo only

SOURCE: Created by Kim Masters Evans for Thomson Gale, 2004

casino games), commercial casinos, minicasinos, card rooms, and games of jai alai (which is similar to handball) occurs in a handful of states.

Industry analysts believe that many sectors of the American gambling market are reaching maturity. In other words, the growth spurt of the past few decades is likely over. Commercial casino gambling has not spread beyond the eleven states in which it operated in 1996.

In November 2003 voters in Maine rejected a referendum that would have allowed tribal casinos in their state. They did approve a racino measure allowing slot machines at horse racetracks. In 2004 New York installed its first video lottery terminals at racetracks, and Oklahoma enacted racino legislation. Allowing machine gambling at existing gambling venues like racetracks is generally more acceptable to voters and politicians than full-fledged casino gambling. However, this is not true in

TABLE 1.2

Public opinion on the acceptability of social issues, May 2004

	Morally acceptable %	Morally wrong %
Divorce	66	26
Gambling	66	30
The death penalty	65	28
Buying and wearing clothing made of animal fur	63	31
Medical testing on animals	62	32
Sex between an unmarried man and woman	60	36
Medical research using stem cells obtained from human embryos	54	37
Doctor-assisted suicide	53	41
Having a baby outside of marriage	49	45
Homosexual behavior	42	54
Abortion	40	50
Cloning animals	32	64
Suicide	15	79
Cloning humans	9	88
Married men and women having an affair	7	91
Polygamy, when one husband has more than one wife at the same time	7	91

SOURCE: Adapted from Lydia Saad, "Summary Table: Moral Acceptability of Issues," in *The Cultural Landscape: What's Morally Acceptable,* The Gallup Organization, June 22, 2004, http://www.gallup.com/content/default.aspx?ci=12061 (accessed June 22, 2004). Copyright © 2004 by The Gallup Organization. Reproduced by permission of The Gallup Organization.

TABLE 1.3

Public opinion on the acceptability of social issues by political ideology, May 2004

	Morally acceptable to conservatives %
The death penalty	74
Medical testing on animals	68
Buying and wearing clothing made of animal fur	68
Gambling	58
Divorce	57

	Morally acceptable to liberals %
Divorce	82
Sex between an unmarried man and woman	79
Homosexual behavior	74
Medical research using stem cells obtained from human embryos	74
Gambling	73

SOURCE: Adapted from Lydia Saad, "Percent Saying Morally Acceptable by Political Ideology," in *The Cultural Landscape: What's Morally Acceptable,* The Gallup Organization, June 22, 2004, http://www.gallup.com/content/default.aspx?ci=12061 (accessed June 22, 2004). Copyright © 2004 by The Gallup Organization. Reproduced by permission of The Gallup Organization.

all states. Throughout the early part of the twenty-first century Kentucky legislators rejected bills that would have expanded gambling at the state's racetracks.

PUBLIC OPINION

In May 2004 the Gallup Organization conducted a nationwide poll to determine the moral acceptability of various social issues. Pollsters interviewed one thousand adults aged eighteen and older regarding their opinions. The results are shown in Table 1.2. Overall, gambling was considered morally acceptable by 66% of those asked. It tied with divorce as the social issue considered most acceptable to people. The acceptability of gambling has risen slightly since 2003 when 63% of Americans polled pronounced it morally acceptable.

The top five issues considered morally acceptable by conservatives and liberals are detailed in Table 1.3. Gambling was considered morally acceptable by 58% of self-described conservatives and 73% of self-described liberals, a difference of 15 percentage points.

Gambling among conservatives was a high-profile issue in 2003 when media reports announced that William J. Bennett had lost as much as $8 million gambling at Las Vegas casinos over the previous decade. Bennett was a well-known conservative politician and author who served as Secretary of Education under President Ronald Reagan (1911–2004) and as drug czar under President George H.W. Bush. Bennett also wrote the best-selling book *The Book of Virtues* with lessons and stories about

teaching children the importance of self-discipline, work, honesty, and other moral characteristics. Liberals and some conservative critics accused Bennett of taking a tough stance against many social and moral issues while indulging his multimillion-dollar gambling habit. In response Bennett publicly admitted that he had gambled too much and pledged to stop gambling.

In August 2003 Gallup polled 517 teenagers aged thirteen to seventeen years about their views regarding various social issues. Gambling was considered morally acceptable by 61% of those asked. This issue ranked third in moral acceptability behind downloading music for free on the Internet (83%) and divorce (67%).

The latest comprehensive poll on gambling attitudes was performed by the Gallup Organization in 1999. A randomly selected national sample of 1,523 adults (aged eighteen and up) and 501 teenagers (aged thirteen to seventeen) were asked a variety of questions about gambling. Results showed that 63% of adults and 52% of teenagers approved of legal gambling or betting in general. Among those adults who approved of legal gambling, 25% expressed strong approval, and among adult gambling opponents, 21% expressed strong disapproval.

The respondents were asked to give the one or two most important reasons for their approval or disapproval of legal gambling. For adults, the freedom and right to choose their leisure activities was the most important reason they approved of gambling, followed closely by the fun and entertainment aspect of gambling. For teenagers who approved of gambling, fun and entertainment were of paramount interest. Adults and teenagers who disapproved of gambling primarily did so because they believed that gambling ruins people's lives and financial well being. The adults in the group also believed strongly that gambling is addictive.

When asked about specific types of gambling, a majority of adults indicated approval for lotteries, bingo, casinos, and offtrack betting on horse races. Gambling on video poker machines at local establishments and betting on professional sports received less support from adults. All six of these gambling activities were approved by a majority of the teenagers.

Adults and teenagers showed far less support for legalized Internet gambling. Only 20% of adults approved of legalized gambling using the Internet. Support was somewhat higher (33%) among teenagers. A vast majority of respondents (76% of adults and 70% of teens) believed it was easy for teenagers to use the Internet to gamble. A majority of adults (57%) and teenagers (63%) thought that the Internet had increased gambling among teenagers.

One argument often leveled against gambling is that it is harmful to the work ethic—the attitude that hard and productive work is a worthwhile endeavor. According to the 1999 Gallup poll, 43% of adults and 58% of teenagers believed that gambling seriously damages people's respect for the value of hard work. Fewer people (36% of adults and 33% of teenagers) believed that the legal gam-bling industry is fundamentally based on taking advantage of poor people.

Americans were nearly evenly split on the philosophi-cal argument that gambling is an issue of freedom. The 1999 Gallup poll showed that 47% of adults and 51% of teenagers believed that gambling should remain legal "to preserve American freedom, regardless of the problems it may cause."

Practical Issues

Besides the moral and ethical ideas that people have about gambling, there are also more down-to-earth issues, such as the role of gambling in crime, government, and pol-itics. Gallup's 1999 poll indicated that many people still linked gambling with organized crime. The survey showed that 50% of adults agreed that legalizing gambling limits the involvement of organized crime. Forty-seven percent disagreed. Teenagers were slightly less prone to believe that organized crime involvement is limited by legalized gam-bling activities—42% agree, while 56% disagree.

The survey respondents were also concerned about a connection between legalized gambling and corruption among government officials. Among adults, 42% feared that the legal gambling industry is responsible for serious government corruption. Half of the teenagers surveyed also shared this view.

CHAPTER 2

SUPPLY AND DEMAND:
WHO OFFERS GAMBLING? WHO GAMBLES?

Like any business in a capitalist society, the gambling industry is driven by the principles of supply and demand. Gambling proponents say that demand drives supply. In other words, the industry grows and spreads into new markets because the public is eager to gamble. Illegal gambling has always flourished, and opinion polls show that most Americans favor legal gambling opportunities—particularly lotteries and casinos. Gambling is one of the most popular leisure activities in the country.

Gambling opponents say that supply drives demand. They argue that people would not be tempted to gamble or to gamble as often if opportunities were not so prevalent and widespread. They see gambling as an irresistible temptation with potentially dangerous consequences. It bothers them that gambling opportunities are presented, promoted, and supported not only by the business world but also by government leaders and politicians—people who are supposed to represent the best interests of the public they serve.

Whatever the driving reason, gambling has become a big business and a popular pastime for many Americans.

SUPPLY—GAMBLING OPPORTUNITIES AND OPPORTUNISTS

Various gambling opportunities are available in this country, both legal and illegal. Gambling is a moneymaking activity for corporations, small businesses, criminals, charities, and governments. The legal gambling industry employs hundreds of thousands of people across the country. In addition, it is supported by a variety of other businesses, including manufacturing companies, distributors, advertising agencies, racehorse breeders, and many more. There would be no gambling if there was no money to be made in the industry.

According to the American Gaming Association (AGA), between 1975 and 2003 the gross revenue taken in by the legal gambling industry increased from $3 billion a year to nearly $73 billion a year; a significant portion of this growth took place during the 1990s, when gross gambling revenue (GGR) doubled. GGR is the money taken in by the industry minus the winnings paid out. In other words, it is equivalent to sales. When operating expenses, wages, benefits, taxes, and salaries are subtracted, the profit to the industry is left.

Commercial casinos, which are nearly all owned by corporations, control 41% of the legal gambling revenue pie, compared to 21% controlled by tribal casinos and 27% by lotteries. In 2003, according to statistics published on the AGA Web site (www.americangaming.org), commercial casinos had $27 billion of GGR after paying winners. This figure is up dramatically from only $9.6 billion in 1992.

Corporations

CASINO OWNERS AND OPERATORS. Corporations have profited the most from legalized gambling since taking over the small casinos of Las Vegas during the late 1960s, when organized crime was pushed out by the government. As gambling became more and more profitable, corporations invested money in new and bigger properties in Las Vegas and around the state of Nevada. In 1978 the first casino hotel opened in Atlantic City, New Jersey. Corporations became increasingly involved in the gambling business over the next few decades. Today, most corporations in the industry own and/or operate several commercial casinos. Some companies, such as Harrah's Entertainment, also manage casinos for Native American tribes. Tribes are increasingly partnering with large well-known corporations to take advantage of their name recognition and corporate experience.

The seven largest and best-known corporations in the gambling industry are listed below.

- Caesars Entertainment, Inc., is one of the world's largest gambling corporations, with twenty-eight gaming properties and 52,000 employees worldwide. It was formed in 1998 as Park Place Entertainment Corporation and adopted its new name in January 2004. Its casino resorts operate under the brand names of Caesars, Bally's, Flamingo, Grand Casinos, Hilton, and Paris. U.S. properties include Caesars Palace, The Flamingo, Bally's, and Paris in Las Vegas, Nevada; The Flamingo in Laughlin, Nevada; The Hilton in Reno, Nevada; Caesars at Lake Tahoe, Nevada; Bally's, Caesars, and Hilton in Atlantic City, New Jersey; Dover Downs racino in Delaware; Bally's and Grand Casino in Tunica, Mississippi; Bally's of New Orleans, Louisiana; Grand Casinos in Gulfport and Biloxi, Mississippi; and Caesars of Indiana. The company also operates Caesars Palace at Sea, shipboard casinos and facilities in Canada, Australia, Asia, and South America, as well as resort and hotel casinos in South Africa, Australia, Uruguay, and Canada. The 2003 corporate revenue of Caesars Entertainment was $4.455 billion, up slightly from $4.437 billion in 2002. The largest single revenue source in 2003 was slot machines, accounting for 50% of the total.

- Harrah's Entertainment has twenty-five U.S. casinos operating under the brand names of Harrah's, Harvey's, Rio, and Showboat. Properties include Harrah's in Atlantic City, New Jersey; Council Bluffs, Iowa; East Chicago, Indiana; Joliet and Metropolis, Illinois; Lake Tahoe, Las Vegas, Laughlin, and Reno, Nevada; Lake Charles and New Orleans, Louisiana; North Kansas City and St. Louis, Missouri; and Tunica and Vicksburg, Mississippi. In addition, four tribal casinos are operated by the company: Harrah's Cherokee in Cherokee, North Carolina; Harrah's Phoenix Ak-Chin in Maricopa, Arizona; Harrah's Prairie Band Casino in Mayetta, Kansas; and Harrah's Rincon–San Diego in Valley Center, California. Other company properties include the Bluffs Run Casino in Council Bluffs, Iowa; Bill's Lake Tahoe and Harvey's Lake Tahoe in Stateline, Nevada; Rio All-Suite Casino in Las Vegas, Nevada; and Showboat in Atlantic City, New Jersey. In addition the corporation operates the Louisiana Downs thoroughbred horseracing track in Bossier City, Louisiana. Harrah's Entertainment employs more than 40,000 people. Net revenues were $4.3 billion in 2003, up from $4.1 billion in 2002. In July 2004 Harrah's finalized purchase of Horseshoe Gaming Holding Corporation with casinos in Bossier City, Louisiana; Tunica, Mississippi; and Hammond, Indiana. Also in July 2004 Harrah's announced plans to purchase Caesars Entertainment. The $9.4 billion deal will include payment of $5.2 billion in cash and stock and assumption of $4.2 billion in debt.

- MGM Mirage owns and/or operates fifteen casinos, including the Bellagio, MGM Grand, New York–New York, the Mirage, the Golden Nugget, and Treasure Island in Las Vegas, Nevada; the Golden Nugget in Laughlin, Nevada; Whiskey Pete's, Buffalo Bill's, and Primm Valley Casinos along the Nevada/California state line; Beau Rivage in Biloxi, Mississippi; and MGM Grand in Detroit, Michigan. The Company owns 50% of the Borgata casino resort in Atlantic City, New Jersey. The company employs more than 45,000 people. The corporate revenue was $3.9 billion in 2003, up 3% from 2002. In June 2004 the company announced plans to purchase Mandalay Resort Group for approximately $7.9 billion.

- Mandalay Bay Resort Group has sixteen casinos that it operates, owns, or in which it has a majority interest. These include Mandalay Bay, Luxor, Excalibur, Circus Circus, and Monte Carlo in Las Vegas, Nevada; Silver Legacy and Circus Circus in Reno, Nevada; Railroad Pass in Henderson, Nevada; Nevada Landing and Gold Strike in Jean, Nevada; Colorado Belle and Edgewater in Laughlin, Nevada; Gold Strike in Tunica, Mississippi; Grand Victoria riverboat casino in Elgin, Illinois; and MotorCity in Detroit, Michigan. The company employed over 26,000 people and had net revenues of $2.5 billion in 2003.

- Boyd Gaming Corporation has eighteen casinos, including Par-A-Dice Casino in East Peoria, Illinois; Blue Chip Casino in Michigan City, Indiana; Treasure Chest Casino, Sam's Town of Shreveport, and Delta Downs racino in Louisiana; Sam's Town in Tunica, Mississippi; and the Barbary Coast, California, El Dorado, Fremont, Gold Coast, Jokers Wild, Main Street Station, Orleans, Sam's Town, South Coast, and Stardust in and around Las Vegas, Nevada. Boyd is a joint-venture partner with MGM Mirage in the Borgata Casino in Atlantic City, New Jersey. The corporation employed nearly 14,000 people in 2003. Net corporate revenue was $1.25 billion in 2003.

- Argosy Gaming Company runs six riverboat casinos in the United States, including the Argosy's Alton Belle in Alton, Illinois; Argosy Casino–Riverside near Kansas City, Missouri; Argosy Casino–Baton Rouge in Louisiana; Argosy Casino–Sioux City Casino in Iowa; Argosy Casino–Lawrenceburg in Indiana; and the Empress Casino–Joliet in Illinois. The company employs more than 6,000 people. Net revenue was $960 million in 2003.

- Station Casinos, Inc., has eleven casinos in and around Las Vegas, Nevada, catering to local markets. The properties include Palace Station, Boulder Station, Fiesta Rancho, Santa Fe Station, Texas Station, Wildfire, Wild Wild West, Fiesta Henderson, Sunset Station, Barley's Casino and Brewery (joint venture) and Green Valley Ranch (joint venture). In addition, the company manages the Thunder Valley Casino for the United

12   Supply and Demand: Who Offers Gambling? Who Gambles?

Gambling: What's at Stake?

Auburn Indian Community in Lincoln, California. The company employed more than 10,000 people in 2003 and had net corporate revenue of $858 million.

Most corporations involved in gambling enterprises, including the ones listed above, are publicly held, meaning that investors can buy shares in the companies on the stock market. In return, investors receive a portion of the profits (if any) made by the company. Publicly held companies are answerable to their shareholders. The U.S. Securities and Exchange Commission (SEC) requires publicly held companies to disclose certain financial and other information to the public. Some casino companies are privately owned. This means they do not offer shares of stock to the public on a stock exchange and therefore do not have to meet the strict SEC disclosure requirements of public companies.

OTHER GAMBLING CORPORATIONS. Different companies play major roles in other realms of the gambling industry. Two publicly traded companies, Churchill Downs and Magna Entertainment, are major organizations in the thoroughbred horse racing business. Churchill Downs operates tracks in California, Florida, Illinois, Indiana, Louisiana, and Kentucky. Magna Entertainment, a Canadian-based corporation with racetracks throughout North America, operated fifteen tracks in 2003. According to Hoovers Online, a financial information source, Churchill Downs had revenues of $424 million in 2003 and Magna Entertainment had revenues of $709 million.

According to the Web site of the National Association of Convenience Stores (www.nacsonline.com), roughly half of all lottery ticket sales during 2003 were in convenience stores. There were more than 130,000 convenience stores in operation in the United States during 2003 and approximately 80% of them sold lottery tickets. 7-Eleven, Inc., is the largest convenience store operator, franchisor, and licensor in the world, with thousands of stores in the United States and abroad. Other large corporations in the convenience store business include Circle K, QuikTrip, and Amerada Hess Corporation.

Many corporations directly support the gambling industry by providing equipment, goods, supplies or services. These may be members of the Gaming Standards Association, an international organization devoted to the development of uniform standards for communication and computer technology used in gambling machines. Some examples of these types of corporations are:

- GTECH Corporation, which introduced the first lottery terminal in 1982. Within two decades it was providing technology services to lotteries in twenty-five states.

- Bally Gaming and Systems, which introduced its first slot machine in 1936 and went on to become a very successful machine manufacturer and distributor.

- Konami Gaming, Inc., a leading producer of high-tech video slot machines and multisite casino management systems.

- WMS Gaming, which is engaged entirely in the manufacture, sale, leasing, and licensing of gambling machines.

GAMBLING AS AN INVESTMENT. The investment firm MUTUALS.com sells shares in the "Vice Fund." This is a mutual fund composed entirely of companies in the alcohol, tobacco, gambling, and defense industries. According to the fund's Web site (www.vicefund.com) as of July 31, 2004, gambling companies comprised 26% of the fund's investments. For the one-year period ending March 31, 2004, the fund had a 57.34% return on investments. This compares with a 35.12% gain for the Standard & Poor's 500 Index and a 32.56% gain for the Dow Jones Industrial Average. According to fund managers, gaming companies including Ameristar Casinos, Inc., Scientific Games Corp., Alliance Gaming Corp., Shuffle Master, Inc., Multimedia Games, Inc., and International Game Technology were major contributors to the fund's growth.

Small Businesses

Small businesses are involved in the gambling industry in a number of ways. Many small casinos and racetracks, minicasinos, and card rooms around the country are owned and/or operated by small companies, families, and entrepreneurs. Other ways in which small businesses are engaged in or serve the gambling industry include:

- The selling of lottery tickets and operation of electronic gaming devices at independently owned convenience stores, markets, service stations, bars, restaurants, bowling alleys, and newsstands

- Internet gambling Web sites

- The manufacture, supply, and distribution of gambling equipment (slot machines, roulette wheels, lottery tickets, dice, cards, etc.)

- Services (advertising, marketing, public relations, accounting, information technology, food services, etc.)

- Horse and greyhound breeding, training, veterinary care, etc.

Most small businesses that offer gambling do so through lottery ticket sales and/or electronic gaming devices (slot machines). These are considered forms of convenience gambling, because patrons do not have to travel to special destinations (like casinos and racetracks) to gamble. Convenience gambling is more controversial than destination gambling. Critics believe that allowing gambling in stores and restaurants and other places that people visit as part of their everyday routine makes it too easy for people to gamble. This is the same criticism leveled against Internet gambling, which patrons can do in their own homes.

Gambling: What's at Stake?

Supply and Demand: Who Offers Gambling? Who Gambles? **13**

Like Internet gambling, some forms of convenience gambling are considered illegal. The legality of elecronic gaming devices (EGDs) is not completely clear in some states. The problem is that many states have exemptions from their gambling laws for machines that dispense small-value merchandise or tickets or tokens that can be exchanged for small-value merchandise. During the late 1990s and early 2000s several states in the Southeast experienced problems with small businesses that began operating electronic games that paid off patrons with small amounts of cash, instead of prizes. Law enforcement officials complained that the machines were not regulated by the state and constituted illegal gambling. Despite court challenges the machines were eventually banned in South Carolina and Georgia.

The operation of video lottery terminals (VLTs) by small businesses has also proved to be controversial. According to the National Council against Legalized Gambling, during 2003 there were six bills that would have allowed lottery ticket machines in stores, that were defeated in six states: Arkansas, Illinois, New Jersey, Pennsylvania, Alaska, and Washington.

INTERNET GAMBLING BUSINESSES. Internet gambling is one of the most controversial markets for small businesses to enter. Industry analysts say that the vast majority of Internet gambling sites are operated by small, virtually unknown companies that operate without regulatory oversight. Most are in offshore locations, mainly the Caribbean. Because Internet gambling is illegal in the United States, little is known about the companies offering these services. However, the U.S. Department of Justice estimates that there were more than 1,800 Internet gambling sites operating around the world at the end of 2003. Industry analyst Christiansen Capital Advisors, LLC, estimates that Internet gambling generated nearly $5.7 billion of revenue in 2003. The company predicts that revenue will exceed $18 billion by 2010.

Criminals

Gambling in America has had a checkered legal history. At various times different gambling activities have been legal, illegal but tolerated, or illegal and actively prosecuted. During times when gambling opportunities have been outlawed, entrepreneurs have stepped in to offer them anyway. These entrepreneurs range from mobsters running million-dollar betting rings to grandmothers running neighborhood bingo games. Either way, the illegal nature of the activity makes these entrepreneurs criminals.

Legal gambling operations can also attract criminals because of the large amounts of cash involved. Gambling opponents use this fact to criticize the industry. Others argue that every moneymaking industry attracts criminals; for example, if there were no banks, there would be no bank robbers.

CASINOS AND CRIME. Casinos, in particular, constantly monitor against dealer fraud, skimming, money laundering, and other criminal activities using sophisticated camera and monitoring systems to watch employees and customers.

In October 2003 a Detroit man was charged with fraud for allegedly tampering with a scratch-and-win ticket purchased at the MotorCity Casino earlier that year. The man presented the ticket to claim a $1-million prize. The casino had the ticket laboratory tested for verification and discovered that it had been altered to appear to be a winning ticket. The man was charged with four felony counts and, if convicted, could face up to sixty years in prison. After the deception was discovered, the casino subjected all other winning tickets to laboratory testing and found that additional tickets had also been altered to win prizes.

HORSE RACING SCANDALS. In December 2003 the New York Racing Association (NYRA) and six of its employees were charged with conspiracy to commit tax fraud. Federal officials accused the NYRA of aiding certain employees in understating their earnings to the Internal Revenue Service. The suit alleges that clerks would remove money from their cash drawers and keep it. Managers then deducted the amounts from the employees' paychecks. This reduced the amount of personal income tax the employees ultimately owed to the government. According to federal prosecutors the scheme went on for at least twenty years with the full knowledge of senior management at the NYRA. It is believed that management participated in the fraud to improve relations with the clerks' union. The NYRA was fined $3 million and forced to undergo massive restructuring within its organization. Several top managers were fired and may face criminal prosecution.

In October 2002 the prestigious Breeders' Cup horse race was held in Arlington Heights, Illinois. A month later, three men were charged with conspiracy to commit wire fraud after winning suspicious bets on the race. One of the three worked for Autotote, a computer company handling wagering for the races. He allegedly changed losing bets to winning bets using his computer terminal. The resulting payoff was more than $3 million. Several long-shot horses won that day, and no other bettor picked all of the winners. Authorities were immediately suspicious and began checking computer records before the money was paid out. The fraud was discovered, and all three men were arrested. Two of them tested positive for cocaine use. In late November 2002 the former Autotote employee pleaded guilty to wire-fraud conspiracy and money-laundering conspiracy. On March 20, 2003, CNN reported that all three men received prison sentences ranging from one to three years.

ORGANIZED CRIME. Organized crime groups have often been associated with—and have often embraced—gambling, a cash business with high demand and good

14   Supply and Demand: Who Offers Gambling? Who Gambles?

Gambling: What's at Stake?

profits. Eastern crime syndicates were among the first to see the potential of Las Vegas, invest in it, and profit from it. At times they have infiltrated other segments of the legal gambling industry, such as horse racing. Strict regulations and crackdowns by law enforcement have been put into place to push them out. The federal Racketeer Influenced and Corrupt Organizations (RICO) Act enacted under the Crime Control Act in 1970 was designed to combat infiltration by organized crime into legitimate businesses, including gambling. Most analysts believe that these efforts have been largely successful at keeping mobsters from establishing or taking over legal gambling businesses.

Although they have been shut out of casino ownership and management roles, some organized crime figures have been caught infiltrating casinos in other ways, such as through labor unions and maintenance or food services. Law enforcement officials also believe that organized crime families have been involved in bribing state officials considering the extension or expansion of gambling options, particularly relating to electronic gambling machines.

The Nevada Gaming Commission and State Gaming Control Board maintains a list of people who are prohibited from gambling in Nevada. The state's "List of Excluded Persons," is more commonly known as "Nevada's Black Book." The list primarily includes crime family bosses, mob associates, and others linked in some way to organized crime. These people are considered so dangerous to the integrity of legal gambling that they are not allowed to set foot in a Nevada casino. The Nevada Gaming Commission and State Gaming Control Board publishes photographs of the people on the list at their Web site (http://gaming.nv.gov/loep_main.htm).

The most lucrative sector of the gambling industry for organized crime has been and continues to be illegal bookmaking and numbers games. Bookmaking is a gambling activity in which a bookmaker takes bets on the odds of a particular event occurring. The vast majority of bookmaking revolves around sporting events—for example, college and professional football and basketball games. Such wagering is extremely popular in the United States. Because sports bookmaking is legal only in Nevada, there is a large illegal market for it across the country. In 1999 the National Gambling Impact Study Commission Final Report estimated that $80 to $380 billion per year is wagered in illegal sports gambling in the United States.

Illegal numbers games are similar to lottery games in that players wager money on particular numbers to be selected in a drawing or by other means. Illegal numbers operators thrive in low-income areas of large cities, even those where legal lotteries are offered.

Gambling with mobsters has advantages and disadvantages. Gambling opportunities abound throughout neighborhoods in local shops and bars. The payoffs are higher than for legal activities, and no taxes are taken out of winnings. Of course, losing bettors face possible physical intimidation and/or bodily harm if they fail to pay their gambling debts. Loan-sharking, or the lending of money at exorbitant interest rates with the threat of violence for non-payment, is also widely practiced by organized crime groups, particularly in areas where legal or illegal gambling occurs. Many gamblers in debt turn to loan sharks after legitimate means of obtaining money are exhausted. Perhaps most important, people who choose to participate in illegal gambling opportunities may have criminal charges filed against them if their activities are discovered.

OFFICE POOLS. Not all bookmaking is done through mobsters. Many enterprising entrepreneurs across the country run small-time illegal gambling books, mostly related to sporting events. Office pools, in which coworkers pool together small wagers on sports or office events (like when a baby is going to be born) are also extremely common. Although society does not generally consider private wagers and small-stakes office pools to be illegal gambling, the laws in most states do.

The Society for Human Resource Management (SHRM) conducted a February 1999 survey of 504 human resources professionals regarding workplace gambling. According to these respondents, football pools were the most common form of gambling in the workplace, with 58% of human resource professionals saying Super Bowl pools occur in their companies and 55% believing regular season football pools occur. Of those respondents who knew that their employees were gambling, a majority (56%) reported no ill effects on worker productivity related to this gambling. However, 25% were not sure of the effects. Another 13% felt that these gambling activities had a positive effect on worker productivity, and only 6% felt the gambling had a negative effect on productivity.

The survey respondents were also asked if their organizations had written policies regarding gambling activities at the workplace—23% of them did and 63% did not. Another 11% did not have written policies but had unwritten or "understood" policies. Of those with gambling policies, 59% indicated that the activities taking place were in violation of those policies. Another 21% said that their policies did not specifically prohibit, but did discourage, gambling activities. Only 16% of workplaces with gambling policies permitted these activities. Punishment for violating gambling policies fell into three categories: no official punishment (38%), formal reprimands (35%), and referral for counseling (19%).

In January 2002 the SHRM Web site released the results of an informal poll of 9,764 human resource professionals around the country. The poll found that 30% of the respondents reported that their organizations did not allow betting pools. Another 14% said that their organizations did allow betting pools. More than half of the respondents

Gambling: What's at Stake?

Supply and Demand: Who Offers Gambling? Who Gambles?   15

(57%) reported they were not worried about whether or not betting pools were taking place at their workplaces.

In "Office Betting Can Be Costly" (*Business Review,* July 2002), Joshua Hurwit reported that office gambling costs companies billions of dollars per year in lost productivity. Many companies are also unsure about the legality of office pools. A spokesperson for the New York attorney general explained that office pools are technically illegal in the state but not criminal "until a player generates a profit." Still, turning a blind eye to office pools can be legally dangerous for companies. The article describes a case in which a man fired by his company for selling stolen goods at work is contesting his firing on the grounds that the company openly permits another illegal activity at work—office pools.

Despite the widespread illegality of gambling, few people are actually arrested for engaging in it. According to the U.S. Department of Justice in *Crime in the United States,* and shown in Table 2.1, there were only 10,506 estimated arrests for gambling during 2002 out of more than 13.7 million total arrests. This is down slightly from 11,112 arrests in 2001.

Charities

REGULATION. Charitable gambling is the most widely practiced form of gambling allowed in the United States. As shown in Table 1.1 in Chapter 1, it was legal in forty-seven states as of September 2004, prohibited only in Arkansas, Hawaii, and Utah. In charitable gambling, a specified portion of the money raised (less prizes, expenses, and any state fees and taxes) goes to qualified charitable organizations. Such organizations include religious groups, fraternal organizations, veterans' groups, volunteer fire departments, parent-teacher organizations, civic and cultural groups, booster clubs, and other nonprofit organizations.

Generally, a charitable organization has to have been in existence for several years and obtain a state license for the gambling activity. Most states will only issue licenses to organizations that have been recognized by the Internal Revenue Service (IRS) as exempt from federal income tax under Tax Code section 501(c). Thousands of charitable organizations are registered to conduct gambling around the country.

In some states charitable gambling activity is unregulated or not under the control of a central regulatory authority. In most states charitable gambling is regulated by state governments, but not uniformly under the same department. Many states regulate charitable gambling under their Department of Revenue, while others use their Department of State, public safety department, state police, alcohol control board, or lottery, gaming, or racing commission. Administrative fees and taxes are levied in most states.

TABLE 2.1

Estimated arrests, 2002

Total[1]	13,741,438
Murder and nonnegligent manslaughter	14,158
Forcible rape	28,288
Robbery	105,774
Aggravated assault	472,290
Burglary	288,291
Larceny-theft	1,160,085
Motor vehicle theft	148,943
Arson	16,635
Violent crime[2]	620,510
Property crime[3]	1,613,954
Crime Index[4]	2,234,464
Other assaults	1,288,682
Forgery and counterfeiting	115,735
Fraud	337,404
Embezzlement	18,552
Stolen property; buying, receiving, possessing	126,422
Vandalism	276,697
Weapons; carrying, possessing, etc.	164,446
Prostitution and commercialized vice	79,733
Sex offenses (except forcible rape and prostitution)	95,066
Drug abuse violations	1,538,813
Gambling	10,506
Offenses against the family and children	140,286
Driving under the influence	1,461,746
Liquor laws	653,819
Drunkenness	572,735
Disorderly conduct	669,938
Vagrancy	27,295
All other offenses	3,662,159
Suspicion	8,899
Curfew and loitering law violations	141,252
Runaways	125,688

[1]Does not include suspicion.
[2]Violent crimes are offenses of murder, forcible rape, robbery, and aggravated assault.
[3]Property crimes are offenses of burglary, larceny-theft, motor vehicle theft, and arson.
[4]Includes arson.

SOURCE: "Table 29. Estimated Arrests, United States, 2002," in *Crime in the United States,* U.S. Department of Justice, Federal Bureau of Investigation, October 27, 2003, http://www.fbi.gov/ucr/cius_02/pdf/4sectionfour.pdf (accessed September 28, 2004)

Due to inconsistencies in state oversight it is difficult to determine the complete extent of charitable gambling in the United States. The American Gaming Association estimates that $2.67 billion was wagered on charitable games in 2003.

Typical games allowed include bingo (the most common), pull tabs, raffles, paddlewheels, tipboards (which are similar to punchboards), and card games like poker or blackjack. Slot machines, roulette, craps, and baccarat are generally not permitted. There are usually limits on the value of cash prizes that can be awarded in each game. Different states differ in which gambling games they allow for charity fundraising; for example, California only allows bingo games.

In 2004 Tennessee became the latest state to permit charitable gambling. During the 1970s and 1980s charitable gambling took place in the state as lawmakers argued about whether it violated the state's constitutional ban on lotteries. In 1987 *The Tennessean* newspaper and other

16   Supply and Demand: Who Offers Gambling? Who Gambles?

Gambling: What's at Stake?

media outlets reported widespread scandal and fraud in the industry. They alleged that professional gamblers were setting up phony charities and bribing legislators to look the other way. The so-called Rocky Top Scandal resulted in federal investigations of bingo operators in 1989 and 1990. Several people were indicted, and two public officials committed suicide. In 1989 the state's supreme court ruled that bingo was a lottery and outlawed it. In 2002 Tennessee voters approved a state lottery and reauthorized gambling for charitable purposes. Legislation regulating charitable gambling activities became final in early 2004.

This leaves only three states that prohibit charitable gambling—Hawaii, Utah, and Arkansas. Hawaii and Utah prohibit all types of gambling. Although charitable gambling is illegal in Arkansas, some conservative ministers have complained that bingo parlors operate openly in the state. Law enforcement officials have stated publicly that enforcement of the bingo ban is low on their priority list.

The National Association of Fundraising Ticket Manufacturers (NAFTM) is a trade association representing companies that manufacture bingo paper, pull tabs, and other supplies used in the charitable gambling industry. In 2003 NAFTM published *Charity Gaming in North America: 2002 Annual Report,* which included statistics on charitable gambling in twenty-nine states. The report stated that $2.8 billion was wagered on charitable gaming in these twenty-nine states during 2002. The top five states were Minnesota ($1.4 billion), Washington ($888 million), Kentucky ($607 million), Indiana ($583 million), and Texas ($556 million). On average prize payouts accounted for 71% of gross receipts. Another 16% went to expenses and 3% to taxes and fees. This left 10% as net profit to charitable organizations.

According to the NAFTM nearly all states charge organizations licensing fees to conduct charitable gambling events. For example, South Carolina charges a one-time fee of $1,000. Some states charge a fee per event, while others charge a set weekly, monthly, or yearly fee. These fees generally run from $10 to $100. A handful of states base the licensing fee on the amount of gross receipts, so these fees can be thousands of dollars. Most states also impose a gaming tax on the proceeds from charitable gambling and/or collect administrative fees. Most states allocate all or a portion of these revenues to their general fund or the agency overseeing charitable gambling. A few states split the money with local law enforcement agencies.

MINNESOTA. It is widely believed that Minnesota has the highest gross receipts from charitable gambling of any state and probably accounts for around half of all money wagered in the United States for this purpose. The activity is regulated by the Minnesota Gambling Control Board. According to the *Annual Report of the Minnesota Gam-* *bling Control Board: Fiscal Year 2003*, charity gambling raised $1.4 billion during fiscal year 2003, down slightly from $1.435 billion in 2002. The amount wagered increased by 12% between 1994 and 2003. Total prizes paid out amounted to $1.164 billion in 2003, making up 82% of gross receipts. Another 9% went to expenses, while 4% went to pay state taxes. This left 5% ($67 million) for the charities.

In January 2004 Joon Kyu Kim, the former president of a Minnesota charitable gambling organization, was arrested for using nearly half a million dollars of the organization's gambling funds to finance personal investments. Minnesota law requires that all proceeds from charitable gambling go to charitable causes, taxes, and operating expenses. Kim faces up to twenty-five years in prison if convicted of the charges.

The Government

The government includes federal, tribal, state, and local agencies that collect money from gambling operations. This happens primarily through the collection of taxes and fees and, in some cases, through the supply of gambling opportunities. Because the money raised is spent on public projects, many Americans are ultimately affected by the government's involvement in gambling.

THE FEDERAL GOVERNMENT. The primary means by which the federal government makes money from the gambling industry is by taxing winning gamblers and gambling operators. Gamblers must declare their gambling winnings when they file their personal income taxes. They get to subtract their gambling losses, but they must keep thorough records and have receipts (if possible) to prove their losses. For racetrack gamblers, this means saving losing betting slips and keeping a gambling diary of dates, events, and amounts. Casino gamblers who use electronic "slot club" cards can get a detailed printout of their playing history from the casino.

Gambling operators, like all companies, are subject to corporate taxes. They are required to report winnings that meet certain criteria to the IRS. (See Table 2.2.) The gambling operator must withhold income tax from winnings of more than $5,000 if the winnings are at least three hundred times the amount of the bet. This applies to sweepstakes, wagering pools, lotteries, and any other wager where the proceeds are at least three hundred times the amount of the bet. The withholding rate is generally 25%. However, 28% is withheld from the winnings of gamblers who do not provide the payer with their social security numbers. Gamblers who win noncash prizes (like cars or other merchandise) have to pay tax on the fair market value of the item.

The federal government is itself in the gambling business. The U.S. Department of Defense (DOD) operates

Gambling: What's at Stake?

Supply and Demand: Who Offers Gambling? Who Gambles? **17**

TABLE 2.2

Gambling winnings that must be reported to the Internal Revenue Service, 2004

Type of game	Amount of prize paid is equal to or greater than:
Lotteries, sweepstakes, horse races, dog races, instant bingo game prizes/pull-tabs, jai alai and other wagering transactions	$600 and prize is at least 300 times wager
Bingo	$1,200
Slot machines	$1,200
Keno	$1,500

SOURCE: Adapted from *2003 Instructions for Forms W-2G and 5754,* Internal Revenue Service, 2004

approximately eight thousand slot machines at U.S. military bases overseas. According to Jeremy Kirk in "Slot Machines Pay MWR Bills, but Some Worry about Effects on Servicemembers" (*Stars and Stripes,* March 18, 2001), 6,200 slot machines were operated in 2001 by the U.S. Army, Navy, and Marines in South Korea, Europe, Okinawa, and mainland Japan that brought in revenues of nearly $91 million a year. In "Base Habit? Air Force Runs 24 'Casinos'" (*Deseret News,* September 23, 2001), Lee Davidson reported that the Air Force operated another 1,580 slot machines in 2001 that made about $29 million per year. Thus, military-operated slot machines bring in revenues of about $120 million per year. Based on an average payout figure of 92.5% (as reported by the DOD), this means the gross amount wagered on the military slot machines is around $1.6 billion per year.

As part of the Fiscal Year 2001 National Defense Authorization Act, Congress required the DOD to prepare a report on the effects of slot machine operations on those who use them. The result was *Report on the Effect of the Ready Availability of Slot Machines on Members of the Armed Forces, Their Dependents, and Others* (November 5, 2001). The DOD report states that slot machines are offered at certain overseas bases unless prohibited by the laws of the host nation. The games are restricted to nickel and quarter denominations. Revenues from the machines fund activity centers, clubs, golf courses, bowling alleys, and other recreational and entertainment projects on overseas and U.S. bases. The report contains no data on the number of machines operated, the amount of revenue they generate, or the number of customers who use them. However, it concludes that the machines are beneficial to the armed services by building morale and providing recreation and have no detrimental effects.

In May 2002 Mark Mazzetti criticized the DOD report in "Uncle Sam's One-Armed Bandits" (*U.S. News & World Report,* May 20, 2002), asserting the report was prepared by the military's Morale, Welfare, and Recreation Department—the very department that receives the revenues from slot machine operations. The article tells the story of an Air Force sergeant stationed at Osan Air Base

in South Korea who wrote $14,000 worth of bad checks to finance her gambling habit at the base's slot machines. The woman said she began gambling to ease her depression and loneliness at being so far from home.

In 2003 military-operated slot machines were criticized by John Kindt, a professor of business and legal policy at the University of Illinois at Urbana-Champaign ("Gambling with Terrorism and U.S. Military Readiness: Time to Ban Video Gambling Devices on U. S. Military Bases and Facilities," *Northern Illinois Law Review,* 2003). Kindt noted that a 2001 DOD survey found that approximately 30,000 military personnel had potentially serious gambling problems. He questioned the wisdom of the U.S. military providing gambling opportunities on bases, even though they are intended for recreational purposes.

STATE GOVERNMENTS. State governments make money from the legal gambling enterprises operated within their borders. These enterprises include lotteries, commercial casinos, horse and dog races, jai alai games, card rooms, charitable gambling, and video machine gambling. Only lotteries are operated by state governments. All other gambling options are operated by other parties.

Forty states operate lotteries. On average, they keep half of all money spent on lottery tickets. This leaves only ten states without lotteries as of mid-2004: Alabama, Alaska, Arkansas, Hawaii, Mississippi, Nevada, North Carolina, Oklahoma, Utah, and Wyoming.

As of August 2004 there were no state-owned casinos in the United States. However, several states have expressed interest in such ventures. In May 2001 Minnesota Senate Minority Leader Dick Day proposed that the state open its own casino to compete with the profitable casinos operated on Native American reservations. Day's proposed legislation called for hiring a private entity to manage the casino, but the state's constitution would first have to be changed. The proposal was opposed by conservative and religious groups and by Native American tribes and was ultimately vetoed. In 2003 the Minnesota legislature declined to pass a plan that would have placed a state-owned casino at one of the state's existing horse race tracks. Native American tribes engaged in gaming in Minnesota argued against the proposal claiming it would take money and jobs away from tribal casinos.

In April 2003 Governor Rod Blagojevich of Illinois proposed that the state take over ownership of the casinos operating commercially in Illinois and hire private firms to manage them. The idea was vigorously opposed by the state's gambling industry. At the time Illinois was facing a $5 billion budget deficit and desperately needed to raise funds.

In January 2004 Governor Kathleen Sebelius of Kansas announced an initiative for five state-owned casinos to be run by a private management firm operating

18   Supply and Demand: Who Offers Gambling? Who Gambles?

Gambling: What's at Stake?

TABLE 2.3

State gambling legislative developments, January–August 23, 2004

State	2004 gambling developments
Alabama	**Failed:** Constitutional amendment to repeal state's ban on lotteries and full-fledged casinos. **Failed:** Electronic bingo at the state's four racetracks.
Alaska	**Failed:** Single casino in Anchorage. **Failed:** Taxation of gambling on cruise ships.
California	**Enacted:** A bill creating new state compacts with five Indian Tribes in California. Agreeing to pay into two state revenue streams, the tribes may now operate an unlimited amount of slot machines and are guaranteed exclusive rights to slots operations in the state.
District of Columbia	**Failed:** Petition drive to include a question on the legalization of slot machines on the November ballot.
Florida	**Failed:** Regulation of gambling arcades. **Failed:** Allow charities, religious and veteran's groups to sell lottery-style bingo tickets.
Georgia	**Failed:** Online lottery.
Indiana	**Failed:** House Bill 1188 would have allowed 1,000 electronic pull-tab machines at each of the state's horse tracks and 1,500 at betting parlors.
Iowa	**Enacted:** Comprehensive gambling bill that allows the introduction of table games at racinos, ends cruise requirements for riverboat casinos, and allows the gaming commission to issue an unlimited number of casino licenses. This bill also prohibits a riverboat casino in downtown Des Moines.
Kansas	**Failed:** At least three different proposals with various combinations of casinos, slots at tracks, slots at fraternal organizations and slots at other locations such as bowling alleys and driving ranges.
Kentucky	**Failed:** A bill providing for a statewide vote on a constitutional amendment allowing expanded gambling at existing racetracks.
Maine	**Enacted:** A bill that provides for the implementation and regulation of slots at racetracks. A ballot initiative allowing slots at racetracks was passed by voters in November, 2003. This bill creates the Gambling Control Board and Advisory Council, and establishes a casino revenue distribution formula.
Maryland	**Failed:** 11,500 video lottery machines at four horse racing tracks, 4,000 at two stand-alone facilities along the Interstate 95 corridor.
Michigan	**Enacted:** House Bill 4612, increases the state wagering tax on Detroit Casinos from 18 to 24 percent. **Failed:** Video Lottery Terminals at racetracks.
Minnesota	**Failed:** Allow racetrack to add casino. **Failed:** Allow existing card club to increase the maximum number of tables from 50 to 100.
Missouri	**Failed:** August ballot proposal expanding legal riverboat casino locations beyond the Missouri and Mississippi rivers.
Nebraska	**Enacted:** Bill allowing ballot measure question on constitutional amendments to allow two casinos in the state. The question will appear as on the November ballot as Amendment 3.
New Jersey	**Enacted:** A bill gradually rolling back an existing 4.25 percent tax on complimentary benefits given by casinos to high wagering guests.
New York	**Implemented:** Video lottery machines in at least two racetracks. **Failed:** Video lottery machines on ferries between Rochester and Toronto. **Failed:** Proposal to expand the availability of the video numbers game "Quick Draw" to more restaurants and taverns by removing food sale percentage requirements in current legislation.
North Dakota	**Implemented:** State joins Powerball.
Ohio	**Failed:** Bill that would put ballot question of a constitutional amendment allowing 2,150 video lottery machines at each of Ohio's seven racetracks to voters.
Oklahoma	**Enacted:** Senate Bill 553 allows electronic bingo terminals at three racetracks.
Pennsylvania	**Enacted:** Legislation allowing up to 61,000 slot machines at seven racetracks, five slots casinos and two resorts.
Rhode Island	**Failed:** A bill for a state-wide referendum on allowing Indian Casino for Narragansett tribe in greater Providence area. After a legislative override of the Governor's veto of the bill, the state Supreme Court ruled that the proposed ballot question violated the state constitution.
Tennessee	**Implemented:** Tennessee Lottery began operations in January 2004. State also became 26th lottery nationwide to join Powerball. **Enacted:** Limited charitable gaming now allowed. **Failed:** Warning labels of gambling addiction possibility on lotto tickets and at distribution points of gambling addiction.
Texas	**Failed:** Up to 40,000 video lottery terminals at seven existing tracks.

SOURCE: Adapted from "Gambling Developments in the States—2004," in *Gambling Developments in the States—2004,* National Conference of State Legislatures, August 23, 2004, http://www.ncsl.org/programs/econ/gamblingdev04.htm (accessed August 26, 2004)

under the direction of the state's lottery commission. The plan calls for voters to make the final decisions about allowing state-owned casinos in their communities. Legislative leaders expressed concerns over the governor's plan with some indicating their opposition to expanding gambling in the state.

The National Conference of State Legislatures (NCSL) is a bipartisan organization that conducts research for state legislators and policymakers. The NCSL publishes at its Web site (www.ncsl.org) updates on gambling legislation at the state level. Table 2.3 summarizes gambling legislation that failed or was enacted and implemented in 2004. The list was current as of August 23, 2004.

TRIBAL GOVERNMENTS. Native American tribes that have been officially recognized by the U.S. government are considered sovereign nations, or free from external control. Tribal sovereignty means that to a certain extent

tribes govern themselves. In 1988 the U.S. Congress passed the Indian Gaming Regulatory Act, which allows federally recognized tribes to open gambling establishments if the state in which they are located already permits certain types of legalized gambling.

Casinos operated by more than two hundred Native American tribes made $16.7 billion during 2003, accounting for 38% of the U.S. casino market. The Indian Gaming Regulatory Act requires that net revenues from tribal gaming be used in five specific areas:

• To fund tribal government operations or programs

• To provide for the general welfare of the tribe and its members

• To promote tribal economic development

• To donate to charitable organizations

• To help fund operations of local government agencies

According to statistics provided on the Web site of the National Indian Gaming Association (www.indiangaming.org), during 2003 three-fourths of the tribes operating casinos allocated all gambling revenue to tribal governmental services, economic and community development, neighboring communities, and charitable purposes. Tribal governments have used gambling revenues to build health clinics, schools, houses, and community centers, and to provide educational scholarships and social services for their members.

LOCAL GOVERNMENTS. Local governments in some states collect taxes and fees from gambling activities operated within their jurisdictions. This is particularly true for casinos and racetracks.

New York City is a particularly active player in the gambling industry. In 1970 the New York City Off-Track Betting (NYCOTB) Corporation was founded as the first legal offtrack pari-mutuel wagering operation in the country. Although the NYCOTB is a government entity, it operates as a private enterprise that turns over profits to the taxpayers.

DEMAND—THE GAMBLERS

Gambling is a leisure activity—people gamble because they enjoy it. Gambling proponents say there is no difference between spending money at a theme park and spending it at a casino. The money is exchanged for a good time in either case. Gambling has a powerful allure in addition to fun, though, and that is the dream of wealth, a very strong motivator. Some gambling options, like the lottery, offer the chance to risk a small investment for an enormous payoff. This potential is too appealing to pass up for many people.

Adults

In December 2003 the Gallup Organization conducted a nationwide poll to determine gambling participation rates. The results showed that 66% of adults asked had gambled during the previous twelve months. As shown in Figure 2.1 lottery play was the most popular gambling activity. Nearly half of those asked (49%) had engaged in it, while 30% had visited a casino. Other forms of gambling were far less common.

According to the Gallup report, three-quarters of the men reported gambling, while only 57% of women did. There were also considerable differences between urban and rural dwellers. While 69% of people living in urban areas had gambled, only 57% of those in rural areas had done so. There were also differences among education levels. People with a postgraduate education were less likely to have gambled than those with less education. However, the participation rate for people with higher incomes (greater than $50,000 per year) was higher than it was for people making less than that. Only 58% of those

FIGURE 2.1

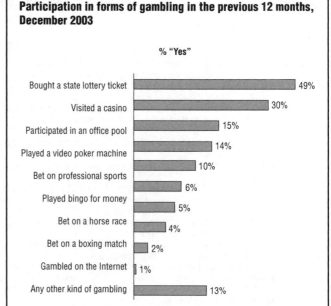

Participation in forms of gambling in the previous 12 months, December 2003

% "Yes"

Bought a state lottery ticket	49%
Visited a casino	30%
Participated in an office pool	15%
Played a video poker machine	14%
Bet on professional sports	10%
Played bingo for money	6%
Bet on a horse race	5%
Bet on a boxing match	4%
Gambled on the Internet	2%
	1%
Any other kind of gambling	13%

SOURCE: Jeffrey M. Jones, "Participation in Forms of Gambling over the Past12 Months," in *Gambling a Common Activity for Americans,* The Gallup Organization, March 24, 2004, http://www.gallup.com/content/default.aspx?ci=11098 (accessed September 28, 2004). Copyright © 2004 by The Gallup Organization. Reproduced by permission of The Gallup Organization.

making less than $30,000 per year reported gambling during the previous twelve months, compared to greater than 70% of those making in excess of $50,000 per year.

Gambling participation rates also varied depending on how often the poll respondents attended church. Those who attended church weekly reported far less gambling activity than those who seldom or never attended church. Midwesterners were more active gamblers than those living in other regions of the country. A slightly larger percentage of nonwhite people than white people reported gambling during the previous year. Age differences were minor as poll participants aged fifty to sixty-four were slightly more active in gambling than those of other ages. Republicans reported gambling slightly less than did Democrats or Independents. Moderates reported gambling slightly more than either conservatives or liberals.

Table 2.4 compares gambling participation rates from 2003 with those reported in Gallup polls conducted between 1989 and 1992. The percentage of people who had visited a casino within the previous year increased by 10% from 20% participation in 1989 to 30% in 2003. Video poker was the only other gambling activity to show an increase in participation, from 11% in 1992 to 14% in 2003. All other gambling activities showed decreased levels of participation. In total, Gallup reported that 70% of those asked during the 1989 poll had gambled in some fashion during the previous twelve months.

TABLE 2.4

Percentage of Americans participating in various forms of gambling, December 2003

	1989 Apr 4–9 %	2003 Dec 11–14 %	Change (in percentage points)
Visited casino	20	30	+10
Played video poker	11‡	14	+3
Bet on horse race	9†	4	−5
Bought state lottery ticket	54	49	−5
Bet on boxing match	8	2	−6
Participated in office pool	22‡	15	−7
Played bingo for money	13	5	−8
Bet on college sports	14	6	−8
Bet on pro sports	22	10	−12

†Feb 15–18, 1990
‡Nov 20–22, 1992

SOURCE: Jeffrey M. Jones, "Percentage of Americans Participating in Various Forms of Gambling," in *Gambling a Common Activity for Americans,* The Gallup Organization, March 24, 2004, http://www.gallup.com/content/default.aspx?ci=11098 (accessed September 28, 2004). Copyright © 2004 by The Gallup Organization. Reproduced by permission of The Gallup Organization.

A national survey, "Gambling Participation in the U.S.—Results from a National Survey," conducted by university researchers in 2002 and reported by the *Journal of Gambling Studies* found that 82% of poll participants had gambled during the previous year.

According to the July/August 2002 issue of *Harvard Magazine,* 81% of adults and 85% of college students in the United States have gambled at some point in their lifetimes. The statistics were based on data from the American Gaming Association (AGA) and analysis of previous gambling studies. The AGA reported, in *2004 State of the States: The AGA Survey of Casino Entertainment,* that lottery games were by far the most popular in 2003, followed by casino gambling, and sports betting pools.

SENIOR CITIZENS. Gallup's December 2003 poll showed that 61% of people aged sixty-five and older reported gambling during the previous year. According to the July/August 2002 issue of *Harvard Magazine,* the percentage of people aged sixty-five and up who have ever gambled increased from 35% in 1975 to 80% in 1999.

In September 2002 the *Wall Street Journal* examined the increasing incidence of gambling problems among older Americans in an article titled "Gambling's Growth." Senior citizens comprise an increasing portion of telephone calls made to problem gambling groups. The California Council on Problem Gambling reports that older adults made up 15% of the callers to their helpline during 2001, up from 12% for the period June 1998 through December 2000. A similar increase occurred in New Jersey, where seniors accounted for 15% of calls in 2001, up from 9% in 2000. The percentages were even higher in Arizona (23%) and Connecticut (32%).

Counselors believe that older adults are experiencing more gambling problems because they increasingly have more disposable income and free time, they live longer and healthier lives, and they have many more gambling options than in years past.

Seniors are very attracted to casino gambling because casinos are warm and friendly places that make them feel safe and welcome. A clinical psychologist in Nebraska reports that one local casino offers a mail-order prescription service with deeply discounted prices, a program extremely appealing to seniors. Casinos also correspond with their patrons, sending them birthday cards and friendly postcards. These little gestures are especially pleasing to older people, who may feel left out of modern society.

Researchers report that women comprise an increasingly larger percentage of the seniors who seek help with gambling problems. This is particularly worrisome because women tend to live longer than men and therefore have a longer period in which to get into financial trouble. In general, seniors with gambling problems tend to reach a financial breaking point faster than younger adults and have fewer options for recouping their money. For example, some are unable to work. The seniors most vulnerable to gambling problems are those who feel isolated, bored, and lonely, particularly the ones suffering from depression or anxiety disorders.

Teenagers and College Students

The minimum legal age for placing a bet at most U.S. gambling activities ranges from eighteen to twenty-one, depending on the state and the activity. The vast majority of states prohibit the sale of lottery tickets to people under eighteen years of age. However, giving lottery tickets as gifts to minors is not generally prohibited. A handful of states limit lottery ticket sales to those twenty-one or older. Pari-mutuel wagering in most states is limited to those aged eighteen and up. One exception is Illinois, which allows seventeen-year-olds to wager at horse races. All commercial casinos have a minimum gambling age of twenty-one as set by state law. Tribal casinos are allowed to set their own minimum gambling age as long as it is at least eighteen. The minimum age to participate in charitable gambling activities, such as bingo games, is eighteen in most states. However, a few states allow people as young as sixteen to wager in charity gambling events.

The January 23, 2002, issue of *The WAGER (The Weekly Addiction Gambling Education Report* of the Harvard Medical School), includes "If You Do Not Gamble, Check This Box," a study on gambling perception and behavior. Researchers asked 449 college students whether they gambled or not, then asked about their participation in various gambling activities. The results are shown in Figure 2.2.

Surprisingly, nearly 150 of the self-characterized nongamblers had purchased scratch tickets at least once.

Gambling: What's at Stake?

Supply and Demand: Who Offers Gambling? Who Gambles?   **21**

FIGURE 2.2

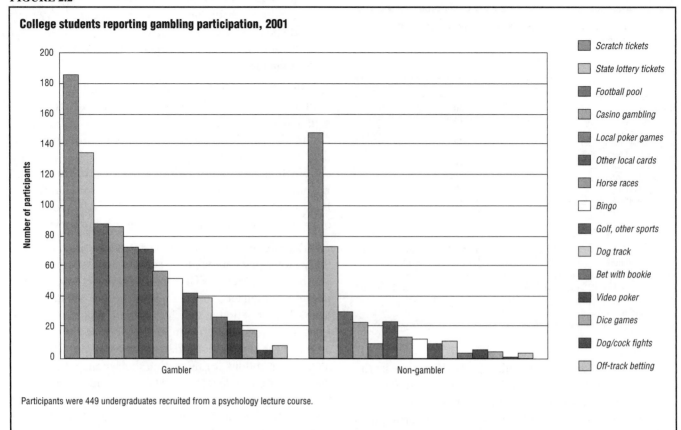

College students reporting gambling participation, 2001

Participants were 449 undergraduates recruited from a psychology lecture course.

SOURCE: "Figure 1: Ever Participated in Gambling Activity at Least Once," in "If You Do Not Gamble, Check This Box," in *The Wager,* vol. 7, no. 4, January 23, 2002, http://www.thewager.org/Backindex/vol7pdf/wager74.pdf (accessed September 2, 2004). Data from Mark Lange, "If You Do Not Gamble, Check This Box," in "Perceptions of Gambling Behavior," *Journal of Gambling Studies,*" vol. 17, no. 30, Kluwer Academic Publishers, Dordrecht, The Netherlands, Fall 2001. With kind permission of Springer Science and Business Media.

Scratch tickets are instant-game tickets offered by most state lotteries. Seventy-four students who considered themselves nongamblers had bought traditional lottery tickets. Smaller numbers had participated in other activities that researchers considered gambling, like casino games and sports betting.

The researchers were puzzled by the responses of the self-proclaimed nongamblers. They concluded that the definition of gambling among young people might be different from that of adults. This is particularly troubling to psychologists and counselors who work with young people because it implies that a young person could have a gambling problem and not even realize it because the person does not consider the activity to be gambling.

The minimum gambling age is twenty-one in Nevada. In 2001 Gemini Research, Ltd., of Northampton, Massachusetts, performed a research study on adolescent gambling for the Nevada Department of Human Resources and published its results in *Gambling and Problem Gambling among Adolescents in Nevada* (March 22, 2002). The report reviews previous studies about adolescent gambling conducted in the United States during the 1980s and 1990s.

The percentage of adolescents who gambled during the previous twelve-month period ranged from 20% to 86% in studies performed between 1984 and 1988, with a median percentage of 45%. A much higher median percentage (66%) is indicated by studies conducted between 1989 and 1999. These studies, conducted between March and May 2001, showed a range of 52% to 71%. These data indicate that adolescent gambling increased significantly as gambling opportunities have expanded in the United States.

For Gemini's 2001 study, a sample group of 1,004 teenagers aged thirteen to seventeen living in the state were interviewed about their gambling habits. Results were compared to studies performed during the late 1990s in four other states: New York, Georgia, Texas, and Washington. As shown in Table 2.5 Georgia had the highest percentage of nongamblers (38.1%), while New York had the highest percentage of weekly gamblers (15.5%). Demographic data from the study indicate that the adolescent gambler is most likely to be a white male aged fifteen who receives an allowance and lives in a household including two adults.

Previous research, also cited in the Gemini study, has shown that the most popular gambling activities for North American adolescents are:

TABLE 2.5

Gambling participation among adolescents in New York, Georgia, Texas, Washington, and Nevada, 1995–2001

	New York %	Georgia %	Texas %	Washington %	Nevada %
	1997 (1103)	1995 (1007)	1995 (3079)	1999 (1000)	2001 (1004)
Non-gamblers	14.0	38.1	19.4	22.4	33.5
Infrequent	10.7	9.8	15.7	12.5	17.8
Past year	59.8	39.9	54.9	57.4	41.8
Weekly	15.5	12.2	10.0	7.7	6.9

SOURCE: Rachel A. Volberg, "Table 23: Gambling Participation among Adolescents in Five States," in *Gambling and Problem Gambling among Adolescents in Nevada,* Nevada Department of Human Resources, March 22, 2002

- Cards, dice, and board games played with family and friends

- Games of personal skill played with friends

- Sporting events

- Bingo

Nevada Adult Residents

In 2000 and 2001 Gemini Research performed a study of gambling in Nevada for the Nevada Department of Human Resources and published its results in *Gambling and Problem Gambling in Nevada* (March 22, 2002). Telephone interviews were conducted with 2,217 adult residents of the state. Many results are compared to those obtained from previous nationwide studies, particularly the 1998 study conducted by the National Opinion Research Center (NORC) for the National Gambling Impact Study Commission (NGISC).

The survey found that Nevada residents are much more likely to have engaged in casino and machine gambling during the previous twelve-month period than the average American. Nevadans are less likely to engage in many other types of gambling, including unlicensed (illegal) forms of gambling. Forty percent of Nevadan respondents gamble regularly, either monthly (21%) or weekly (19%). Fewer than one-third of the respondents (29%) had gambled in the past year but not regularly, while 14% had never gambled. The remaining 17% had gambled at least once in their lifetimes but had not gambled in the previous year.

The most common reasons given for gambling are as follows:

- Entertainment or fun (72%)

- Win money (67%)

- Socialize (37%)

- Excitement or challenge (35%)

Men were somewhat more likely than women to gamble for the excitement or challenge. Blacks were much less likely than all other ethnic groups to choose entertainment or socializing as a reason for gambling—winning money was the most important reason given.

The reasons given by nongamblers for not gambling also differed along ethnic lines. Approximately 70% of white and black nongamblers did not gamble for financial reasons. Only 44% of Hispanic nongamblers listed financial reasons. Moral reasons for not gambling were also named by one-third to one-half of the nongamblers.

Problem Gamblers

Problem gambling is a broad term that covers all gambling behaviors that are harmful to people in some way—financially, emotionally, socially, and/or legally. The harmful effects of problem gambling include the following:

- Financial difficulties, such as unpaid bills, loss of employment, large debts, and even bankruptcy

- Emotional problems, such as depression, anxiety, addictions, and suicidal tendencies

- Social problems, as evidenced by strained or broken relationships with one's spouse, family, friends, and coworkers

- Legal problems related to neglect of children or commission of criminal acts to obtain money

In the Gallup Organization's December 2003 poll regarding gambling activities the pollsters found that 6% of those asked said gambling had been a source of problems for their families. (See Table 2.6.) This value is up slightly from the percentages reported in 1989, 1992, and 1996, but down slightly from the percentage reported in 1999. The 2003 survey showed a marked difference in answers by age. Only 4% of those aged fifty and up said gambling had been a problem for their family, compared with 12% of adults aged eighteen to twenty-nine years. In comparison, a July 2003 Gallup poll found that 31% of all adults reported that alcohol had been a source of problems for their families.

In general, scientists characterize gambling behavior by the level of harm that it causes. People who experience no harmful effects are called nonproblem gamblers, or social, casual, or recreational gamblers. People who gamble regularly and may be prone to a gambling problem are called at-risk gamblers. Those who experience minor to moderate harm from their gambling behavior are called problem gamblers. Those who suffer severe harm from their gambling behavior are called pathological gamblers.

Scientists use a screening process to determine which category fits a particular gambler. One of the most common is the South Oaks Gambling Screen (SOGS), a sixteen-item

Gambling: What's at Stake?

Supply and Demand: Who Offers Gambling? Who Gambles?   **23**

TABLE 2.6

Poll results regarding family problems related to gambling, selected years, 1989–2003

HAS GAMBLING EVER BEEN A SOURCE OF PROBLEMS WITHIN YOUR FAMILY?

	Yes %	No %	No opinion %
2003 Dec 11–14	6	94	*
1999 Apr 30–May 23	9	91	*
1996 Jun 27–30	5	95	*
1992 Nov 20–2	5	94	1
1989 Apr 4–9	4	96	*

*Less than 0.5%

SOURCE: Jeffrey M. Jones, "Has gambling ever been a source for problems within your family?" in *Gambling a Common Activity for Americans,* The Gallup Organization, March 24, 2004, http://www.gallup.com/content/default.aspx?ci=11098 (accessed August 14, 2004). Copyright © 2004 by The Gallup Organization. Reproduced by permission of The Gallup Organization.

questionnaire developed in the 1980s by Dr. Henry Lesieur and Dr. Sheila Blume. A detailed description of SOGS and its development was first given in the article "SOGS: A New Instrument for the Identification of Pathological Gamblers," published in the *American Journal of Psychiatry* in September 1987. The authors used information from 1,616 subjects to develop the SOGS screen, including patients with substance abuse and pathological gambling problems, members of Gamblers Anonymous, university students, and hospital employees.

One version of the SOGS questionnaire is shown in Table 2.7. The scoring system is shown in Table 2.8. Of course, since the SOGS screen is a questionnaire filled out by potential problem gamblers themselves, the score depends entirely on the truthfulness of the person answering the questions.

Gamblers Anonymous (GA) is a self-help organization for gamblers that was begun in 1957. GA uses the term "compulsive gambling" to describe the illness that problem gamblers experience. On its Web site (www.gamblersanonymous.org), the organization lists the following general characteristics of compulsive gamblers:

- An "inability and unwillingness to accept reality"
- A belief that they have a "system" that will eventually pay off
- A lot of time spent daydreaming about what they will do when they finally make a big win
- Feelings of emotional insecurity when they are not gambling
- Immaturity and a desire to escape from responsibility
- Wanting all the good things in life without expending much effort for them
- Desire to be a "big shot" in the eyes of other people

TABLE 2.7

South Oaks Gambling Screen (SOGS)

1. Please indicate which of the following types of gambling you have done in your lifetime. For each type, mark one answer: "**Not at All**," "**Less than Once a Week**", or "**Once a Week or More**."

Please Check one answer for each statement:	NOT AT ALL	Less than once a week	Once a week or more
a. Played cards for money.	___	___	___
b. Bet on horses, dogs, or other animals (at OTB, the track, or with a bookie).	___	___	___
c. Bet on sports (parlay cards, with bookie, at Jai Alai).	___	___	___
d. Played dice games, including craps, over and under or other dice games.	___	___	___
e. Went to casinos (legal or otherwise).	___	___	___
f. Played the numbers or bet on lotteries.	___	___	___
g. Played bingo.	___	___	___
h. Played the stock and/or commodities market.	___	___	___
i. Played slot machines, poker machines, or other gambling machines.	___	___	___
j. Bowled, shot pool, played golf, or some other game of skill for money.	___	___	___
k. Played pull tabs or "paper" games other than lotteries.	___	___	___
l. Some form of gambling not listed above (please specify):	___	___	___

2. What is the largest amount of money you have ever gambled with on any one-day?
___ Never Gambled   ___ More than $100.00 up to $1,000
___ $1.00 or less   ___ More than $1,000 up to $10,000
___ More than $1.00 up to $10.00   ___ More than $10,000
___ More than $10.00 up to $100.00

3. Check which of the following people in your life has (or had) a gambling problem.
___ Father   ___ Mother
___ Brother/Sister   ___ My spouse/partner
___ My child(ren)   ___ Another relative
___ A Friend or someone important in my life

4. When you gamble, how often do you go back another day to win back money you have lost?
___ Never   ___ Most of the time
___ Some of the time   ___ Every time that I lose
(less than half of time I lose).

5. Have you ever claimed to be winning money gambling, but weren't really? In fact you lost?
___ Never
___ Yes, less than half the time I lost
___ Yes, most of the time

6. Do you feel you have ever had a problem with betting or money gambling?
___ No   ___ Yes   ___ Yes, in the past, but not now.

7. Did you ever gamble more than you intended to?
___ Yes   ___ No

8. Have people criticized your betting or told you that you had a problem, regardless of whether or not you thought it was true?
___ Yes   ___ No

9. Have you ever felt guilty about the way you gamble, or what happens when you gamble?
___ Yes   ___ No

10. Have you ever felt like you would like to stop betting money on gambling, but did not think that you could?
___ Yes   ___ No

11. Have you ever hidden betting slips, lottery tickets, gambling money, IOUs, or other signs of betting or gambling from your spouse, children or other important people in your life?
___ Yes   ___ No

12. Have you ever argued with people you live with over how you handle money?
___ Yes   ___ No

13. (If you answered "yes": to question 12) Have money arguments ever centered on your gambling?
___ Yes   ___ No

14. Have you ever borrowed from someone and not paid them back as a result of your gambling?
___ Yes   ___ No

15. Have you ever lost time from work (or school) due to betting money or gambling?
___ Yes   ___ No

TABLE 2.7

South Oaks Gambling Screen (SOGS) [CONTINUED]

16. If you borrowed money to gamble or to pay gambling debts, who or where did you borrow from (check "Yes" or "No" for each):

a. From household money   _____ Yes   _____ No
b. From your spouse/partner   _____ Yes   _____ No
c. From relatives or in-laws   _____ Yes   _____ No
d. From banks, loan companies, or credit unions   _____ Yes   _____ No
e. From credit cards   _____ Yes   _____ No
f. From loan sharks   _____ Yes   _____ No
g. You cashed in stocks, bonds or other securities   _____ Yes   _____ No
h. You sold personal or family property   _____ Yes   _____ No
i. You borrowed on your checking accounts (passed bad checks)   _____ Yes   _____ No
j. You have (had) a credit line with a bookie   _____ Yes   _____ No
k. You have (had) a credit line with a casino   _____ Yes   _____ No

The SOGS may be reproduced as long as the language is used as printed and the scored items are not revised without permission of the authors.

SOURCE: Henry R. Lesieur and Shelia B. Blume, "The South Oaks Gambling Screen (the SOGS): A New Instrument for the Identification of Pathological Gamblers," *American Journal of Psychiatry,* vol. 144, 1987, pp. 1184–88, and Henry R. Lesieur and Sheila B. Blume, "Revising the South Oaks Gambling Screen in Different Settings," *Journal of Gambling Studies,* vol. 9, 1993, pp. 213–23.

GA has a list of twenty questions that it suggests gamblers answer to determine if they have a compulsive gambling problem. The questions are presented in Table 2.9. GA indicates that compulsive gamblers are likely to answer yes to at least seven of these questions.

PATHOLOGICAL GAMBLERS. Pathological gamblers are the most seriously troubled problem gamblers. In general, pathological gambling is a disorder characterized by irrational thinking in which people continuously (or periodically) lose control over their gambling behavior. Pathological gamblers become preoccupied with gambling, constantly thinking about their next bet or how to raise more money with which they can gamble. This behavior continues even if the gambler suffers adverse consequences, such as financial difficulties or strained relationships with family and friends. The consequences of pathological gambling can be quite severe, both to gamblers and to those around them.

In 1975 the first nationwide prevalence study on gambling in the United States was conducted by the University of Michigan Survey Research Center for the Commission on the Review of the National Policy Toward Gambling. Responses were obtained from 1,736 adults. As there was no scientific basis for determining whether or not someone was a problem gambler at that time, researchers used a questionnaire based on GA's twenty questions. Results indicated that 0.77% of Americans were "probable compulsive gamblers" and another 2.33% were "potential compulsive gamblers." The percentages for Nevada residents were approximately three times higher than for the national sample.

The American Psychiatric Association (APA) first officially recognized pathological gambling as a mental

TABLE 2.8

South Oaks Gambling Screen (SOGS) score sheet

Scores on the SOGS are determined by scoring one point for each question that shows the "at risk" response indicated and adding the total points.

Question 1 Not counted		
Question 2 Not counted		
Question 3 Not counted		
Question 4	_____	Most of the time I lose, or Yes, every time I lose
Question 5	_____	Yes, less than half the time I lose or Yes, most of the time
Question 6	_____	Yes, in the past but not now or Yes
Question 7	_____	Yes
Question 8	_____	Yes
Question 9	_____	Yes
Question 10	_____	Yes
Question 11	_____	Yes
Question 12 Not counted		
Question 13	_____	Yes
Question 14	_____	Yes
Question 15	_____	Yes
Question 16a	_____	Yes
Question 16b	_____	Yes
Question 16c	_____	Yes
Question 16d	_____	Yes
Question 16e	_____	Yes
Question 16f	_____	Yes
Question 16g	_____	Yes
Question 16h	_____	Yes
Question 16i	_____	Yes
Question 16j Not counted		
Question 16k Not counted		

TOTAL: _____
(maximum score = 20)

Interpreting the score:
0 No problem with gambling
3–4 Some have used this score to indicate problem gambling
5 or more Probable pathological gambler

SOURCE: Henry R. Lesieur and Shelia B. Blume, "The South Oaks Gambling Screen (the SOGS): A New Instrument for the Identification of Pathological Gamblers," *American Journal of Psychiatry,* vol. 144, 1987, pp. 1184–88, and Henry R. Lesieur and Sheila B. Blume, "Revising the South Oaks Gambling Screen in Different Settings," *Journal of Gambling Studies,* vol. 9, 1993, pp. 213–23

health disorder in 1980 and listed it in their publication *Diagnostic and Statistical Manual of Mental Disorders* (DSM). The latest edition of the manual, published in 2000, is known as DSM-IV-TR. Table 2.10 shows the diagnostic criteria used by the APA in DSM-IV to define pathological gambling. The SOGS questionnaire was designed to correlate with the DSM criteria for pathological gambling.

In July 1984 Dr. Henry Lesieur and Dr. Robert L. Custer published "Pathological Gambling: Roots, Phases, and Treatment" in the *Annals of the American Academy of Political and Social Science.* The researchers reported that pathological gamblers have tendencies to be hyperactive and to be able to tolerate high levels of stress.

In 1996 the National Center for Responsible Gaming provided a grant to researchers at the Harvard Medical School to perform another large-scale study of the prevalence of problem gambling. The results were published in

Gambling: What's at Stake?

Supply and Demand: Who Offers Gambling? Who Gambles?   **25**

TABLE 2.9

Twenty questions that may help indicate that an individual is a compulsive gambler

Gamblers Anonymous offers the following questions to anyone who may have a gambling problem. These questions are provided to help the individual decide if he or she is a compulsive gambler and wants to stop gambling.

1. Did you ever lose time from work or school due to gambling?
2. Has gambling ever made your home life unhappy?
3. Did gambling affect your reputation?
4. Have you ever felt remorse after gambling?
5. Did you ever gamble to get money with which to pay debts or otherwise solve financial difficulties?
6. Did gambling cause a decrease in your ambition or efficiency?
7. After losing did you feel you must return as soon as possible and win back your losses?
8. After a win did you have a strong urge to return and win more?
9. Did you often gamble until your last dollar was gone?
10. Did you ever borrow to finance your gambling?
11. Have you ever sold anything to finance gambling?
12. Were you reluctant to use "gambling money" for normal expenditures?
13. Did gambling make you careless of the welfare of yourself or your family?
14. Did you ever gamble longer than you had planned?
15. Have you ever gambled to escape worry or trouble?
16. Have you ever committed, or considered committing, an illegal act to finance gambling?
17. Did gambling cause you to have difficulty in sleeping?
18. Do arguments, disappointments or frustrations create within you an urge to gamble?
19. Did you ever have an urge to celebrate any good fortune by a few hours of gambling?
20. Have you ever considered self destruction or suicide as a result of your gambling?

Most compulsive gamblers will answer yes to at least seven of these questions.

SOURCE: "Twenty Questions," in *Gamblers Anonymous,* Gamblers Anonymous, 2002, http://www.gamblersanonymous.org/20questions.html (accessed August 28, 2004)

Estimating the Prevalence of Disordered Gambling in the U.S. and Canada: A Meta-Analysis (1997). A meta-analysis is an analysis of previously collected data. The researchers examined hundreds of scientific studies on gambling in the United States and Canada. They developed a new ranking system to define levels of problem gambling:

• Level 0—Nongamblers

• Level 1—Social gamblers with no gambling problems

• Level 2—Problem gamblers

• Level 3—Pathological gamblers

The lifetime prevalence rate of Level 3 (pathological) gambling in the adult North American population was calculated to be 1.6%.

In 1999 *Pathological Gambling: A Critical Review* was published by National Academies Press. The book identified and analyzed all available scientific research studies dealing with pathological and problem gambling. The studies were reviewed by dozens of researchers on behalf of the National Research Council, an organization administered by the National Academy of Sciences, the National Academy of Engineering, and the Institute of Medicine. The effort was supported by the NGISC. The

book estimates that 1.5% of U.S. adults are pathological gamblers at some point in their lives. In any given year, 0.9% of U.S. adults (approximately 1.8 million people) and 1.1 million adolescents aged twelve to eighteen are pathological gamblers. The following general conclusions are drawn:

• Men are more likely than women to be pathological gamblers.

• Pathological gambling often occurs concurrently with other behavioral problems, such as drug and alcohol abuse and mood and personality disorders.

• The earlier in life a person starts to gamble, the more likely he or she is to become a pathological gambler.

• Pathological gamblers are more likely than those without a gambling problem to have pathological gamblers as parents.

• Pathological gamblers who seek treatment generally get better.

The researchers complained that the research literature on pathological gambling available at that time was of limited scientific value. For example, they were unable to determine whether any particular treatment technique was more effective than most others or even if some pathological gamblers are able to recover on their own. They were also unable to determine whether particular groups, such as the elderly and the poor, have disproportionately high rates of pathological gambling. They recommended that the Centers for Disease Control and Prevention (CDC) and the National Institutes of Health (NIH) monitor pathological gambling as part of their annual surveys on the nation's health status.

Another nationwide study published during 1999 was titled *Gambling Impact and Behavior Study: Report to the National Gambling Impact Study Commission.* This study was conducted by the NORC at the University of Chicago. The study found the lifetime prevalence rate for pathological adult gamblers to be 0.9%. The past-year prevalence rate was 0.6%.

There have also been statewide studies of the prevalence of problem gambling. The report *Gambling and Problem Gambling in Nevada* (March 22, 2002) summarized the findings of the most recent studies for various states in Figure 2.3. The prevalence of problem gambling in Nevada in 2000 was 6.4%, the largest of any state. Nevada also had the highest percentage of probable pathological gamblers—3.5%. Despite the widespread availability of casinos in Nevada, the type of gambling with the highest prevalence of problem gamblers is not casino gambling (at 8.7%) but card room gambling (at 33.7%). This is followed by horse/dog racing (18.8%),

TABLE 2.10

Diagnostic criteria for pathological gambling

Persistent and recurrent maladaptive gambling behavior as indicated by five (or more) of the following:	
Preoccupation	Preoccupied with gambling (e.g. preoccupied with reliving past gambling experiences, handicapping or planning the next venture, or thinking of ways to get money with which to gamble)
Tolerance	Needs to gamble with increasing amounts of money in order to achieve the desired excitement
Withdrawal	Restlessness or irritability when attempting to cut down or stop gambling
Escape	Gambling as a way of escaping from problems or relieving dysphoric mood (e.g. feelings of helplessness, guilt, anxiety or depression)
Chasing losses	After losing money gambling, often return another day in order to get even ("chasing one's losses")
Lying	Lies to family members, therapists or others to conceal the extent of involvement with gambling
Loss of control	Made repeated unsuccessful efforts to control, cut back or stop gambling
Illegal acts	Committed illegal acts, such as forgery, fraud, theft or embezzlement, in order to finance gambling
Risked significant relationship	Jeopardized or lost a significant relationship, job, educational or career opportunity because of gambling
Bailout	Reliance on others to provide money to relieve a desperate financial situation caused by gambling

The gambling behavior is not better accounted for by a Manic Episode.

SOURCE: Rachel A. Volberg, "Table 1: Diagnostic Criteria for Pathological Gambling," in *Gambling and Problem Gambling in Nevada,* Nevada Department of Human Resources, March 22, 2002

FIGURE 2.3

Comparing prevalence rates of problem gambling in selected states, 1996–2000

SOURCE: Rachel A. Volberg, "Figure 2: Comparing Prevalence Rates in the United States," in *Gambling and Problem Gambling in Nevada,* Nevada Department of Human Resources, March 22, 2002

private gambling (17.2%), and gambling on machines not located at casinos (12.0%).

Gemini Research, Ltd., examined the prevalence of problem gambling among teenagers in *Gambling and Problem Gambling among Adolescents in Nevada.* Table 2.11 shows the percentage of nonproblem, at-risk, and problem gamblers identified among adolescent gamblers in five states from 1995 to 2000. Georgia had the highest percentage of problem adolescent gamblers (2.8%). The percentages were determined using SOGS-RA, a version of the SOGS questionnaire specially developed for adolescents.

TREATMENT ORGANIZATIONS. A variety of treatment methods are available to problem gamblers through organizations and private counselors. Major organizations devoted solely to problem gambling include GA, the National Council on Problem Gambling, and the Institute for Problem Gambling.

GA is a self-help organization open to all people who want to stop gambling. Meetings are held throughout the United States at which gamblers can remain anonymous by using their first names only. At the meetings, gamblers talk about their past experiences and the problems in their lives caused by gambling. The group method offers compulsive gamblers moral support and an accepting environment in which they can talk about their problems openly and honestly. Gambling is not treated as a vice but as a progressive illness.

GA contends that compulsive gamblers are sick people who can recover if they follow to the best of their ability the organization's 12-step recovery program. (See Table 2.12.) These steps are similar to those employed by other support groups like Alcoholics Anonymous. Although the steps have a spiritual aspect, GA is not affil-

Gambling: What's at Stake?

Supply and Demand: Who Offers Gambling? Who Gambles? **27**

TABLE 2.11

Problem gambling among adolescents in New York, Georgia, Texas, Washington, and Nevada, 1995–2001

	New York %	Georgia %	Texas %	Washington %	Nevada %
	(1103)	(1007)	(3079)	(1000)	(1004)
Non-problem	83.6	86.8	88.2	91.6	91.9
At risk	14.0	10.4	9.9	7.5	6.2
Problem	2.4	2.8	2.3	0.9	1.9

SOURCE: Rachel A. Volberg, "Table 24: Problem Gambling among Adolescents in Five States," in *Gambling and Problem Gambling among Adolescents in Nevada,* Nevada Department of Human Resources, March 22, 2002

iated with any religious group or institution, and the organization is funded by donations. GA believes that a recovering compulsive gambler cannot gamble at all without succumbing to the gambling compulsion. In other words, GA advocates a "cold turkey" approach to quitting gambling rather than a gradual step-down.

The National Council on Problem Gambling (NCPG) is a nonprofit organization founded in 1972 to increase public awareness about pathological gambling and to encourage development of educational, research, and treatment programs. NCPG was known as the Council on Compulsive Gambling from 1972 to 1976 and as the National Council on Compulsive Gambling from 1976 to 1989.

NCPG sponsors the *Journal of Gambling Studies,* an academic journal dedicated to scientific research on problem gambling. The NCPG has 34 state affiliate chapters and operates a national 24-hour confidential hotline (1-800-522-4700) that can refer people for further help. The hotline received more than 145,000 calls during 2003.

NCPG also operates the National Certified Gambling Counselor program, a certification program for professional counselors who treat problem gamblers. On its Web site (www.ncpgambling.org), NCPG offers an extensive database of more than two hundred counselors around the United States who have completed its certification program. Other organizations that certify gambling counselors include the American Compulsive Gambling Certification Board and the American Academy of Health Care Providers in the Addictive Disorders.

The Institute for Problem Gambling (IPG) is a not-for-profit organization founded in 1997 that primarily assists government leaders in dealing with problem gamblers. IPG provides the resource of scientific information on the study, prevention, and treatment of problem gambling. It also collects and develops public service announcements, educational videos, and instruction manuals useful to treatment programs.

ASPECTS OF TREATMENT. Effective treatment of a problem gambler requires recognition of the problem by

TABLE 2.12

Gamblers Anonymous 12-step program of recovery

1. We admitted we were powerless over gambling - that our lives had become unmanageable.
2. Came to believe that a Power greater than ourselves could restore us to a normal way of thinking and living.
3. Made a decision to turn our will and our lives over to the care of this Power of our own understanding.
4. Made a searching and fearless moral and financial inventory of ourselves.
5. Admitted to ourselves and to another human being the exact nature of our wrongs.
6. Were entirely ready to have these defects of character removed.
7. Humbly asked God (of our understanding) to remove our shortcomings.
8. Made a list of all persons we had harmed and became willing to make amends to them all.
9. Make direct amends to such people wherever possible, except when to do so would injure them or others.
10. Continued to take personal inventory and when we were wrong, promptly admitted it.
11. Sought through prayer and meditation to improve our conscious contact with God as we understood Him, praying only for knowledge of His will for us and the power to carry that out.
12. Having made an effort to practice these principles in all our affairs, we tried to carry this message to other compulsive gamblers.

SOURCE: "The Recovery Program," *Gamblers Anonymous,* Gamblers Anonymous, 2002, http://www.gamblersanonymous.org/recovery.html (accessed August 28, 2004)

the gambler. Most problem gamblers deny that they even have a gambling problem. Those who enter treatment often do so under pressure from a spouse or family member and are driven by their fear of losing that relationship. The most common treatment method used by professional counselors in group or individual counseling sessions is called cognitive behavior therapy. The cognitive portion of the therapy focuses attention on the person's thoughts, beliefs, and assumptions about gambling. The primary goal is recognizing and changing faulty thinking patterns. Behavior therapy focuses on changing harmful behaviors.

The major components of cognitive behavior therapy for problem gambling include:

• Acknowledgment that gambling is causing problems

• Indication that a change in circumstances is desired

• Examination of decision-making processes related to gambling

• Discussion of gambling misconceptions

• Identification of any behavior triggers

• Development of coping strategies

Most programs favor complete abstinence from gambling as the only sure method to prevent relapses.

One thing that makes the treatment of pathological gambling difficult is the likelihood that it is accompanied by other psychological problems. In 1987 Dr. Henry Lesieur and Dr. Sheila Blume, the developers of SOGS, reported that existing studies at that time showed clear

28 Supply and Demand: Who Offers Gambling? Who Gambles?

Gambling: What's at Stake?

connections between pathological gambling and substance abuse. These researchers also found a much higher rate of pathological gambling among psychiatric hospital patients and prison inmates than among the general population. A 1995 article in *Annals of Clinical Psychiatry* reported a significantly higher rate of impulse control disorders and attention deficit disorders among pathological gamblers than among a control group. One of the most prevalent impulse control disorders among pathological gamblers was compulsive sexual behavior.

The National Research Council reported to the U.S. Senate in 2001 that "gambling is highly associated with other behavioral disorders, particularly depression, alcoholism, and drug addiction." These other disorders accelerate and intensify gambling-related problems like financial crises, strained relationships with family and friends, problems at work, and criminal activities to repay gambling debts.

THE GAMBLER'S FALLACY. Scientific literature about problem gamblers often mentions the gambler's fallacy. A fallacy is a false or mistaken idea. The gambler's fallacy is the mistaken belief that a string of losses makes it more likely that the next bet will be a winner. For example, the gambler's fallacy says that if a coin is tossed and comes up heads five times, the chances are extremely good that the sixth toss will come up tails. This is not so. The probability of each individual coin toss coming up heads or tails is 50-50. The long-run probability says that over many coin tosses the number of heads and tails will come out even. The proportion of heads to tails will approach 50-50 the more times the coin is tossed, but it may take many thousands of tosses. Ignorance about long-run probability causes many gamblers to make poor betting decisions.

In the March 22, 2002, issue of *Science,* researchers at the University of Michigan published a study on the role of the brain in processing win and loss information during gambling. Twelve subjects (six men and six women) aged nineteen to thirty performed 768 trials of a gambling game while their brain activity was monitored with an electroencephalogram (EEG).

During each game, two boxes appeared on a computer screen, one marked 5 cents and the other 25 cents. The player had to choose one of the boxes. After a short delay, each box would turn green or red. If the player's chosen box turned green, the player won the amount listed in the box. Choosing a box that turned red resulted in a loss of the amount listed in the box. Sometimes both boxes turned green or both turned red.

The researchers found that the medial frontal cortex of the brain responded whether the choice was a win or a loss, as evidenced by a dip in the EEG tracing. However, the dip was larger after a loss. Researchers suspect that the brain shows greater activity when it realizes that an emotionally painful error has been made. The dip became even more pronounced after subsequent losses, suggesting that each additional loss is more painful. The researchers noticed that after losses, players were more likely to take bigger risks during the next game. The researchers concluded that earlier gains and losses affect risk-taking behavior and brain activity, suggesting that the two are linked. In other words, the brain's automatic response to a loss may be to make a riskier bet the next time.

Gambling: What's at Stake?

Supply and Demand: Who Offers Gambling? Who Gambles? **29**

CHAPTER 3
CASINOS, PART 1: AN INTRODUCTION

When most people think about gambling, they think about a casino. But what is a casino? According to Merriam Webster's dictionary, a casino is a "building or room used for social amusements, specifically gambling." This definition is much broader than what the average American would consider a casino to be. Most people would picture one of the megaresorts in Las Vegas—a massive hotel and entertainment complex, blazing with neon lights, fun, and games. While this description does fit some casinos, many others are small businesses defined more by the types of gambling they offer than by glitz and glamour.

The federal government classifies all businesses and industries operated within the United States with a six-digit code called the North American Industry Classification System (NAICS) code. The NAICS code for casinos is 713210. The official definition of code 713210 is as follows: "This industry comprises establishments primarily engaged in operating gambling facilities that offer table wagering games along with other gambling activities, such as slot machines and sports betting. These establishments often provide food and beverage services." Casino hotels fall under NAICS code 721120. These are hotels with a casino on the premises. They typically offer a variety of amenities, including dining, entertainment, swimming pools, and conference and convention rooms.

For practical purposes, casino gambling encompasses games of chance and skill played at tables and machines. Therefore, casino games take place in massive resorts, as well as in small card rooms. There are floating casinos operating on boats and barges on various waterways across the country. Casino game machines have been introduced at racetracks to create "racinos." Also, some casino game machines are allowed in truck stops, bars, grocery stores, and other small businesses. By and large, the industry is composed of land- and water-based gambling halls that offer both table games and slot machines.

Like any industry in a capitalist society, casinos are in business to make money. Successful ones rake in billions of dollars each year for the companies, corporations, investors, and Native American tribes that own and operate them. State and local governments also reap casino revenues in the form of taxes, fees, and other payments.

THE HISTORICAL AND CURRENT STATUS OF CASINOS

Gambling was illegal for most of the nation's history. This did not keep casino games from occurring, sometimes openly and with the complicity of local law enforcement, but it did keep them from developing into a legitimate industry. Even after casino gambling was legalized in Nevada in 1931, its growth outside that state was stifled for decades. It was another forty-five years before a second state, New Jersey, decided to allow casino gambling within its borders. Even that move did not open a floodgate of casino gambling.

As Atlantic City, New Jersey, began permitting casinos during the late 1970s, a groundswell of change was about to sweep the country from an unlikely source—Native American tribes. A string of legal victories allowed Native American tribes to convert the small-time bingo halls they had been operating into full-scale casinos. Suddenly, other states wanted to get in on the action. Between 1989 and 1996, another nine states authorized commercial casino gambling—South Dakota, Iowa, Illinois, Mississippi, Colorado, Louisiana, Missouri, Indiana, and Michigan.

Based on estimates from gambling industry trade groups and media reports, U.S. casinos had revenues around $45 billion in 2003. The research firm Christiansen Capital Advisors estimates that commercial casinos and racinos accounted for approximately $29 billion of this total. Tribal casino revenues are estimated by various sources as ranging from $15.9 to $16.7 billion in 2003.

Approximately eight hundred casinos were in operation nationwide in 2003. Just over half (443) were commercial operations, while the remainder were tribal operations.

In 2004 commercial casinos operated in Colorado, Illinois, Indiana, Iowa, Louisiana, Michigan, Mississippi, Missouri, New Jersey, Nevada, and South Dakota, while Native American casinos operated in twenty-eight states. Besides the full-scale casinos, there were racetrack casinos, or "racinos," in eight states—Delaware, Iowa, Louisiana, Maine, New Mexico, New York, Rhode Island, and West Virginia. These facilities are actually racetracks that also offer slot machines.

CASINO ACCEPTABILITY

The American Gaming Association (AGA) is a national trade organization that represents the commercial casino industry. Each year the AGA releases results of surveys conducted for it by Peter D. Hart Research Associates, Inc., and the Luntz Research Companies regarding gambling acceptability in the United States. The latest survey was published in *2004 State of the States: The AGA Survey of Casino Entertainment.* The survey, conducted during February and March 2004, interviewed 1,200 American adults about their opinions regarding casinos. Most of the interviews (59%) were conducted in nongaming states. The results indicate that casino gambling is considered acceptable by a vast majority of Americans. In the 2004 survey 54% of respondents found casino gambling to be perfectly acceptable for anyone. Another 27 percent considered casino gambling to be acceptable for others, but not for themselves. Only 16% of respondents in 2004 felt that casino gambling was not acceptable for anyone.

Casino gambling acceptability (believing that it is acceptable for anyone) was split by gender, with more men than women feeling that casino gambling is acceptable for anyone. However, women surveyed by the AGA were more likely to see casino gambling as acceptable for others, if not themselves. Acceptability was highest among those living in the Northeast and Pacific states (87%) and lowest among those living in southern states (76%). Acceptability of casino gambling for anyone was highest among Americans in upper income brackets. Acceptability was greatest among those who attend church rarely or not at all. Weekly churchgoers were far less accepting of casino gambling with 27% saying it was unacceptable for anyone.

Despite the apparent widespread acceptability that casinos enjoy, they are not welcome everywhere. In February 2002 the New Hampshire and Hawaii legislatures voted to drop all bills that would have legalized casino gambling in their states. In November 2003 Maine voters voted down a referendum that would have allowed development of a tribal casino in the southern part of the state. The casino drive was supported by labor unions, but opposed by the state's governor and many business and civic leaders.

CASINO GAMES

Casinos offer a variety of games, including card games, dice games, domino games, slot machines, and gambling devices (such as the roulette wheel). Some games are banked games, meaning that the house has a stake in the outcome of the game and bets against the players. Banked games include blackjack, craps, keno, roulette, and traditional slot machines. A nonbanked game is one in which the payout and the house cut depend on the number of players or the amount bet, not the outcome of the game. In percentage games, the house collects a share of the amount bet.

For example, in "traditional" poker, players bank their own games. Each player puts money into the pot and competes against the other players to win the pot. A portion of the winning pot is taken by the house. In house-banked games, the players play against the house rather than each other. Another type of house-banked game is one in which there is a posted payout schedule for winning hands rather than a pot.

Gaming machines are by far the most popular type of casino activity. They are simple to operate and offer large payouts for small wagers. The first commercial gambling machines were introduced in 1896. They were called "slot machines" because the gambler inserted a coin into a slot to begin play. Each slot machine consisted of a metal box housing three reels that spun randomly when a handle was pulled. The reels were decorated all around with symbols (usually types of fruit or card markings such as spades, hearts, diamonds, and clubs). Stoppers within the machine slowed each reel to a stop after a time. If the sequence of symbols that appeared across the reels matched a posted winning sequence (usually three of a kind), the player was a winner. Because each reel featured multiple symbols, there were literally thousands of possible outcomes. Because of their ease of play, low odds of winning, and the single handle used to activate them, slot machines came to be known as "one-armed bandits."

Some casinos still offer old-fashioned slot machines, but most gaming machines today are electronic and computer controlled. They are manufactured to strict technical specifications and use a computer programming technique called random number generation. A preprogrammed computer chip inserted into the machines tracks accounting and progressive play information and determines the percentage of payout. The machines are similar to high-tech video games, offering sophisticated graphics and sound. Many electronic slot machines are designed to mimic the look and feel of reel-type machines. Patrons may have a choice of a modern push button or an old-fashioned handle to activate play.

Electronic slot machines offer many different games; poker is one of the most popular. For this reason, the machines are called by a variety of names: electronic gaming devices, video gaming terminals, video gaming devices, video poker machines, or just slots. Slot machines can be played for a variety of denominations—from a penny up to hundreds of dollars. The quarter slot machine is the most popular.

Some casinos have slot machines with progressive jackpots—in other words, the jackpot grows with continued play. Most progressive jackpot machines are connected with one another in a computerized network. Play on any one machine within the group causes the jackpot to increase. On March 21, 2003, a man playing a progressive slot machine at the Excalibur Hotel–Casino in Las Vegas won $38.7 million, the largest slot machine payout in U.S. history.

Odds against Gamblers

Since casinos are businesses, and as such must make money in order to survive, the mathematical odds are always against game players in casino games. For example, according to PBS *Frontline,* a person betting $100 an hour on roulette will lose an average of $5.26 an hour in the long run. The "long run" is an important concept that is often overlooked by gamblers.

For example, most roulette wheels have two colors—red and black. Many people assume that if several consecutive spins have come up red, then black is overdue and will bet on black. However, the law of probabilities says that each spin has an equal chance of being red or black. Only when averaged over the course of many spins will red and black come up equally.

The same effect holds true for slot machines. The Colorado Division of Gaming explains this concept in an undated brochure titled "Understanding How A Slot Machine Works." The brochure notes that a slot machine with a 97% payout would "theoretically" be expected to pay back 97% of all money taken in over the lifetime of the machine, typically seven years. Therefore, a gambler would have to gamble on that machine continuously for seven years to attain a 97% payout.

THE CASINO GAMBLER

In December 2003 the Gallup Organization conducted a poll on gambling activities. The results indicated that 30% of poll participants had visited a casino within the previous twelve months. (See Figure 2.1 in Chapter 2.) As shown in Figure 3.1 casino visitation rates have increased from a low of 20% reported in Gallup's 1989 poll.

Demographics

Harrah's Entertainment, Inc., is one of the major corporations operating commercial casinos in the United

FIGURE 3.1

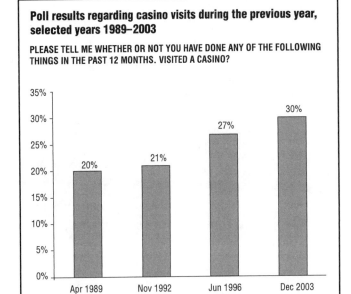

Poll results regarding casino visits during the previous year, selected years 1989–2003

PLEASE TELL ME WHETHER OR NOT YOU HAVE DONE ANY OF THE FOLLOWING THINGS IN THE PAST 12 MONTHS. VISITED A CASINO?

SOURCE: Adapted from Jeffrey M. Jones, "Please tell me whether or not you have done any of the following things in the past 12 months. Visited a Casino?," in *Gambling a Common Activity for Americans,* The Gallup Organization, March 24, 2004, http://www.gallup.com/content/default .aspx?ci=11098 (accessed August 14, 2004). Copyright © 2004 by The Gallup Organization. Reproduced by permission of The Gallup Organization.

States. In September 2003 the company presented results of a survey conducted for it by Roper ASW and NFO WorldGroup, Inc., in *Harrah's Survey 2003: Profile of the American Casino Gambler.* The survey was twofold: 2,000 American adults were interviewed face-to-face, and a survey questionnaire was mailed to a panel of 100,000 adults (of which 64,753 responded).

The survey results indicated that 51.2 million people gambled at a casino in 2002—about 26% of the American adult population age twenty-one and above. The typical casino gambler is a forty-seven-year-old female from a household with an above-average income. According to the 2004 edition of the Harrah's survey, 19% of casino gamblers had a college degree and an additional 8% had education beyond a four-year degree, while 28% had some college credits, and 45% had not attended college. This compares very closely with education levels on a national basis. (See Figure 3.2.)

According to *Harrah's Survey '04: Profile of the American Casino Gambler,* there were 310 million casino visits in 2003, with the average gambler visiting a casino six times during the year. Adults age fifty-one to sixty-five, who often have more free time and available spending money than younger adults, made up the largest group of casino gamblers in 2004—29% of the total. (See Table 3.1.)

The 2004 survey found that 32% of Americans with annual household incomes in excess of $95,000 were

FIGURE 3.2

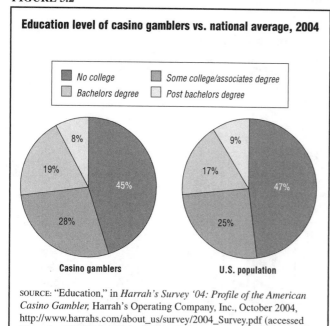

Education level of casino gamblers vs. national average, 2004

| ■ No college | ■ Some college/associates degree |
| ■ Bachelors degree | ■ Post bachelors degree |

Casino gamblers: 45%, 8%, 19%, 28%

U.S. population: 47%, 9%, 17%, 25%

SOURCE: "Education," in *Harrah's Survey '04: Profile of the American Casino Gambler,* Harrah's Operating Company, Inc., October 2004, http://www.harrahs.com/about_us/survey/2004_Survey.pdf (accessed November 15, 2004). Used with permission.

TABLE 3.1

Casino participation rate by age, 2004

21–35 years old	24%
36–50	24%
51–65	29%
66 and above	26%

SOURCE: "Age Differences in Casino Participation," in *Harrah's Survey '04: Profile of the American Casino Gambler,* Harrah's Operating Company, Inc., October 2004, http://www.harrahs.com/about_us/survey/2004_Survey.pdf (accessed November 15, 2004). Used with permission.

TABLE 3.2

Casino participation rate by income, 2004

Under $35,000	20%
$35,001–$55,000	26%
$55,001–$75,000	29%
$75,001–$95,000	30%
Over $95,000	32%

SOURCE: "Income Differences in Casino Participation," in *Harrah's Survey '04: Profile of the American Casino Gambler,* Harrah's Operating Company, Inc., October 2004, http://www.harrahs.com/about_us/survey/2004_Survey.pdf (accessed November 15, 2004). Used with permission.

casino gamblers. (See Table 3.2.) Participation in casino gambling dropped with decreasing income, with only 20% of Americans with incomes less than $35,000 per year participating. Casino gamblers were more likely to be residents of western states (35%) than of the north-central (27%), northeast (27%), or southern (18%) regions of the country. The states whose residents accounted for the largest shares of all casino trips in 2003 were California (19%), Nevada (6%), Illinois (5%), and New York (5%). States accounting for the smallest percentages of all gambling trips were Idaho, New Hampshire, North Dakota, Oklahoma, South Carolina, South Dakota, and West Virginia, each of which accounted for less than 1% of all gambling trips. (See Table 3.3.)

Slot machines were the most popular casino game among casino gamblers in 2004. (See Table 3.4.) A large majority, 75% of casino gamblers, indicated that they play slot machines and other electronic gaming devices. The quarter slot machine was the most popular among this category. Table games, such as blackjack/21, roulette, and craps, were less popular, drawing only 13% of casino gamblers.

In the 2004 Harrah's survey, female casino gamblers showed a marked preference for electronic gaming, with 81% of those surveyed indicating that it was their favorite type of game, compared to 66% for men. Nearly half (48%) of women preferred machines in the $.25 to $.50 per play range. Men were more likely to participate in table games (20%) than were women (8%). Game preference also varied by age, with younger gamblers showing a preference for table games and senior citizens preferring electronic games. (See Table 3.5.)

In March 2002 Gemini Research released a report on the gambling habits of Nevada citizens. *Gambling and Problem Gambling in Nevada* was prepared for the Nevada Department of Human Resources. Respondents who acknowledged participation in casino gambling at least once a month during the previous year were asked which casino games they most liked to play. The largest portion (50%) selected slot machines. Card games, such as blackjack and poker, were the favorite of 30% of respondents. All other games were far less popular. Bingo and keno were the favorite games of only 6% of the gamblers. Table games (such as roulette and craps) and gambling on sporting/racing events each garnered only 5%.

Motivation—How Do Casinos Persuade People to Gamble?

Casino gambling is different from other forms of gambling, such as lotteries and Internet gambling, because of its social aspect. Players are either directly interacting with others, as in craps or poker, or surrounded by other people as they play the slot machines. A casino floor usually contains many tables at which small groups play various games. Excited players shout out encouragement. The atmosphere is boisterous and partylike. Alcoholic drinks are easily accessible and delivered directly to gamblers by waiters and waitresses circulating throughout the casino. Nonalcoholic drinks and snacks are sometimes provided free of charge. The casino atmosphere is designed around noise, light, and excitement.

TABLE 3.3

State profiles of commercial casino participation, 2004

State	2003 U.S. census population (21+)	2003 Casino participation rate	2003 Number of casino gamblers	2003 Average trip frequency (per year)	2003 Number of gambling trips	2003 Share of U.S. gambling trips	Top casino destinations (in alphabetical order)
Alabama	3,225,152	20%	645,000	4.9	3,161,000	1%	Gulf Coast MS Mississippi Indian Tunica, MS
Arizona	3,907,855	41%	1,602,000	5.9	9,453,000	3%	Arizona Indian Las Vegas/ Laughlin
Arkansas	1,956,085	22%	430,000	4.8	2,066,000	1%	Shreveport/ Bossier City, LA Tunica, MS
California	24,394,117	38%	9,270,000	5.7	52,838,000	19%	Las Vegas N. California Indian S. California Indian
Colorado	3,284,975	34%	1,117,000	6	6,701,000	2%	Colorado Las Vegas
Connecticut	2,468,888	40%	988,000	5.7	5,629,000	2%	Atlantic City Connecticut Indian Las Vegas
Delaware	582,288	28%	163,000	9.2	1,500,000	1%	Atlantic City Delaware Las Vegas
Florida	12,572,881	17%	2,137,000	4.2	8,978,000	3%	Cruise ships Florida Indian Gulf Coast, MS Las Vegas
Georgia	6,133,858	13%	797,000	2.6	2,073,000	1%	Cherokee, NC Gulf Coast Las Vegas
Idaho	929,197	25%	232,000	3	697,000	<1%	Idaho Indian Las Vegas Other Nevada
Illinois	8,865,588	28%	2,482,000	5.9	14,646,000	5%	Chicago area Las Vegas St. Louis
Indiana	4,364,554	22%	960,000	4.3	4,129,000	1%	Chicago area Las Vegas Southern IL/IN
Iowa	2,101,363	26%	546,000	6.5	3,551,000	1%	Iowa Indian Other Iowa riverboats Quad Cities/Council Bluffs
Kansas	1,906,819	26%	496,000	5.2	2,578,000	1%	Kansas City, MO Kansas Indian Las Vegas
Kentucky	2,976,801	19%	566,000	4	2,262,000	1%	Southern IL/IN Tunica, MS
Louisiana	3,118,119	39%	1,216,000	8.6	10,458,000	4%	Gulf Coast, MS Lake Charles New Orleans Shreveport/Bossier City
Maine	958,705	12%	115,000	small sample	small sample	small sample	small sample
Maryland	3,878,464	17%	659,000	4.1	2,703,000	1%	Atlantic City Delaware
Massachusetts	4,648,548	31%	1,441,000	4.1	5,908,000	2%	Connecticut Indian Rhode Island
Michigan	7,092,971	32%	2,270,000	5.4	12,257,000	4%	Detroit/Windsor Michigan Indian
Minnesota	3,568,202	34%	1,213,000	6.6	8,007,000	3%	Las Vegas Minnesota Indian
Mississippi	2,002,356	35%	701,000	8.9	6,237,000	2%	Gulf Coast, MS Tunica, MS

According to a poll conducted for the American Gaming Association in 2002 by Peter D. Hart Research Associates, Inc. and the Luntz Research Companies, 92% of survey respondents go casino gambling in the company of their spouses, families, and friends or as part of organized groups. Casino gambling was considered "a fun night out" by 82% of those asked.

TABLE 3.3

State profiles of commercial casino participation, 2004 [CONTINUED]

State	2003 U.S. census population (21+)	2003 Casino participation rate	2003 Number of casino gamblers	2003 Average trip frequency (per year)	2003 Number of gambling trips	2003 Share of U.S. gambling trips	Top casino destinations (in alphabetical order)
Missouri	4,043,835	30%	1,213,000	7.8	9,463,000	3%	Kansas City, MO St. Louis
Montana	654,204	18%	118,000	small sample	small sample	small sample	small sample
Nebraska	1,216,955	35%	426,000	8.1	3,450,000	1%	Quad Cities/Council Bluffs South Dakota Indian
Nevada	1,622,669	40%	649,000	24.3	15,772,000	6%	Las Vegas Reno
New Hampshire	916,239	20%	183,000	4.4	806,000	<1%	Atlantic City Connecticut Indian
New Jersey	6,170,667	36%	2,221,000	5.6	12,440,000	4%	Atlantic City Las Vegas
New Mexico	1,282,715	32%	410,000	7.1	2,914,000	1%	Las Vegas New Mexico Indian
New York	13,708,258	27%	3,701,000	3.9	14,435,000	5%	Atlantic City Connecticut Indian
North Carolina	6,090,949	8%	487,000	2.9	1,413,000	1%	Atlantic City Cherokee, NC
North Dakota	452,569	31%	140,000	4.3	603,000	<1%	Minnesota Indian North Dakota Indian
Ohio	8,121,037	19%	1,543,000	3	4,629,000	2%	Detroit/Windsor Las Vegas Southern IL/IN West Virginia
Oklahoma	2,476,698	16%	396,000	3.4	1,347,000	<1%	Las Vegas Oklahoma Indian Tunica, MS
Oregon	2,552,233	28%	715,000	4.3	3,073,000	1%	Las Vegas Oregon Indian
Pennsylvania	8,983,452	21%	1,887,000	4.1	7,735,000	3%	Atlantic City West Virginia
Rhode Island	764,255	36%	275,000	6.2	1,706,000	1%	Connecticut Indian Rhode Island
South Carolina	2,967,842	8%	237,000	3.1	736,000	<1%	Cherokee, NC Las Vegas
South Dakota	533,666	32%	171,000	5	854,000	<1%	North Dakota Indian South Dakota Indian
Tennessee	4,232,699	20%	847,000	5.1	4,317,000	2%	Cherokee, NC Southern IL/IN Tunica, MS
Texas	14,967,435	21%	3,212,000	3.9	12,526,000	4%	Lake Charles, LA Las Vegas Shreveport/ Bossier City, LA
Utah	1,488,279	27%	402,000	3.6	1,447,000	1%	Las Vegas Other Nevada
Vermont	449,402	9%	40,000	small sample	small sample	small sample	small sample
Virginia	5,291,982	12%	650,000	3	1,949,000	1%	Atlantic City Las Vegas West Virginia
Washington	4,343,446	28%	1,216,000	5.5	6,689,000	2%	Las Vegas Washington Indian
West Virginia	1,347,674	7%	92,000	3.6	331,000	<1%	Las Vegas West Virginia
Wisconsin	3,889,572	29%	1,128,000	6.2	6,994,000	2%	Las Vegas Wisconsin Indian
Wyoming	353,136	17%	60,000	small sample	small sample	small sample	small sample

The casinos go to great lengths to lure gamblers into their facilities and keep them gambling as long and as happily as possible. Large companies invest millions of dollars in determining what colors, sounds, and scents are most appealing to patrons.

The legend that casinos pump in oxygen to keep their customers alert and peppy is untrue. Such a practice would be an extreme fire hazard. However, many casinos do furnish their gambling halls with bright and sometimes gaudy floor and wall coverings because these have been

TABLE 3.3

State profiles of commercial casino participation, 2004 [CONTINUED]

DMA	2003 U.S. census population (21+)	2003 Casino participation rate	2003 Number of casino gamblers	2003 Average trip frequency (per year)	2003 Number of gambling trips	Top casino destinations (in alphabetical order)
Atlanta	3,955,496	14%	560,000	2.7	1,511,000	Cherokee, NC Cruise ships Gulf Coast, MS Las Vegas New Orleans Tunica, MS
Baltimore	2,005,768	18%	361,000	3.9	1,408,000	Atlantic City Delaware
Boston	4,476,819	30%	1,351,000	3.9	5,267,000	Connecticut Indian
Buffalo	1,181,766	30%	355,000	4.9	1,742,000	Canada Las Vegas New York Indian
Cincinnati	1,569,703	26%	402,000	4.9	1,972,000	Chicago Area Las Vegas Southern IL/IN
Cleveland	2,795,707	23%	643,000	2.7	1,737,000	Detroit/Windsor Las Vegas West Virginia
Columbus, OH	1,500,351	13%	193,000	2.7	522,000	Detroit/Windsor Las Vegas Southern IL/IN
Little Rock/Pine Bluff	980,824	22%	218,000	5.3	1,157,000	Tunica, MS
Louisville	1,133,306	27%	307,000	3.8	1,168,000	Las Vegas Southern IL/IN
Los Angeles	11,585,293	40%	4,606,000	4.4	20,265,000	Las Vegas Laughlin So. California Indian
Miami/Ft. Lauderdale	3,020,024	19%	569,000	3.3	1,877,000	Cruise ships Florida Indian Las Vegas
Minneapolis/St. Paul	2,992,281	37%	1,112,000	6.9	7,675,000	Las Vegas Minnesota Indian Wisconsin Indian
Mobile/Pensacola	920,072	35%	320,000	4.7	1,505,000	Gulf Coast, MS
New York City	14,715,137	33%	4,850,000	4.4	21,338,000	Atlantic City Connecticut Indian

SOURCE: "State Profiles," in *Harrah's Survey '04: Profile of the American Casino Gambler,* Harrah's Operating Company, Inc., October 2004, http://www.harrahs.com/about_us/survey/2004_Survey.pdf (accessed November 15, 2004). Used with permission.

shown to have a stimulating and cheering effect on people. Red is extremely popular as a decorating color in casinos for the same reason and because it is thought to make people lose track of time. There are no clocks on casino walls either. Most casinos have no windows or mirrors in order to minimize distractions and keep the focus on the gambling action.

According to "The Tech Of: A Casino," a TechTV program broadcast in June 2002, casinos use a variety of tricks to attract gamblers. Slot machines and gaming tables are arranged in a mazelike fashion so that wandering patrons are continuously enticed by more gambling options. Slot machines are designed by computers to be appealing to the senses of sight, sound, and touch. Bells, lights, whistles, and the "cling clang" noise of dropping coins during a payout are all part of the sensory experience. The machine noises are electronically tuned to the musical key of C to be pleasing to the ear and fit into the ambient noise of the rest of the casino. Humans are

attracted to bright lights, so, more than 15,000 miles of neon tubing are used to light the casinos along the Las Vegas Strip.

In addition to stimulating atmospheres, casinos also focus on customer service. They provide perks designed to encourage gamblers to spend more and to reward those who do. Most casinos offer "comps," which is short for complimentaries, or free items. During the 1970s, Las Vegas casinos were famous for their deeply discounted travel packages, cheap buffets, and free show tickets. The strategy at that time was to maximize the volume of people coming and staying at the casino. Gambling revenue was driven by filling hotel rooms and the casino floor with as many people as possible.

Today, casinos are more choosy. They prefer to concentrate their investments on gamblers who spend much more than average—the so-called "high rollers" or "big spenders." Such people receive VIP treatment. They

TABLE 3.4

Casino games played most often, 2004

Slots/video poker (net)	**75%**
$ .01 – .02	1%
$ .05 – .10	18%
$ .25 – .50	45%
$ 1.00 – 4.00	9%
$ 5.00+	1%
Table games (net)	**13%**
Blackjack/21	9%
Roulette	2%
Craps	2%
Other	3%
Don't know	8%

SOURCE: "Games Played Most Often by Americans," in *Harrah's Survey '04: Profile of the American Casino Gambler,* Harrah's Operating Company, Inc., October 2004, http://www.harrahs.com/about_us/survey/2004_Survey.pdf (accessed November 15, 2004). Used with permission.

TABLE 3.5

Casino games played most often by age group, 2004

	21–35	36–50	51–65	66+
Slots/video poker (net)	**69%**	**73%**	**77%**	**79%**
$ .01 – .02	1%	1%	2%	1%
$ .05 – .10	19%	18%	18%	19%
$ .25 – .50	41%	45%	47%	49%
$ 1.00 – 4.00	8%	9%	10%	8%
$ 5.00+	1%	1%	1%	1%
Table games (net)	**18%**	**15%**	**11%**	**8%**
Blackjack/21	12%	11%	7%	5%
Roulette	2%	2%	1%	1%
Craps	3%	2%	2%	2%
Other	5%	5%	5%	5%
Don't know	8%	7%	7%	8%

SOURCE: "Age and Games Played Most Often," in *Harrah's Survey '04: Profile of the American Casino Gambler,* Harrah's Entertainment, Inc., October 2004, http://www.harrahs.com/about_us/survey/2004_Survey.pdf (accessed November 15, 2004)

often gamble in special rooms, separate from the main casino floor, where the stakes (amount bet) can be in the thousands of dollars. Casinos make much of their profit from these high-stakes gamblers. Therefore, the high rollers receive comps worth a great deal of money during their visits, such as free luxury suites and lavish personal attention.

Less expensive comps are available to smaller spenders. Most casinos offer clubs that are similar to air-line frequent-flyer programs. Gamblers who join receive a card that can be swiped electronically before they play a game. Casino computers track their usage and spending habits and tally up "points" that can be exchanged for free or discounted meals, drinks, or shows, or coupons for free slot play. The comp programs also serve as a valuable marketing tool for the casinos. They develop a patron database that can be used for mail advertising and to track trends in game preference and spending.

CHAPTER 4

CASINOS, PART 2: COMMERCIAL CASINOS

THE MARKET

Commercial casinos are those owned and operated by large and small companies. They are heavily regulated by state governments. Each state sets different limits on the types and locations of casinos permitted. Some states allow land-based casinos, while others restrict casino games to floating gambling halls on barges or riverboats. A handful of states allow slot machines at noncasino locations, such as horse and dog racetracks or other commercial establishments. Most states specify exactly which table games can be played in casinos. Some states place a limit on the amount that can be wagered, in so-called "limited-stakes" gambling.

In gambling terminology, the "handle" is the gross amount of money wagered by gamblers. As reported by Dan Seligman in "In Defense of Gambling" (*Forbes,* June 23, 2003), approximately $600 billion was gambled at U.S. casinos during 2003. The American Gaming Association (AGA) reported in *2004 State of the States: The AGA Survey of Casino Entertainment* that commercial casinos kept $27 billion of this amount in 2003. This is called the gross gaming revenue or "casino win." The remaining $573 billion was taken home by gamblers and is called the "payout." The casino industry considers its revenue to be consumer spending, as gamblers "spent" that money while gambling. In *2004 State of the States,* the AGA reported that consumer spending on gambling ($27 billion) was far less than consumer spending on fast-food meals ($137.8 billion) but greater than spending on other leisure activities, such as amusement and theme parks ($10.3 billion) and movies ($9.49 billion).

2004 State of the States reported that there were eighty-three riverboat/dockside casinos operating during 2003 in Illinois (nine), Indiana (ten), Iowa (ten), Louisiana (fourteen), Mississippi (twenty-nine), and Missouri (eleven). Major markets for floating casinos included Chicago, Illinois; Tunica, Mississippi; the Mississippi

Gulf Coast; and Bossier City, Shreveport, and Lake Charles, Louisiana. Some of the largest gaming companies, including Harrah's Entertainment, Inc., MGM Mirage, Park Place Entertainment, and Mandalay Resort Group, operated floating casinos.

According to the AGA, there were 432 major commercial casinos operating in eleven states during 2002. (Note: This total does not include casinos in Nevada with annual revenues less than $1 million.) The eleven states listed are also those in which full-scale casinos that offer table games and machines are legal:

- Nevada
- New Jersey
- Mississippi
- Indiana
- Louisiana
- Illinois
- Missouri
- Michigan
- Iowa
- Colorado
- South Dakota

NEVADA

Gambling has a long history in Nevada. It was widely practiced in the frontier towns of the Old West but was outlawed around the end of the nineteenth century, during a time when conservative values predominated. However, illegal gambling was widely tolerated throughout the state. In 1931 gambling was legalized again in Nevada. At the time, the country was in a deep economic depression.

Casino development was slow at first. Many businesspeople were not convinced that the rural desert towns of Nevada could attract sufficient tourists to make the opera-

FIGURE 4.1

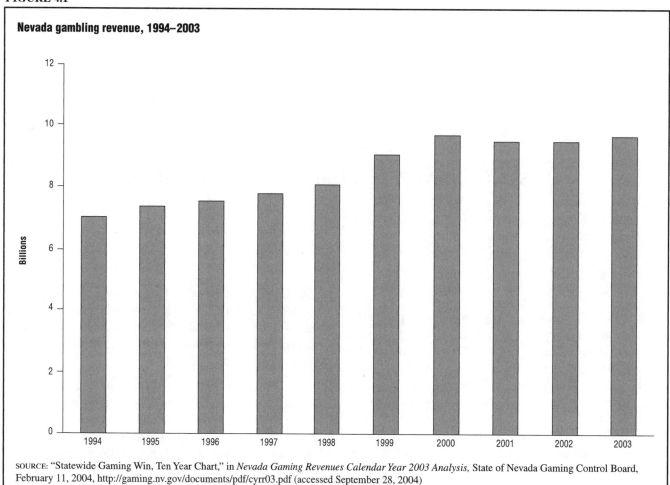

Nevada gambling revenue, 1994–2003

SOURCE: "Statewide Gaming Win, Ten Year Chart," in *Nevada Gaming Revenues Calendar Year 2003 Analysis,* State of Nevada Gaming Control Board, February 11, 2004, http://gaming.nv.gov/documents/pdf/cyrr03.pdf (accessed September 28, 2004)

tions profitable. In 1941 the El Rancho Vegas opened in Las Vegas. Five years later, notorious mobster Bugsy Siegel opened the Flamingo Hotel, also in Las Vegas. Although Siegel was eventually murdered by his business partners for cost overruns, the Mafia became more and more invested in Las Vegas casinos. It was a relationship that lasted for another thirty years and tainted casino gambling in many people's minds.

Although the state of Nevada began collecting gaming taxes during the 1940s, regulation of the casinos was lax until the 1970s. Organized crime figures were gradually pushed out of the casino business as corporations moved in. In 1975 gaming revenues in the state reached $1 billion, according to the official Web site of the Las Vegas Convention and Visitors Authority (www.lasvegas24hours.com). In 2004 the gambling industry is the largest employer in Nevada and accounts for more than one-third of all taxes paid into the state's general fund.

There are many different forms of legal gambling in Nevada, including live bingo, keno, and horse racing; card rooms; casino games; and off-track and phone betting on sports events and horse races. "Restricted" slots are those located in establishments restricted to fewer than fifteen machines, such as bars, restaurants, and stores. "Nonrestricted" slots are primarily located in casinos, which are allowed to have more than fifteen machines.

During 2003 there were 256 commercial casinos operating in Nevada—by far, the most of any state. According to the Nevada Gaming Control Board, the state's commercial casinos (i.e., those not operated by Native American tribes) generated $9.6 billion dollars of revenue from gambling operations during 2003, up 1.9% from 2002. As shown in Figure 4.1 casino revenues leveled off at the beginning of the twenty-first century after climbing steadily during the 1990s.

Nevada casino revenue (or "total win") for calendar year 2003 is broken down by area and gambling category in Table 4.1. Slot machines accounted for 67% of the casinos' gaming revenue in 2003, the highest percentage ever. Revenue from games and tables was down by 0.82%, while that from slot machines was up by 3.25% from the previous year.

Patrons gambled nearly $118 billion at Nevada slot machines in 2003 and nearly $21 billion at games and tables. The quarter slot machine was most popular, accounting for $35 billion (30%) of the total wagered at

TABLE 4.1

Total win; win from games and tables; and win from slot machines, Nevada casinos, 2003 and percent change from 2002

Counties/areas	Total win		
	Calendar dollar	Increase/-Decrease	
		dollar	percent
Clark	7,830,675,556	200,713,331	2.63
S. Lake Tahoe area	335,497,875	−903,170	−0.27
Elko	219,587,344	−8,782,307	−3.85
Carson Valley area	102,957,197	5,770,865	5.94
Washoe	1,010,452,464	−24,383,325	−2.36
All others	126,131,745	5,532,834	4.59
Total	**9,625,302,181**	**177,948,228**	**1.88**

Counties/areas	Win from games and tables		
	Calendar dollar	Increase/-Decrease	
		dollar	percent
Clark	2,724,312,079	−3,590,436	−0.13
S. Lake Tahoe area	118,747,121	−3,245,311	−2.66
Elko	46,451,652	−456,731	−0.97
Carson Valley area	8,945,596	−30,780	−0.34
Washoe	245,246,960	−19,057,963	−7.21
All others	4,741,946	344,010	7.82
Total	**3,148,445,354**	**−26,037,211**	**−0.82**

Counties/areas	Win from slot machines		
	Calendar dollar	Increase/-Decrease	
		dollar	percent
Clark	5,106,363,477	204,303,766	4.17
S. Lake Tahoe area	216,750,754	2,342,142	1.09
Elko	173,135,692	−8,325,576	−4.59
Carson Valley area	94,011,601	5,801,644	6.58
Washoe	765,205,504	−5,325,362	−0.69
All others	121,389,799	5,188,824	4.47
Total	**6,476,856,827**	**203,985,438**	**3.25**

SOURCE: Adapted from "Quarterly Statistics Report," in *State of Nevada, Nevada Gaming Commission and State Gaming Control Board: Quarterly Report for the Quarter Ended December 31, 2003; Fiscal Year to Date July 1, 2003 through December 31, 2003; Calendar Year to Date January 1, 2003 through December 31, 2003,* State of Nevada Gaming Control Board, February 3, 2004

slot machines. Among tables and games, Twenty-One had the highest amount wagered ($8.6 billion or 41% of the total). However, Three-Card Poker had the greatest increase in play from the year before. The amount wagered at this game increased by 30% to $478 million in 2003. Mini-Baccarat wagers were up by 16% to $1.3 billion.

Although casinos are located throughout the state, the major gambling markets in Nevada are in the southern part of the state in Clark County (home of Las Vegas and Laughlin) and along the California border in Washoe County (home of Reno) and the Lake Tahoe resort area.

Las Vegas

Perhaps no other city is more associated with casinos than Las Vegas. According to the Las Vegas Convention and Visitors Authority (LVCVA) the city had 35.5 million visitors in 2003, and they spent nearly $33 billion. The number of visitors was up 1.3% from the previous year. The city had 130,482 hotel/motel rooms in 2003. The hotel/motel occupancy rate was 85%. This compares with a national occupancy rate of only 59%. The LVCVA reported that the average Las Vegas visitor in 2003 was fifty years old and stayed 3.4 nights in the city. During 2003 Las Vegas was the site of more than 24,000 conventions that attracted more than five million people.

A four-mile stretch of Las Vegas Boulevard south of downtown Las Vegas is known universally as "the Strip." According to the AGA, the casinos on the Las Vegas Strip made up the number one commercial casino market in the country in 2002.

There are more than forty hotel/casinos along the Strip, several of which are among the largest hotels in the country. These megaresorts offer guests such amenities as lavish decorating themes, spas, pools, multiple restaurants, and top-notch entertainment. The large companies operating megaresorts in Las Vegas generate a substantial amount of revenue from nongambling sources, including lodging, dining, and entertainment.

According to the LVCVA casinos in Las Vegas made $6.1 billion in gaming revenue in 2003. Casinos along the Strip accounted for $4.8 of this total. All Las Vegas casinos account for 63% of the state's entire gambling revenue.

Beyond the well-known casinos of the Strip, other casinos are located throughout Clark County. Casinos located off-Strip in Las Vegas are geared toward local markets. They are less flashy and feature more casual dining and entertainment options. In total, the 150 casinos in Clark County, both on the Strip and off, accounted for $7.8 billion in gaming revenue during 2003, according to "Nevada Gaming Revenues Calendar Year 2003 Analysis" (Carson City, NV: State of Nevada Gaming Control Board, Tax and License Division, February 11, 2004). This is 81% of the state's total casino gambling revenues for that year.

Casino gambling has had an enormous effect on Clark County's growth. The population of the county went from 48,289 in 1950 to nearly 1.4 million in 2000. During the 1990s alone, the county's population increased by 86%. This compares with a national average of 13.1%. Clark County residents make up 70% of the state's entire population. Traffic congestion has become such a problem on the Strip in Las Vegas that a four-mile monorail was built to move people around. The monorail began operation in 2004 and makes stops at various resorts and the city's convention center. It is expected to carry nineteen million passengers per year.

NEW JERSEY

In June 1976 casino gambling in Atlantic City, New Jersey, was legalized by the state's voters, making it the second state (after Nevada) to permit casino gambling. New Jersey casinos are regulated under the state's Casino Control Act.

Atlantic City

Atlantic City was an immensely popular resort destination throughout the late 1800s and early 1900s. It was easily accessible by rail, and people visited the beautiful beaches and elegant hotels along the nearly five-mile boardwalk. During the 1960s the city lost most of its tourist trade to beaches further south, mainly in Florida and the Caribbean, and the city fell into an economic slump. Casinos were seen as a way to revitalize the city and attract tourists again. The first casino, Resorts International, opened in 1978, followed by Caesars Atlantic and Bally's Park Place in 1979. By 1991 casino gambling was permitted twenty-four hours a day.

Although it has only thirteen casinos, Atlantic City is the second-largest gambling market in the country according to the AGA, with a gross revenue of $4.48 billion in 2003, up 3% from 2002. (See Table 4.2.) All Atlantic City casinos are land-based. According to the *New Jersey Casino Control Commission 2003 Annual Report,* as of December 31, 2003 they offered 1,370 table games, sixteen keno windows, and 42,378 slot machines. Atlantic City casinos employed 46,159 people in 2003 and paid wages of $1.1 million. They paid taxes of $358 million.

Atlantic City differs from Las Vegas in many ways. There are far fewer hotel rooms (only about 13,000) with fewer amenities. Atlantic City is considered a "day-tripper market," meaning that it attracts people mostly within driving or train distance who visit for the day (many of them from New York City and Philadelphia). Casino development has been sluggish in Atlantic City. No new casinos were built during the 1990s. The Boyd Gaming Corp. and MGM Mirage collaborated to open the city's newest casino/hotel named Borgata in July 2003 in the marina district of the city.

In Atlantic City each casino is assessed an 8% tax on its gross revenue (i.e., casino revenue after all bets are paid but before taxes and other expenses are paid). These payments go into a fund that is distributed among various programs throughout the state, primarily for physical and mental health programs for the elderly and people with disabilities. According to the New Jersey Casino Control Commission, in fiscal year 2003 (July 2002–June 2003) fund expenditures totaled $435 million and were distributed as follows:

- Physical and Mental Health Programs—90%

- Transportation Programs—5%

- Educational, Cultural, and Intellectual Development—4%

- Economic Planning, Development, and Security—1%

TABLE 4.2

New Jersey casino industry statistics, 2002–03

($ in thousands)

Casino hotel		Gross revenue	Tax	Market share of casino win
AC Hilton	2003	$ 308,651	$ 24,692	6.9%
	2002	$ 306,296	$ 24,504	7.0%
Bally's Atlantic City	2003	677,286	54,183	15.1%
	2002	525,017	42,001	12.0%
Borgata	2003	266,857	21,349	5.9%
	2002	–	–	n/a
Caesars	2003	517,760	41,421	11.6%
	2002	524,241	41,939	12.0%
Claridge	2003	–	–	n/a
	2002	159,286	12,743	3.7%
Harrah's Marina	2003	451,013	36,081	10.1%
	2002	450,842	36,067	10.3%
Resorts	2003	232,599	18,608	5.2%
	2002	260,741	20,859	6.0%
Sands	2003	184,541	14,763	4.1%
	2002	207,447	16,596	4.8%
Showboat	2003	377,706	30,217	8.4%
	2002	368,504	29,480	8.4%
Tropicana	2003	372,142	29,771	8.3%
	2002	405,302	32,424	9.3%
Trump Marina	2003	258,934	20,715	5.8%
	2002	280,976	22,478	6.5%
Trump Plaza	2003	317,908	25,433	7.1%
	2002	338,655	27,092	7.8%
Trump Taj Mahal	2003	515,495	41,240	11.5%
	2002	532,002	42,560	12.2%
Totals	**2003**	**$ 4,480,892**	**$ 358,473**	**100.0%**
	2002	**$ 4,359,309**	**$ 348,743**	**100.0%**

SOURCE: Adapted from "New Jersey Casino Industry Gross Revenue Statistics for the Two Years Ended December 31, 2003, and 2002," in *New Jersey Casino Control Commission 2003 Annual Report,* New Jersey Casino Control Commission, January 28, 2004

The casinos of Atlantic City have not changed the town into a trendy tourist destination as was originally hoped. In fact, Atlantic City has the reputation of being "a slum with casinos." Industry experts point to two primary factors for this perception. First is the town's reliance on day-trippers rather than long-term vacationers. Second is the way in which casino tax revenues have been invested. The tax revenues generated by the casino industry have largely funded physical and mental health programs throughout the state rather than being invested in local infrastructure and economic development programs.

MISSISSIPPI

Gambling along the Mississippi River and its connecting waterways was widespread during the early 1800s. The rivers were the modern-day equivalent of the interstate highway system, carrying cash-laden farmers, merchants, and tourists to bustling towns along the riverbank. Many of these towns developed gambling halls, notorious establishments that attracted many professional gamblers. These sharps, chiefly cardsharps, soon had an unsavory reputation for cheating visitors out of their money.

By the 1830s the cardsharps had worn out their welcome in riverbank towns. According to Richard Dunstan in *Gambling in California* (Sacramento, CA: California Research Bureau, 1997), five cardsharps were lynched in Mississippi in 1835, and the professional gamblers moved to the riverboats cruising up and down the rivers. Gambling between riverboat passengers was a popular pastime during the 1840s and 1850s. The onset of the Civil War (1861–65) and then the antigambling movement around the turn of the twentieth century dampened, but did not destroy, open gambling in the state.

During and after World War II (1939–45), the Mississippi coast experienced a resurgence in illegal casino gambling, particularly in Harrison County, home of the city of Biloxi and Keesler Air Force Base. The officers' club at the base is reputed to have openly operated slot machines. During the 1960s the Alcohol Beverage Control Board began refusing licenses to public facilities allowing gambling. A few private clubs and lodges continued to offer card games and slot machines, but they were eventually shut down by the mid-1980s.

In 1987 the ship *Europa Star* and several other ships from Biloxi ports began taking gamblers on "cruises to nowhere"—cruises to international waters in the Gulf of Mexico where onboard gambling could take place legally. Although supported by the city of Biloxi, the state initially opposed these cruises until it became apparent that they were reviving tourism in port towns. The state was in desperate economic times, having been proclaimed the poorest state in the country by the 1980 census. In 1989 Mississippi became the first state to permit cruises to conduct gambling in state waters when the ships were on their way to or from international waters.

Dockside casino gambling was legalized by the Mississippi legislature in 1990 with passage of House Bill 2. The bill established the Mississippi Gaming Control Act and the three-commissioner Mississippi Gaming Commission to regulate dockside casinos and charitable gaming. Each parish (county) was allowed to decide whether it would allow gambling. Fourteen parishes along the Gulf Coast and Mississippi River held referendums regarding dockside casinos, and all voted them down. The next year, a city-by-city vote was held, and voters in Biloxi, which was nearly bankrupt at the time, approved the referendum. In 1992 nine dockside casinos opened in Biloxi.

There are three major casino regions in the state: the northern region centered in Tunica, the central region based in Vicksburg and Natchez, and the coastal region centered in Biloxi, Gulfport, and Bay St. Louis. According to the AGA the casino markets in Tunica and Biloxi were ranked among the top ten markets in the country during 2002.

Mississippi has not set a limit on the number of casinos that can be built in the state, instead allowing competition to determine the market size. By law, casinos must be permanently docked in the water along the Mississippi River and the Mississippi Gulf Coast. The gambling halls of the casinos actually sit on the water, while their associated lodging, dining, and entertainment facilities are on land. Along the Mississippi River, the gambling halls sit in slips cut into the riverbank. The Choctaw Indians operate the only land-based casinos in the state.

As of March 2004 there were twenty-nine commercial casinos operating in Mississippi. (See Table 4.3.) In total, they employed 28,794 people and offered nearly 1.5 million square feet of gaming space, nearly 40,000 slot machines, more than one thousand table games, and one hundred poker games. Games offered include blackjack, craps, roulette, baccarat, mini-baccarat, big six wheel, keno, and various forms of poker and other card games. The state allows round-the-clock gambling with no bet limits. Gross casino revenue for the state was $2.7 billion in calendar year 2003, virtually unchanged from 2002. (See Figure 4.2.) In fact, commercial casino revenue leveled off during the early twenty-first century after growing steadily through the 1990s. The casinos had more than 14,000 hotel rooms and received nearly fifty-four million visitors during 2003.

According to statistics provided by the Mississippi Gaming Commission, the casino industry produces 10% of the state's annual budget, generating in excess of $300 million in wagering, sales, and income taxes. For fiscal year 2004 (July 2003–June 2004), casinos paid $332 million in taxes; half went to the state's general fund, one-third went to local governments, and the remainder went into the Bond Sinking Fund and Highway Fund. In total, $2 billion was collected in casino taxes in Mississippi between July 1992 and June 2004.

LOUISIANA

Louisiana has a long gambling history, according to *The Rivergate,* a documentary on the destruction of the Port of New Orleans Exhibition Center to make way for a Harrah's casino. In 1823, eleven years after Louisiana became a state, its legislature legalized several forms of gambling and licensed six "temples of chance" in the city of New Orleans. Each was to pay $5,000 per year to fund the Charity Hospital and the College of Orleans. The casinos attracted many patrons, including professional gamblers, swindlers, and thieves. In 1835 the legislature repealed the licensing act and passed laws making gambling hall owners subject to prison terms or large fines.

However, casino-type gambling continued and even prospered throughout the southern part of the state. By 1840 New Orleans contained an estimated five hundred gambling halls employing more than four thousand people, but these halls paid no revenue to the city. Riverboat

TABLE 4.3

Mississippi commercial casino statistics, January–March 2004

Quarterly Survey Information: January 1, 2004–March 31, 2004

Coastal Region	Number of employees	Gaming sq. footage	# slot games	# table games	# poker games	Activities in addition to gaming
Beau Rivage - Biloxi	2,459	71,669	2,234	91	—	12 restaurants, retail promenade, marina, convention center, showroom, spa, and hotel
Boomtown - Biloxi	913	33,632	1,120	21	—	Motion theater, buffet, restaurant, cabaret, fun center
Casino Magic - Bay St. Louis	1,107	39,500	1,210	30	—	Golf course, hotel, RV park, restaurants, sporting events, Camp Magic, charter boats, spa
Casino Magic - Biloxi	915	49,260	1,234	30	—	Eclipse Showroom entertainment, restaurants
Copa Casino - Gulfport	697	43,025	1,143	32	—	Gift shop and restaurants
Grand Casino - Biloxi	2,109	134,200	2,624	85	21	Restaurants, theatre, hotels, arcade, and Kid's Quest
Grand Casino - Gulfport	1,665	85,000	2,131	72	15	Restaurants, entertainment barge, hotels, Lazy River, arcade, and Kid's Quest
Imperial Palace	486	70,000	1,633	31	—	Spa, pool, movie theaters, restaurants, shops, and showroom
Isle of Capri - Biloxi	835	32,500	1,127	28	—	Restaurants and live entertainment
President - Biloxi	271	38,297	843	34	7	Live entertainment, restaurants, arcade, fishing, valet parking and golf
The New Palace - Biloxi	900	58,500	1,333	37	—	Theater, hotel, gift shop, spa, salon, pool, and restaurants
Treasure Bay - Biloxi	898	41,000	978	41	—	Arcades, gift shop, restaurants, tanning bed, and travel agency
Region Totals	**13,255**	**696,583**	**17,610**	**532**	**43**	

North River Region	Number of employees	Gaming sq. footage	# slot games	# table games	# poker games	Activities in addition to gaming
Bally's - Robinsonville	731	40,000	1,311	37	—	Restaurants, hotel
Fitzgerald's - Robinsonville	936	36,000	1,345	34	—	Hotel, restaurant, slot and table game tournaments
Gold Strike - Robinsonville	1,350	50,486	1,388	49	14	Restaurants, Millenium theater, arcade, and hotel
Grand Casino -Tunica	2,329	136,000	2,544	82	11	Restaurants, RV park, arcade, golf gourse, Kid's Quest, and clay shooting
Harrah's - Tunica	793	35,000	1,172	23	—	Live entertainment, restaurants, and golf
Hollywood - Robinsonville	985	54,000	1,626	33	6	Restaurants, RV park, arcade, hotel, and pool
Horseshoe - Robinsonville	2,554	63,000	2,115	76	12	Live entertainment, restaurants, health club, and Blues Museum
Isle of Capri - Lula	763	63,500	1,569	29	—	Movies, concerts, and dining
Sam's Town - Tunica	1,144	74,210	1,318	42	10	Gift shop, restaurants and hotel
Sheraton - Robinsonville	798	32,800	1,389	37	—	Restaurants, hotel
Region Totals	**12,383**	**584,996**	**15,777**	**442**	**53**	

South River Region	Number of employees	Gaming sq. footage	# slot games	# table games	# poker games	Activities in addition to gaming
Ameristar - Vicksburg	938	42,500	1,360	36	—	Showroom and restaurants
Harrah's - Vicksburg	330	20,000	657	13	4	Restaurants and lodging
Isle of Capri - Vicksburg	535	24,000	788	19	—	Live entertainment, restaurants, and hotel
Jubilee - Greenville	293	28,500	875	13	—	Live entertainment and restaurants
Isle of Capri - Natchez	363	15,783	648	11	—	Live entertainment and restaurants
Lighthouse - Greenville	260	22,000	801	10	—	Restaurants and live entertainment
Rainbow - Vicksburg	437	25,000	930	12	—	Restaurants, gift shop, and hotel
Region Totals	**3,156**	**177,783**	**6,059**	**114**	**4**	
STATE TOTALS	**28,794**	**1,459,362**	**39,446**	**1,088**	**100**	

SOURCE: Adapted from "Quarterly Survey Information: January 1, 2004–March 31, 2004," in *Mississippi Gaming Commission—Public Information*, Mississippi Gaming Commission, April 23, 2004, http://www .mgc.state.ms.us/pdf/QRpt1Q04-Property.pdf (accessed September 28, 2004)

FIGURE 4.2

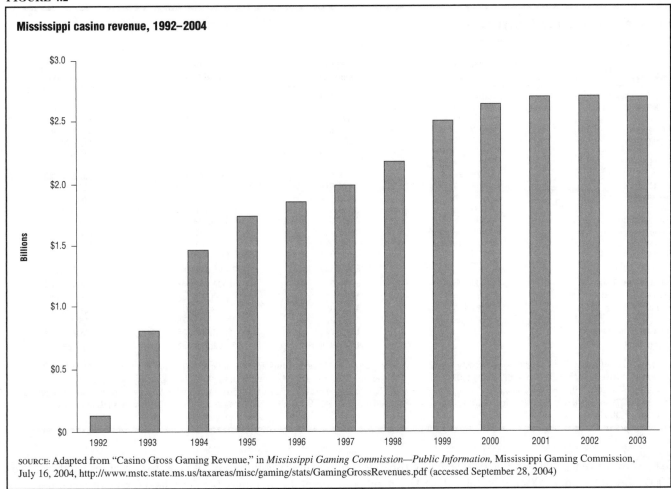

Mississippi casino revenue, 1992–2004

SOURCE: Adapted from "Casino Gross Gaming Revenue," in *Mississippi Gaming Commission—Public Information,* Mississippi Gaming Commission, July 16, 2004, http://www.mstc.state.ms.us/taxareas/misc/gaming/stats/GamingGrossRevenues.pdf (accessed September 28, 2004)

casinos frequented by hundreds of professional gamblers floated up and down the Mississippi River between St. Louis and New Orleans. When the Civil War broke out, the riverboats were pressed into military service. In 1869 the legislature legalized casino gambling once again, requiring each casino to pay the state a $5,000 tax.

In *Bad Bet on the Bayou* (New York: Farrar, Straus, and Giroux, 2001), author Tyler Bridges credits Louisiana gamblers for popularizing craps and poker in the United States during the nineteenth century. Both were games of chance that had originated in Europe. The Louisiana state lottery began in 1868 but was outlawed in 1892, along with other forms of gambling, after a massive fraud scandal. Casino gambling went underground and continued to flourish well into the 1960s, thanks to mobsters and political corruption. Two of the state's governors, Earl Long and Edwin Edwards, were well-known gamblers. Edwards reportedly hosted high-stakes gambling games at the governor's mansion.

During the early 1990s the state legalized gambling once again, authorizing a lottery, casinos, and the operation of video poker machines in restaurants, bars, and truck stops. In 1991 the legislature authorized operation of up to fifteen riverboat casinos in the state; all but those

along the Red River were required to make regularly scheduled cruises. The riverboat casinos were required to be at least 150 feet long and decorated to look like nineteenth-century paddleboats. The first riverboat casino, the *Showboat Star,* began operating in the fall of 1993.

In 1993 New Orleans received special permission from the legislature to allow a limited number of land-based casinos. In January 1995 Harrah's began construction on one in the heart of the city. By November 1995, the casino had declared bankruptcy. Following years of negotiations with the state and city, it reopened in 1999 but threatened bankruptcy again in 2001, blaming the state's $100 million minimum tax. The legislature cut the tax to $50 million for 2001 and $60 million for subsequent years to help keep the casino in business.

On April 1, 2001, the legislature ended the so-called phantom cruises of the riverboat casinos, ruling that it would actually be illegal for them to leave the docks. All riverboats were allowed to begin dockside gambling. However, their tax rate was increased from 18.5% to 21.5%.

Up to fifteen floating casinos are allowed in Louisiana. According to revenue reports published by the Louisiana Gaming Control Board, the state's riverboat casinos admit-

TABLE 4.4

Louisiana casino statistics, fiscal year 2004

Licensees	Opening date	FYTD admissions	FYTD total AGR	FYTD fee/state tax
Boomtown Bossier	10/4/1996	2,420,594	$107,263,349	$23,061,620
Harrahs Shrev.	4/18/1994	2,989,249	$145,402,026	$31,261,436
Hollywood	12/20/2000	3,911,081	$135,048,412	$29,035,409
Horseshoe	7/9/1994	3,077,665	$253,418,980	$54,485,081
Isle-Bossier	5/20/1994	1,544,626	$112,046,556	$24,090,010
Sam's Town	5/20/2004	387,535	$17,954,565	$3,860,231
Grand Palais	7/12/1996	2,133,894	$137,550,608	$29,573,381
Ilse-LC	7/29/1995	949,816	$34,640,556	$7,447,720
Harrahs Pride	12/8/1993	1,889,679	$101,722,786	$21,870,399
Harrahs Star	10/24/1993	1,024,142	$49,878,501	$10,723,878
Ballys	7/7/1995	1,342,236	$60,565,045	$11,328,563
Boomtown N.O.	8/6/1994	2,337,596	$113,639,322	$24,432,454
Treasure Chest	9/5/1994	1,602,186	$110,715,810	$23,803,899
Argosy	9/30/1994	1,148,023	$82,039,244	$17,638,438
Casino Rouge	12/28/1994	1,508,814	$104,769,736	$22,525,493
Riverboat total		**28,267,136**	**$1,566,655,498**	**$335,138,011**
Harrah's New Orleans	**10/26/1999**	**6,593,077**	**$300,251,946**	**$62,354,386**
Delta Downs (slots)	2/13/2002	1,597,158	$130,986,745	$19,870,690
Harrahs LA Downs (slots)	5/21/2003	1,726,632	$63,860,519	$9,687,641
Evangeline Downs (slots)	12/19/2003	1,177,956	$37,820,975	$5,737,442
Racetrack total (slots)		**4,501,746**	**$232,668,239**	**$35,295,773**
Casino total		**39,361,959**	**$2,099,575,683**	**$432,788,170**

SOURCE: Adapted from "Fiscal Year-to-Date Activity Summary—Landbased for the Period of July 1, 2003–June 30, 2004 and Fiscal Year-to-Date Activity Summary—Riverboats for the Period of July 1, 2003–June 30, 2004 and Fiscal Year-to-Date Activity Summary—Slots at Racetracks for the Period of July 1, 2003–June 30, 2004," in *Louisiana Gaming Control Board Revenue Report,* Louisiana Gaming Control Board, July 2004, http://web01.dps.louisiana.gov/lgcb.nsf/b4569279468fa0c086256e9b0049dbd8/42f80c95dcb5321886256ed7007287aa/$FILE/June%202004%20Landbased%20Revenues.pdf (accessed September 28, 2004)

ted just over twenty-eight million people during fiscal year 2004 (July 2003–June 2004). (See Table 4.4.) This number is down from thirty-one million people admitted during fiscal year 2002. Total adjusted gross revenue for the riverboats in fiscal year 2004 was $1.57 billion. The state's one land-based casino in New Orleans admitted nearly 6.6 million people and had gross revenue of $300 million. Although attendance was slightly down from previous years, the casino made more money. Its gross revenue increased by 14.5% between 2002 and 2004.

Three racinos grossed nearly $233 million in slots revenue during fiscal year 2004. Slot machines at racetracks are relatively new in Louisiana. The first racino began operating in 2002 and was joined in 2003 by two more establishments.

Total gross casino revenue in Louisiana for fiscal year 2004 was $2.1 billion, up from $1.8 billion during fiscal year 2001 and $1.4 billion during fiscal year 1999. (See Figure 4.3.) The state took in approximately $433 million in taxes from the casinos/racinos during fiscal year 2004. This is up from $400 million collected during fiscal year 2001.

There are four major markets in the state: Shreveport–Bossier City, New Orleans, Lake Charles, and Baton Rouge. The Shreveport market was the tenth-largest casino market in the United States in 2002, according to the AGA. A wide variety of games are allowed at Louisiana casinos, including blackjack, poker, craps, roulette, baccarat, keno, bingo, big six wheel, and slot machines. The state's video gaming division reports that there were 14,296 slot machines at noncasino locations as of June 2004, primarily truck stops, bars, and restaurants.

INDIANA

The state of Indiana legalized riverboat gambling in 1993 with passage of the Riverboat Gambling Act, which was enacted by Public Law 277-1993 and codified as Indiana Code 4-33. The act established the Indiana Gaming Commission and gave it authority to issue up to eleven riverboat licenses in specific areas of the state—in the northwest corner along Lake Michigan, at the southern border along the Ohio River, and around Patoka Lake in the southern part of the state. The Patoka Lake site initially received a riverboat license, but it was later vetoed by the U.S. Army Corps of Engineers.

The first riverboat began operation in December 1995 in Evansville. By December 1996, six riverboats were operating. By 2002 there were ten in operation, leaving one unused riverboat license. In February 2002 the Indiana Senate passed legislation permitting dockside operation of the riverboats in counties that would accept it. Permanent mooring allows patrons to access the casinos anytime during operating hours rather than just during cruise boarding times. The Senate passed the measure to

FIGURE 4.3

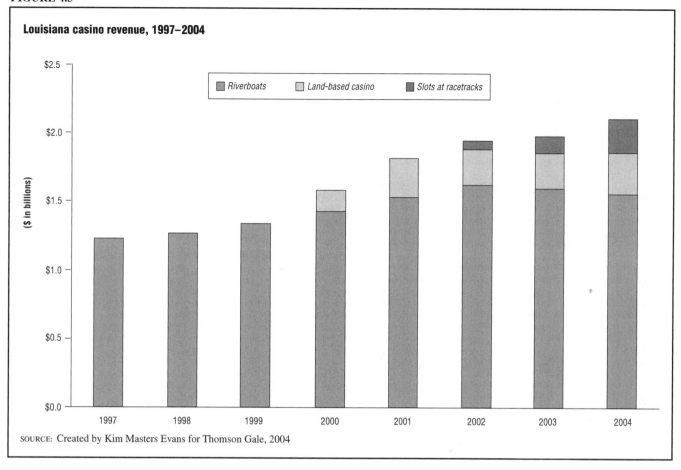

Louisiana casino revenue, 1997–2004

SOURCE: Created by Kim Masters Evans for Thomson Gale, 2004

make Indiana casinos more competitive with those in Illinois. The Indiana legislature approved the measure in June 2002. However, a provision that would have transferred the inactive riverboat license from Patoka Lake to Orange County was vetoed. Orange County politicians had hoped to use gambling revenues to renovate two historic hotels and boost employment in the south-central Indiana county.

All ten riverboats were allowed to become dockside casinos in July 2002. The change was accompanied by a change in the wagering tax structure from a 22.5% flat tax on adjusted gross receipts to a graduated tax rate of 15%–35%. A portion of the increased tax revenue is distributed to counties that do not have casinos. The admissions tax remained unchanged at $3 per person. The admissions tax is split three ways, with one dollar each going to the state, county, and city.

In fiscal year 2003 (July 2002–June 2003) there were ten riverboats operating in Indiana as shown in Table 4.5. Five of the casinos were along Lake Michigan and five along the Ohio River. Together, the ten riverboats had 17,601 slot machines and 620 table games in 2003. Games allowed include blackjack, craps, roulette, baccarat, big six, and poker. Eight of the riverboats are docked at locations with associated land-based hotels, restaurants, and entertainment venues. The other two are docked at pavilions offering only dining and shopping.

According to the *Indiana Gaming Commission Annual Report to the Governor: Fiscal Year 2004,* total riverboat admissions in Indiana were 26,545,058 from July 2003 to June 2004. This number is down dramatically from 41,373,160 during 2001. The total win for riverboat casinos during fiscal year 2004 was $2.31 billion, up from $1.84 billion in 2001. In 2002 southeastern Indiana made up the ninth-largest casino market in the United States in terms of gross revenue, and the combined northwest Indiana/northeast Illinois market was third largest, according to statistics published on the AGA Web site (www.americangaming.org).

As stated in the *Indiana Gaming Commission Annual Report,* total admission and wagering taxes paid in fiscal year 2004 were $742 million. Total admission and wagering taxes paid from the inception of riverboat gambling in 1995 through 2004 were nearly $3.8 billion.

In November 2003 Orange County voters approved a measure that would allow development of a riverboat casino in their county. As of August 2004 several development proposals were under consideration by state and local authorities.

TABLE 4.5

Indiana casino statistics, fiscal year 2003

	Total admissions	Number of table games	Table game drop	Table game win	Number of electronic gaming devices (EGD)	Coin in	EGD win	Total win	Wagering tax	Admission tax	Total tax
Argosy	3,935,342	95	386,383,201	$74,629,592	2,298	$5,339,912,259	$317,361,185	$391,990,777	$118,405,747	$11,806,026	$130,211,773
Belterra	1,747,023	41	114,546,072	$19,517,399	1,554	$1,492,603,789	$106,223,908	$125,741,307	$29,439,561	$5,241,069	$34,680,630
Blue Chip	2,670,288	50	175,259,282	$30,895,780	1,671	$2,572,735,530	$187,358,828	$218,254,608	$59,321,198	$8,010,864	$67,332,062
Caesars	3,578,173	141	350,765,826	$62,416,589	2,346	$3,076,118,803	$212,517,716	$274,934,305	$78,634,356	$10,734,519	$89,368,875
Aztar	1,526,453	47	87,777,579	$18,333,010	1,351	$1,167,729,048	$93,849,398	$112,182,408	$25,419,359	$4,579,359	$29,998,718
Grand Victoria	1,592,754	39	88,031,707	$16,378,021	1,420	$1,618,004,261	$121,583,730	$137,961,751	$33,112,075	$4,778,262	$37,890,337
Harrah's	3,868,094	65	291,422,006	$52,901,166	1,983	$2,864,127,018	$237,032,820	$289,933,986	$83,434,807	$11,604,282	$95,039,089
Horseshoe	3,778,642	47	445,520,403	$71,565,091	1,687	$3,659,466,338	$267,984,781	$339,549,872	$100,741,633	$11,335,926	$112,077,559
Majestic Star	1,797,564	50	141,729,518	$21,970,273	1,551	$1,525,803,411	$116,724,902	$138,695,175	$33,121,110	$5,392,692	$38,513,802
Trump	1,795,318	45	116,778,298	$18,374,471	1,740	$1,405,090,250	$110,470,197	$128,844,668	$30,132,239	$5,385,954	$35,518,193
Total	**26,289,651**	**620**	**$2,198,213,892**	**$386,981,392**	**17,601**	**$24,721,590,707**	**$1,771,107,465**	**$2,158,088,857**	**$591,762,085**	**$78,868,953**	**$670,631,038**

SOURCE: Indiana Casino Statistics, in *Indiana Gaming Commission Annual Report to the Governor, Fiscal Year 2003*, Indiana Gaming Commission, September 1, 2003, http://www.state.in.us/gaming/reports/annual/FY2003-Annual.pdf (accessed September 28, 2004)

TABLE 4.6

Illinois casino statistics, 1999–2003

	1999	2000	2001	2002	2003
Licensees	*10	*10	*10	*10	*10
AGR	$1,362,931,231	$1,658,004,361	$1,783, 958,166	$1,831,550,836	$1,709,943,480
Table games	$288,169,419	$308,794,704	$291,01 4,759	$286,980,831	$251,895,773
EGD	$1,074,761,812	$1,349,209,657	$1,492, 943,407	$1,544,570,005	$1,458,047,707
Admissions**	21,991,689**	19,014,939**	18,808,281**	18,821,582**	16,597,552**
AGR per adm	$61.97	$87.19	$94.85	$97.31	$103.02
Total tax	**$418,797,333**	**$512,213,123**	**$555,20 4,313**	**$666,101,823**	**$719,858,219**
Wagering tax	$374,813,955	$474,183,245	$517,58 7,751	$619,255,784	$659,882,032
Admissions tax	$43,983,378	$38,029,878	$37,616,562	$46,846,039	$59,976,187
State share	$328,665,137	$410,328,901	$447,22 8,898	$555,702,432	$617,797,595
Local share	$90,132,196	$101,884,222	$107,97 5,415	$110,399,391	$102,060,624

*Jo Daviess Silver Eagle ceased operations July 29, 1997.
**On June 26, 1999 DOCKSIDE GAMBLING began in Illinois. On that date the definition of admissions changed to reflect the count of patrons entering the gaming areas. This report reflects that change.

SOURCE: "Five Year History," in *2003 Illinois Gaming Board Annual Report,* Illinois Gaming Board, 2004, http://www.igb.state.il.us/annualreport/2003igb.pdf (accessed September 28, 2004)

ILLINOIS

Illinois legalized riverboat gambling in 1990, only the second state to do so. The Illinois Gaming Board was authorized under the Riverboat Gambling Act to grant up to ten casino licenses. Each license allows up to two vessels to be operated at a single specific docksite. Each docksite can have no more than 1,200 gaming positions, and all wagering is cashless. The first riverboat casino opened on September 11, 1991. The tenth license was issued in 1994. It went to a casino called the Silver Eagle owned by Emerald Casino, Inc. The casino closed in 1997, and the owners asked in 1999 to relocate it to another location. This move was opposed by other casino owners who hoped to obtain the tenth license. A long court battle began that still was not resolved as of mid-2004.

Originally, riverboats were required to cruise during gambling, but dockside gaming was approved in 1999. The first full year of dockside casino gambling occurred during 2000.

According to the American Gaming Association, in 2004 nine riverboat casinos were operating within the state: two on the Fox River and two on the Des Plaines River near Chicago in the northeast part of the state, one on the Illinois River in the central part of the state, one on the Ohio River in the south, and three on the Mississippi River to the west. Illinois riverboat casinos generated $1.71 billion of adjusted gross revenue (gross receipts less winnings) in 2003, a 6.6% decrease from 2002. (See Table 4.6.) The vast majority (85%) of 2003 revenue was from electronic gambling devices. The remainder was from table games. Admissions were 16.6 million in 2003, down 11.8% from 2002.

Illinois casinos are levied an admissions tax and a wagering tax. In 2002 the state legislature increased the admissions tax from $2 per patron to $3 per patron. In 2003 the admissions tax was increased to $4 per patron for casinos admitting 1–2.3 million patrons per year and to $5 per patron for casinos admitting more than 2.3 million patrons per year. Also in 2003 the legislature established a new rate structure for wagering taxes based on adjusted gross revenue (AGR). The rate begins at 15% for casinos with AGR less than or equal to $25 million and increases with increasing AGR. Casino taxes are shared by the state and local communities in which casinos are located. According to the *2003 Illinois Gaming Board Annual Report,* during 2003 the casino industry paid $617.8 million in state taxes and $102 million in local taxes.

The state's tenth casino license has been dormant since 1997. Although Emerald Casino, Inc. has applied for renewal several times, the applications have been denied for a variety of legal and regulatory reasons. In 2001 the Illinois Gaming Board denied the company's latest bid for renewal following allegations that company owners were associated with known members of organized crime. The company was also accused of violating Board rules and providing false information about its operations. In 2003 the company was forced to file for bankruptcy. As part of its reorganization plan it was agreed that the casino would be sold and top company managers would be banned from the state's casino industry.

The controversy did not end there. In March 2004 the Illinois Gaming Board agreed to allow Emerald Casino to sell its gaming license for $518 million to Isle of Capri Casinos, Inc. The new company announced plans to build a casino in the town of Rosemont, a suburb of Chicago. Although the mayors of Rosemont and Chicago were in favor of the deal, it was vigorously opposed by state officials. The Illinois attorney general launched an investigation amid allegations that the licensing deal was approved by Gaming Board directors despite strong objections from Board staff members. The attorney general sued the Board seeking a halt to the license review process. As of November 2004 the issue had not been resolved.

In May 2004 Chicago Mayor Richard Daley announced his plan to ask the state legislature for permission to build a city-owned land-based casino in downtown Chicago. In response, Governor Rod Blagojevich announced that he would veto any such legislation.

MISSOURI

In November 1992 a referendum to allow riverboat gambling was approved by 64% of Missouri voters. The initiative read as follows: "Authorizes riverboat gambling excursions on the Mississippi and Missouri Rivers, regulated by the State Tourism Commission. Excursions may originate where locally approved by the voters. Five hundred dollar maximum loss limit per person per excursion. The proposal is intended to produce increased General Revenue."

What followed was eighteen months of policy changes and legal maneuvers. Following complaints in the media about loose regulation, the General Assembly repealed sections of the referendum. In April 1993 Senate Bills 10 and 11 were passed, which placed casino riverboats under the authority of a five-member board called the Missouri Gaming Commission and ordered that the boats be continuously docked if in the best interest of public safety. In February 1994 the Missouri Supreme Court ruled in *Harris v. Missouri Gaming Commission* that the legislature did not have the authority to allow games of chance on riverboats, only games of skill. The court ruled that by repealing portions of the referendum and issuing bills, the general assembly was acting of its own accord rather than of the people's accord, a violation of the state constitution.

In response, the legislature drafted a constitutional amendment as follows: "The general assembly is authorized to permit only upon the Missouri and Mississippi Rivers, lotteries, gift enterprises, and games of skill or chance to be conducted on excursion gambling boats and floating facilities." However, the measure was defeated by the state's voters in April 1994. The general assembly responded with Senate Bill 740, which defined games of skill and authorized riverboats to be located in artificial basins. In May 1994 the commission granted the first two licenses for riverboat casinos. However, because the casinos could not offer games of chance, chiefly slot machines, competition from Illinois riverboats kept customers away and the casinos were not profitable.

A petition effort brought the issue to a vote yet again. In November 1994 voters considered the following new initiative: "Shall the General Assembly be authorized to permit only upon the Mississippi River and the Missouri River, lotteries, gift enterprises, and games of chance to be conducted on excursion gambling boats and floating facilities? This proposal would increase state revenues from existing gaming boats approximately $30,000,000 per year. Impact on local governments unknown." The initiative was approved by a vote of 943,652 in favor to 807,707 against.

The result was significant. Revenues from casino riverboats during the first quarter of fiscal year 1996 were more than twice what they had been during the first quarter of the previous year. Initially, the casinos were only allowed to hold two-hour gambling "excursions." This was changed in 2000, when a law was passed allowing continuous boardings. However, the original $500 loss limit per excursion approved in 1992 still applies. Patrons are allowed to purchase only $500 worth of chips or tokens in any two-hour period, preventing them from losing more than that amount within the "excursion" period. The commission has repeatedly complained that the loss limit hurts the competitiveness of Missouri riverboat casinos compared to those in neighboring states.

According to the *Missouri Gaming Commission Annual Report to the General Assembly: Fiscal Year 2003*, eleven riverboat casinos operated in Missouri during fiscal year 2003 (July 2002–June 2003). The state has six general markets: St. Louis, Kansas City, Caruthersville, St. Joseph, LaGrange, and Boonville. All of the riverboats remain dockside. Games allowed include slots; blackjack, Red Dog, Pai Gow, mini-baccarat, poker, and other card games; craps; roulette; and several wheel games. Missouri gaming revenue topped $1 billion for the first time during 2001, and reached $1.3 billion during 2003. (See Figure 4.4.) Just over fifty-one million people were admitted to the state's casinos during fiscal year 2003.

Casino operators pay an 18% tax on adjusted gross receipts to the state and a 2% local tax to the home dock city or county. In addition, a $2 admission fee is paid for each patron per excursion. This fee is split evenly between the state and the local jurisdiction. The casinos also pay costs associated with Missouri Gaming Commission (MGC) agents assigned to each casino. According to the MGC the average annual cost was $568,000 per casino during 2003.

During fiscal year 2003 (July 2002–June 2003) total admission fees were $102 million and gaming taxes collected were $261 million. According to the Missouri Riverboat Gaming Association gaming fees and taxes were the fifth-largest source of tax dollars for the state.

The MGC is not limited in the number of licenses it can issue. However, the state's constitution limits riverboat casinos to locations along the Mississippi and Missouri rivers. In 2004 the town of Rockaway Beach in southwestern Missouri was behind a ballot initiative to change the constitution to allow riverboat casinos along

FIGURE 4.4

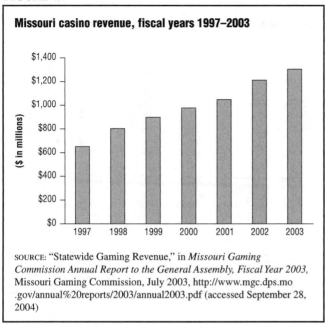

Missouri casino revenue, fiscal years 1997–2003

SOURCE: "Statewide Gaming Revenue," in *Missouri Gaming Commission Annual Report to the General Assembly, Fiscal Year 2003,* Missouri Gaming Commission, July 2003, http://www.mgc.dps.mo .gov/annual%20reports/2003/annual2003.pdf (accessed September 28, 2004)

the White River. The town of fewer than six hundred residents was suffering from economic depression and had hoped that a riverboat casino would bring in much-needed jobs and income. Despite an expensive media campaign waged by the casino's backers, the initiative was rejected by the state's voters in August 2004.

MICHIGAN

Pari-mutuel horse racing was legalized in 1933 in Michigan. During the 1970s, the state lottery was legalized, and a concerted effort began to bring casino gambling to Detroit. These efforts were unsuccessful until 1994, when the Windsor Casino opened just across the river from Detroit in Windsor, Canada. By this time, more than a dozen tribal casinos were operating around the state of Michigan, and Detroit was in an economic downturn. Attitudes toward casino gaming changed, and in November 1996 Michigan voters narrowly approved ballot Proposal E, authorizing the operation of up to three casinos in any city that met the following conditions:

- A population of 800,000 people or more

- Located within 100 miles of any other state or country in which gaming is permitted

- Casino gaming is approved by a majority of voters in the city

Proposal E was approved by a 51.5% majority of voters and subsequently modified and signed into law as the Michigan Gaming Control & Revenue Act (Public Act 69 of 1997; MCL 432.201). The Michigan Gaming Control Board was given authority to license, regulate, and control the casinos and to enforce the act. Eleven casino proposals were submitted, which were narrowed to three in

1997: Atwater/Circus Circus Casino (later called MotorCity Casino), owned by Detroit Entertainment; Greektown Casino, owned by the Sault Ste. Marie Tribe of Chippewa Indians; and the MGM Grand, owned by MGM Grand Detroit Casino. The casinos were granted permission to open at temporary locations while an upscale casino district was developed along the downtown Detroit waterfront.

The first casino, the MGM Grand, opened in July 1999 in a former IRS building. The MotorCity Casino opened in December 1999 in a former bread factory. The Greektown Casino opened in November 2000 in the heart of the city, becoming the first tribally owned casino to open off of a reservation. Detroit became the largest city in the country to allow casino gambling.

Plans for permanent Detroit casino locations incorporating large hotel complexes have faltered again and again. Although the casino companies began purchasing land along the waterfront, rising costs and local opposition forced them to abandon the idea of a casino district there. Hotel plans were scaled back after marketing studies showed that many casino customers were regional and did not need overnight lodging. The mayor and city council have bickered over permanent arrangements for the casinos, although city leaders and tourism officials are very eager for the casino/hotel complexes to be open by January 2006, when Detroit hosts the National Football League's Super Bowl.

In August 2002 the Detroit City Council approved agreements negotiated by Mayor Kwame Kilpatrick for permanent locations for the three casinos. Each of the permanent casinos is to have four hundred hotel rooms.

However, the fate of Detroit casinos remained uncertain as of 2004. The Lac Vieux Desert Band of Lake Superior Chippewa Indians filed a lawsuit against the casinos in 1997, alleging that preferential treatment was given to Atwater/Circus Circus (now MotorCity) and Greektown during the casino selection process, because the two campaigned heavily in the original statewide election on bringing casinos to Detroit. The suit has dragged on for years. The Sixth U.S. Circuit Court of Appeals in Cincinnati ruled in January 2002 that the selection process was unconstitutional. The city of Detroit tried to appeal to the U.S. Supreme Court, but the court refused to hear the appeal. In July 2002 U.S. District Judge Robert Bell denied the tribe's request for a halt to permanent casino development agreements and for reopening of the bidding process, saying "the egg cannot be unscrambled at this late date." However, only two months later, a U.S. appeals court ruled that the city must delay issuing building permits for the permanent casinos until the tribe's suit is completely reviewed.

In April 2004 the Lac Vieux tribe accepted a $79 million settlement with two of the casinos, MotorCity and

Greektown. As of August 2004 the lawsuit against the MGM Grand has not been resolved, meaning that plans for permanent casinos in Detroit are still on hold. In addition, Michigan's legislature and senate approved separate measures during 2004 that would allow slot machines at racetracks, creating so-called racinos. A final compromise on the legislation still has to be worked out.

According to the *Michigan Gaming and Control Board Annual Report to the Governor: Calendar Year 2003,* the Detroit casinos together grossed $1.130 billion in calendar year 2003 (see Figure 4.5), up very slightly from 2002. For 2003 each casino paid 8.1% of adjusted gross receipts as a state wagering tax. The entire amount went into a statewide School Aid Fund for K–12. More than $91 million was paid into the fund during 2003. During that same year, the casinos paid an additional 9.9% of adjusted gross receipts as a local wagering tax to the city of Detroit. This money was used for public safety, anti-gang and youth development programs, taxpayer relief, capital and road improvements, and other programs designed to improve the quality of life in the city. In total, adjusted gross receipts were taxed at 18%.

In addition, each of the three casinos pays an annual state services fee equal to one-third of $25 million adjusted by the Detroit consumer price index and a yearly licensing fee of $25,000. The casinos together pay an additional $4 million annually as a municipal services fee. The Compulsive Gaming Prevention Fund receives $2 million each year from the state services fee for treatment, prevention, education, training, research, and evaluation of pathological gamblers and their families under the Michigan Department of Community Health.

In 2004 the Michigan House of Representatives passed a bill that would have doubled the casino wagering tax rate to 36%. Detroit's casino industry was vigorously opposed to the increase and warned that it could force them to lay off personnel and prevent them from building the new permanent casinos. An editorial in the *Detroit News* suggested the proposed tax hike was a "back-door ploy" to encourage the casinos to drop their opposition to slot machines at the racetracks. However, the state's senate voted to raise the tax rate to 24%, and in August 2004, the Michigan legislature voted to approve the gaming revenue taxes at 24%, which took effect September 1, 2004. The breakdown of the new tax rate allocated 12.1% of revenue to the State Casino Gambling Fund and 12.1% to the city of Detroit. According to the *Michigan Gaming Law* Web site, the Greektown Casino cut 182 casino jobs that August, and the MGM Grand laid off 150 employees in September.

Unlike casinos in some other states, Detroit casinos are not permitted under the Michigan Liquor Control Code (Public Act 58 of 1998; MCL 436.2025) to provide free alcoholic drinks.

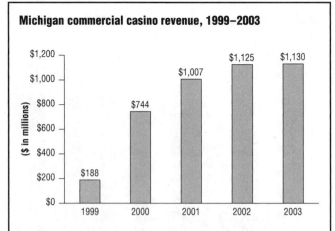

FIGURE 4.5

Michigan commercial casino revenue, 1999–2003

SOURCE: Adapted from "Casino Revenues," in *Michigan Gaming Control Board Annual Report to the Governor, Calendar Year 2003,* Michigan Gaming Commission, April 15, 2004, http://www.michigan .gov/documents/annrep03_88990_7.pdf (accessed September 28, 2004)

IOWA

Gambling was outlawed in the state of Iowa from the time of its statehood in 1846 until 1972, when a provision in the state constitution prohibiting lotteries was repealed. In 1973 the general assembly authorized bingo and raffles by specific parties. A decade later in 1983, pari-mutuel wagering at dog and horse tracks was legalized. A state lottery was authorized in 1985. In 1989 gambling aboard excursion boats was authorized for counties in which voters approved gambling referendums. Between 1989 and 1995 referendums authorizing riverboat gambling were approved in more than a dozen counties. The Iowa Racing and Gaming Commission granted licenses allowing riverboat gambling in ten counties: Clarke, Clayton, Clinton, Des Moines, Dubuque, Lee, Polk, Pottawattamie, Scott, and Woodbury. By law, the residents of these counties vote every eight years on a referendum to allow riverboat gambling to continue. In 1994 pari-mutuel racetracks were permitted to operate slot machines.

In 2003 there were ten riverboat casinos and three racetrack casinos operating in Iowa. As stated in the *Iowa Racing and Gaming Commission 2003 Annual Report,* admissions were 12.7 million to the riverboats and 6.7 million to the racinos. The riverboats are required by law to meet space requirements for nongamblers and to provide shopping and tourism options. Slots are allowed at racetracks only if a specific number of live races are held during each racing season. The renewal or extension of a particular gambling license is decided by referendum every eight years.

As shown in Figure 4.6 total adjusted gross revenues during calendar year 2003 topped $1 billion for the first time. This was a 5% increase from the year before. During 2003 casino revenues accounted for 68% of the total, and racino revenues accounted for 32%. According to *2004 State of the States: The AGA Survey of Casino Entertain-*

FIGURE 4.6

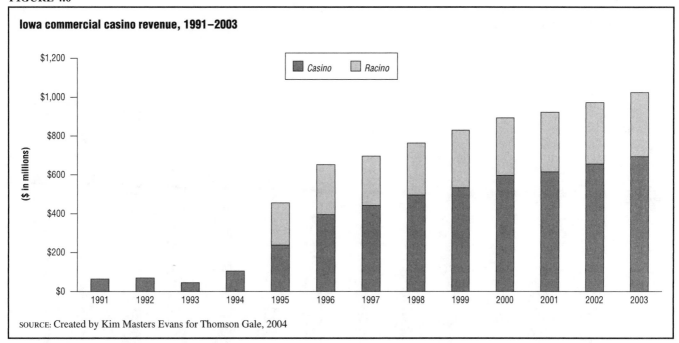

Iowa commercial casino revenue, 1991–2003

SOURCE: Created by Kim Masters Evans for Thomson Gale, 2004

ment, nearly $210 million was collected in city, county, and state taxes. Iowa's gaming tax rate ranges from 5% to 20% depending on revenue. The city and county each get 0.5% of this amount. Another 0.3% goes to gambler treatment programs, and the remainder goes to designated state funds.

Allocation of tax revenues collected by the state is dictated under Iowa Code section 8.57(5)(e). Beginning in the fiscal year extending from July 1995 through June 1996, the first $60 million in tax revenues collected by the state from all casinos was allocated to the state's general fund. Revenues in excess of that amount were allocated to the Rebuild Iowa Infrastructure Fund. Beginning in the fiscal year extending from July 2000 to June 2001, revenues in excess of $60 million were allocated to the Vision Iowa Fund, the School Infrastructure Fund, and the Rebuild Iowa Infrastructure Fund. The Vision Iowa Fund is used for recreation, education, entertainment, and cultural projects. According to the Iowa Gaming Association, in fiscal year 2004, gaming revenues topped $240 million, with appropriations going to the general fund ($60 million), Vision Iowa Fund ($15 million), School Infrastructure Fund ($5 million), gambling treatment ($3 million), Endowment for Healthy Iowans ($70 million), local city and county taxes ($10.5 million), Rebuild Iowa Infrastructure Fund ($41.6 million), and the Environment First Fund ($35 million).

COLORADO

During the 1800s gambling halls and saloons with card games were prevalent throughout the mining towns of Colorado. However, gambling was outlawed in the state around the turn of the twentieth century.

In November 1990, Colorado voters approved a constitutional amendment permitting limited-stakes gaming in the towns of Black Hawk and Central City, near Denver, and Cripple Creek, located near Colorado Springs. The first Colorado casinos opened in October 1991 and had gross revenues of nearly $8.4 million during their first month of operation. Only blackjack, poker, and slot machines are permitted, with a maximum single bet of $5. Any increase in betting limits, additional types of games, or new gambling locations would require a statewide vote authorizing change in the constitutional amendment. Since 1992, there have been seven votes on whether to expand casino gaming to additional locations; each time, expansion has been defeated by at least a two-to-one margin. The most recent vote was held during November 2003. Voters rejected by an 81% to 19% margin a proposal to allow slot machines at the state's horse and dog racetracks.

According to the Colorado Gaming Commission there were forty-four casinos operating in the state during 2003. They had gross revenues of $711 million during fiscal year 2004 (July 2003–June 2004). As shown in Figure 4.7 annual revenue grew steadily from 1992 through 2002 and then leveled off. The Black Hawk casinos have historically been the most successful in the state, accounting for 70% to 75% of casino gaming revenue each year. The Cripple Creek market is second in gross revenue, accounting for 20% to 25% of the annual total. The Central City casinos typically account for 5% to 10%.

According to *Gaming in Colorado: Fact Book & 2003 Abstract,* a publication of the Colorado Division of Gaming, total adjusted gross revenue earned between the inception of casino gambling and February 2004 added up to $5.8 billion. The casinos have paid $780 million in gaming taxes to the state over that time period. The

FIGURE 4.7

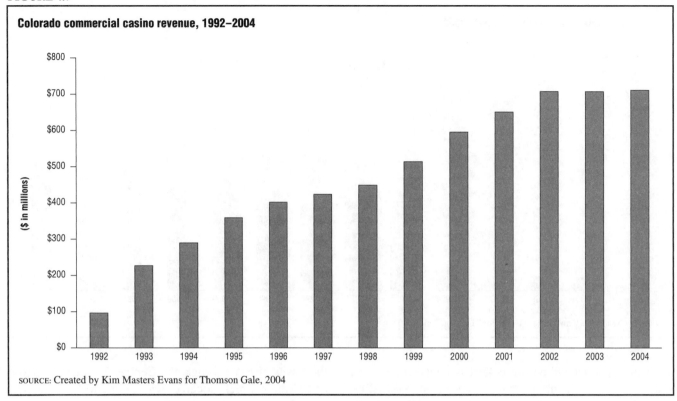

Colorado commercial casino revenue, 1992–2004

($ in millions)

SOURCE: Created by Kim Masters Evans for Thomson Gale, 2004

money has been used to fund historical restoration projects in Colorado and to offset the costs of casino gaming to state and local governments (including regulatory costs associated with the casino industry).

The casinos are overseen by the Colorado Division of Gaming, a division of the Colorado Department of Revenue. The Division of Gaming, which is responsible for regulation and enforcement, is headquartered in Lakewood, near Denver. It investigates gaming license applicants and monitors existing license holders for problems, such as ties to organized crime. Division investigators patrol the casinos to watch for any violations of gaming laws, rules, and regulations.

Casino rules and regulations are promulgated by the Colorado Limited Gaming Control Commission, a five-member group appointed by the governor. The commission establishes the gaming tax rate and has final authority over all gaming licenses issued in the state.

The gaming tax rate is graduated depending on each casino's adjusted gross proceeds (AGP), the amount of money wagered minus the amount paid out in prizes. The tax rate is set by the commission on an annual basis. In June 2003 the commission decided to retain the tax structure in place since July 1999 as follows:

- 0.25% on $0–$2 million AGP
- 2% on $2–$4 million AGP
- 4% on $4–$5 million AGP
- 11% on $5–$10 million AGP
- 16% on $10–$15 million AGP
- 20% on AGP greater than $15 million

In addition the casinos pay an annual state device fee of $75 per slot machine and game table. They also pay annual device fees ranging from $750 to $1,265 per year to their local jurisdictions. The Colorado Gaming Commission newsletter reported in October 2004 that there were 15,663 slot machines and 175 table games operating in the state. The slot machines range in denominations from pennies to $5 per play. All machines are legally required to pay back at least 80% of all money taken in by the machine over the long term.

SOUTH DAKOTA

Commercial casino gambling in South Dakota is restricted to the town of Deadwood in Lawrence County. Deadwood, located approximately sixty miles from Mount Rushmore, is a rustic mountain town that was designated as a National Historic Landmark and is listed on both the National and South Dakota Register of Historic Places. The town features more than eighty historic casinos, with a total of 112 casinos in all. Games allowed are blackjack, poker, and slot machines.

The rocky history of gambling in Deadwood is described in *The Last Gamble: Betting on the Future in Four Rocky Mountain Mining Towns* by Katherine R. Jensen and Audie L. Blevins (Tucson, AZ: University of Arizona Press, 1998). The gold rush of 1876 brought large

FIGURE 4.8

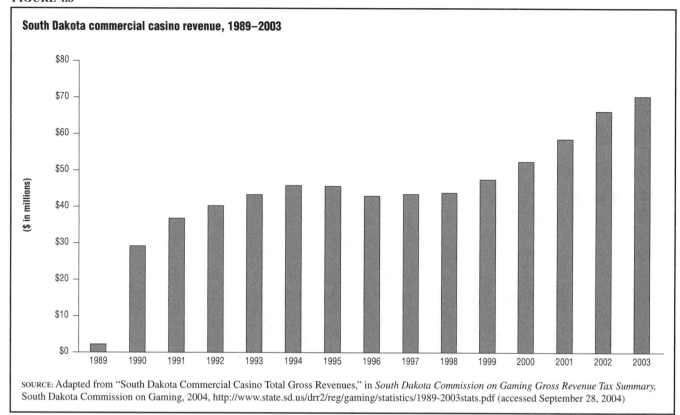

South Dakota commercial casino revenue, 1989–2003

($ in millions)

SOURCE: Adapted from "South Dakota Commercial Casino Total Gross Revenues," in *South Dakota Commission on Gaming Gross Revenue Tax Summary*, South Dakota Commission on Gaming, 2004, http://www.state.sd.us/drr2/reg/gaming/statistics/1989-2003stats.pdf (accessed September 28, 2004)

numbers of people into the town, and it soon became packed with saloons and gambling halls. The town became associated with such notorious characters as Wild Bill Hickok, Poker Alice, and Calamity Jane.

Although gambling was outlawed in the Dakota Territory in 1881, it continued quite openly in Deadwood with the apparent complicity of the local sheriff. In 1907 gambling opponents complained that the town's gambling halls "operated as openly as grocery stores, running twenty-four hours a day." On a busy Saturday night in 1947, South Dakota's attorney general sent sixteen raiders into the bars of Deadwood to show the town that the state meant business. The blatant days of gambling were over in Deadwood, although locals say that the establishments continued to operate quietly for the next four decades.

In 1984 a group of Deadwood businessmen and community leaders began working to bring legalized gambling back to Deadwood, primarily to raise money to preserve the town's historic buildings. The group developed the slogan "Deadwood You Bet" and had it printed on hundreds of buttons. Despite widespread local support, though, the state's voters and legislators were not keen on the idea. It failed at the ballot box in 1984 and was voted down by the legislature in 1988. The measure made it onto the ballot anyway in November 1988 following a massive petition effort. In 1989 South Dakota voters approved limited-stakes casino gambling for Deadwood, making South Dakota the third state (after Nevada and New Jersey) to legalize casino gambling again. Originally,

the casinos could only offer a $5 maximum bet. This limit was raised to $100 in 2000.

Deadwood's casinos are regulated by the South Dakota Commission on Gaming. According to the *South Dakota Commission on Gaming Annual Report Fiscal Year 2004*, Deadwood casinos pay an 8% gaming tax on their adjusted gross revenue and an annual fee of $2,000 per card game or slot machine. The gaming tax is allocated as follows: 50% to the Commission Fund, 40% to the Department of Tourism, and 10% to Lawrence County. The annual device fees also go into the Commission Fund.

In calendar year 2003, Deadwood casinos had total gross revenues of $70.4 million, a 6% increase from 2002. (See Figure 4.8.) South Dakota casino revenues held steady for most of the 1990s. Unlike casinos in many other states, however, they have experienced robust growth during the early twenty-first century. There were nearly three thousand licensed gambling devices and more than eighty table games operating in Deadwood during 2003. The average overall payout to patrons during December 2003 was 90%. Since the reintroduction of legalized casino gambling through December 2003, gross revenues totaled $669 million.

Nearly $5.5 million in gaming taxes was collected during 2003. Between 1989 and 2003 a total of nearly $52 million was collected. Of this amount $26 million went to the state's gaming commission fund, $21 million was allocated to promote tourism, and $5 million was turned over to Lawrence County.

CHAPTER 5

CASINOS, PART 3: NATIVE AMERICAN TRIBAL CASINOS

Indian Gaming: Final Impact Analysis (2004), a report issued by the National Indian Gaming Association (NIGA), reported that casinos operated by Native American tribes made $16.7 billion during 2003. Commercial casinos during that same year made $27 billion, as reported by the American Gaming Association (AGA) in *2004 State of the States: The AGA Survey of Casino Entertainment.* Tribal casinos, therefore, had 38% of the casino market during 2003. This percentage is expected to continue to grow throughout the first decade of the twenty-first century.

According to the U.S Census conducted in 2000, more than four million people in the United States (approximately 1.5% of the total population) identify themselves as Native Americans. These individuals belonged to more than five hundred federally recognized tribes. In 2003 more than two hundred tribes were engaged in gaming enterprises. The NIGA reported in *Indian Gaming* that more than eighteen million Americans visited tribal gaming facilities in 2002. According to *Harrah's Survey 2003: Profile of the American Casino Gambler,* Native American casinos were the top casino destination for residents of Arizona, California, Connecticut, Florida, Massachusetts, Minnesota, New Hampshire, New Mexico, North Carolina, North Dakota, Oklahoma, Oregon, Rhode Island, South Carolina, South Dakota, Washington, and Wisconsin.

Although tribal casinos are being operated throughout much of the United States, they are not welcome everywhere. In 2003 the Passamaquoddy and Penobscot tribes of Maine held a successful petition drive to put a casino referendum on the November 2003 ballot. The referendum was defeated by Maine voters by a two-to-one margin.

HISTORY

The growth of tribal casinos can be traced to the late 1970s, when Native American tribes began to operate bingo halls to raise funds for tribal purposes. Tribes in Florida and Wisconsin tried to open high-stakes bingo games on their reservations. Bingo games were legal in those states but subject to restrictions on the size of the jackpot and how often games could be held. The Oneida Tribe of Wisconsin and the Seminole Tribe of Florida took their respective states to court, claiming that the tribes were sovereign nations and not subject to state limitations on gambling.

In 1981 the Fifth Circuit Federal Court of Appeals ruled in *Seminole Tribe of Florida v. Butterworth* (658 F.2d 310) that the tribe could operate a high-stakes bingo parlor because the state of Florida did not have regulatory power over the tribe. In other words, the tribe is a sovereign governing entity that is exempt from state regulations. A similar ruling was issued in *Oneida Tribe of Indians v. Wisconsin* (518 F. Supp. 712). Both cases concluded that the states' gambling laws were regulatory (civil) in nature rather than criminal, because the states already allowed bingo games to take place.

Other tribes also sued, and the issue eventually reached the U.S. Supreme Court, which ruled in February 1987. In *California v. Cabazon Band of Mission Indians* (480 U.S. 202), the court decided that California could not prohibit a tribe from conducting activities (in this case, high-stakes bingo and poker games) that were legal elsewhere in the state.

In 1989 the Bay Mills Indian Community opened the King's Club in Brimley, Michigan; it was the first Native American gambling hall to offer slots and blackjack games instead of just bingo.

GAMBLING CLASSES

The U.S. Congress passed the Indian Gaming Regulatory Act in 1988. This act allows only federally recognized Indian tribes to open gambling establishments on their reservations if the state in which they are located already permits legalized gambling. It set up a regulatory system and three classes of gambling activities:

- Class I—Social gaming for minimal prizes and traditional gaming (for example, in tribal ceremonies or celebrations)

- Class II—Bingo and bingolike games, lotto, pull tabs (two-ply laminated paper tickets with perforated windows concealing symbols or numbers), tip jars (lottery-like games played with preprinted tickets), punch boards (thick cardboard drilled with holes, each of which is covered with foil and contains paper imprinted with symbols or numbers), and nonbanking card games (such as poker, which is played against other players instead of the house)

- Class III—Banking card games, casino games, slot machines, pari-mutuel betting, horse and dog racing, jai alai, electronic facsimiles of any game of chance, and any other forms of gaming not included in Class I or II

Class I gaming is regulated exclusively by the tribes and requires no financial reporting to other authorities. Class II games are allowed only if the state in which the tribe is located permits such gaming for any purpose by anyone. Class III games are allowed only if such games are already permitted in the state where the tribe is located. According to the U.S. General Accounting Office (GAO), the investigatory branch of Congress, court rulings have maintained that tribes can operate casinos in states that only offer state-run lotteries and charitable casino nights.

Both Class II and III operations require that the tribe adopt a gaming ordinance that is approved by the National Indian Gaming Commission (NIGC). In addition, Class III gaming requires that the tribe and state have an agreement, called a tribal-state compact (or treaty), that is approved by the secretary of the interior. A compact is supposed to balance the interests of the state and the tribe in regard to standards for operation and maintenance, the applicability of state and tribal laws and regulations, and the amount needed by the state to defray its regulatory costs. Tribes may have compacts with more than one state and may have different compacts for different types of gambling operations.

REGULATION

Tribal casinos are regulated at three levels of government: federal, state, and tribal. Federal regulation is performed by the NIGC, which "oversees the licensing of gaming employees and management and reviews tribal gaming ordinances." The NIGC also has enforcement powers. In fact, in June 2004 the NIGC issued an order of temporary closure against the Coyote Valley Band of Pomo Indians in Redwood Valley, California. The casino was allegedly operating Class III gambling devices without a compact in place with the state of California.

The federal government also has criminal jurisdiction over cases involving embezzlement, cheating, and fraud at tribal gaming operations, because such crimes are federal offenses.

State regulation is spelled out in the tribal-state compacts negotiated between the respective governments. Compacts cover such matters as the number of slot machines that may be operated, limits on types and quantities of card games that can be offered, minimum gambling ages in the casinos, authorization for casino workers to unionize, frameworks for how state and tribal regulators will work together, the length of the compact, public health and safety issues, compulsive gambling issues, the effects of tribal gaming on other state enterprises, infrastructure needs, dispute resolution, and how much revenue should be paid to the state and how often.

The tribes themselves are the primary regulators of tribal gaming. The NIGA, a trade organization for Native American casinos, reported in 2004 that more than 2,800 regulatory and enforcement personnel are employed by tribes and that more than $203 million was spent by the tribes on regulation of their industry during 2003.

FEDERAL RECOGNITION

Native American casinos must be a tribal endeavor, not an individual endeavor. In other words, a random group of Native Americans cannot legally start a casino. Only a tribe's status as a sovereign entity allows it to conduct gaming. A Native American tribe must be granted official federal recognition in order to be a sovereign entity.

The list of federally recognized tribes is maintained by the Bureau of Indian Affairs (BIA), an agency of the U.S. Department of the Interior. The most current list includes the names of 562 tribes. It was published on December 5, 2003, under the title "Indian Entities Recognized and Eligible to Receive Services from the United States Bureau of Indian Affairs," in the *Federal Register.*

Throughout history, tribes have received federal recognition through treaties with the U.S. government, via congressional actions, or through BIA decisions. Most tribes were officially recognized during the eighteenth and nineteenth centuries. Today, recognition can be achieved either through an act of Congress or through a series of actions known as the "Federal Acknowledgement Process." This can be very long and laborious, sometimes taking decades. Under federal regulation 25 CFR Part 83 a–g, there are seven criteria that a group of Native Americans must meet to be federally recognized as a tribe:

- They must have been identified as an American Indian entity on a substantially continuous basis since 1900.

- A predominant portion of the group must comprise a distinct community and have existed as a community from historical times to the present.

- They must have maintained political influence or authority over their members as an autonomous entity from historical times until the present.

- They must submit a copy of the group's present governing documents, including membership criteria.

- The group's membership must consist of individuals who descended from a historical Indian tribe or from historical Indian tribes that combined and functioned as a single autonomous political entity.

- The membership of the group must be composed primarily of people who are not members of an existing acknowledged North American Indian tribe.

- The tribe must not be the subject of congressional legislation that has terminated or forbidden a federal relationship.

Federal recognition is extremely important to Native American tribes because tribes must be federally recognized to be sovereign entities and to be eligible for billions of dollars in federal assistance. The federal government has about fifty-four million acres of land held in trust for federally recognized Indian tribes and their members. In general, exemptions from state and local jurisdiction apply to land held in trust by federally recognized tribes. Even if a tribe does not have a land base, the federal government can take land in trust for the tribe once it receives recognition. This land is no longer subject to local jurisdiction, including items such as property taxes and zoning ordinances.

Within a tribe, there are rules for membership. Most tribes require that a person have a particular degree of Native American heritage (usually 25%) to be an enrolled member. Some tribes require proof of lineage for membership. According to the GAO, federally recognized tribes had a membership of approximately 1.7 million as of May 2001.

One of the most contentious issues related to tribal casinos is the authenticity of the tribes themselves. Critics charge that some Native American groups want federal recognition only as a means to enter the lucrative gambling business. In 2001 the GAO examined this issue in a report titled *Improvements Needed in Tribal Recognition Process* (November 2001). According to the GAO there were 193 tribes with gambling facilities at that time. The report noted that 170 of the tribes (88%) could trace their federal recognition at least back to the time of the Indian Reorganization Act (IRA) of 1934 or similar legislation from the 1930s. In addition, 59% of IRA-era tribes were engaged in

gambling operations in 2001, while 45% of tribes recognized since 1960 were engaged in gambling operations.

The GAO report complained that the regulatory process established by the BIA in 1978 to ensure a uniform and objective recognition process has become too lengthy and inconsistent, leading to more and more lawsuits in federal courts.

The number of petitions for recognition received annually by the BIA began to climb during the 1990s. Although the increase was not dramatic, a backlog began to grow. As of August 2001, the BIA had received 250 petitions for recognition under the program. However, only fifty-five of those petitions had completed the documentation required for consideration. Of those, the BIA recognized fourteen tribes, denied recognition to fifteen tribes, and was considering or was scheduled to consider the other twenty-six.

As noted by the GAO, a significant amount of time is required by the BIA for a final decision on official tribal status due to limited budget and personnel, an ineffective structure for making decisions, and involvement in numerous lawsuits. A petition must be supported by substantial documentation. Once all documentation has been received and the petition is determined to be complete, it is called in "ready status." At this point, the petition is ready to be considered. The date of entering "ready status" determines the order in which a petition comes up for consideration. The GAO reported that six of the ten petitions in "ready status" in 2001 had been waiting for consideration for at least five years. During consideration, a petition is in "active status."

According to the GAO, there was a spike in petitions entering "ready status" during the mid-1990s. The BIA had placed fifty-five petitions in "ready status" since the program's inception in 1978. Twenty-three of those petitions (or 42%) were placed in "ready status" between 1993 and 1997. Although active consideration of a completed petition is supposed to take approximately two years, the BIA reported to the GAO that it could take fifteen years for the agency to resolve all of the petitions awaiting active consideration as of 2001.

REVENUES

Because tribes are sovereign governments they are not required by law to make public their revenues. Financial information on individual tribal casinos is not publicly released. Each year the NIGC announces total gaming revenue for the previous year for all tribal gaming facilities combined. It also breaks down the revenue by U.S. region and revenue class. On July 13, 2004, the NIGC released financial information showing that tribal casinos made $16.7 billion during 2003, an increase of 13.7% over

TABLE 5.1

Tribal gaming revenues by region, fiscal years 2002 and 2003

(In thousands)

| | Fiscal year 2003 | | Fiscal year 2002 | | Increase | (decrease) |
	Number of operations	Gaming revenues	Number of operations	Gaming revenues	Number of operations	Gaming revenues
Region I	43	1,439,516	47	1,230,194	−4	209,322
Region II	54	4,699,889	51	3,678,095	3	1,021,794
Region III	43	1,898,522	40	1,782,874	3	115,648
Region IV	91	3,547,360	109	3,537,227	−18	10,133
Region V	75	822,727	79	651,841	−4	170,886
Region VI	24	4,322,134	22	3,835,825	2	486,309
Totals	**330**	**16,730,148**	**348**	**14,716,056**	**−18**	**2,014,092**

Region I	Alaska, Idaho, Oregon, and Washington.
Region II	California, northern Nevada.
Region III	Arizona, Colorado, New Mexico, and southern Nevada.
Region IV	Iowa, Michigan, Minnesota, Montana, North Dakota, Nebraska, South Dakota, and Wisconsin
Region V	Kansas, Oklahoma, and Texas.
Region VI	Alabama, Connecticut, Florida, Louisiana, Mississippi, North Carolina and New York.

Note: Compiled from gaming operation audit reports received and entered by the National Indian Gaming Commission through June 30, 2004.

SOURCE: National Indian Gaming Commission Tribal Gaming Revenues (in Thousands) by Region, Fiscal Year 2003 and 2002, in *NIGC Announces Indian Gaming Revenue for 2003,* National Indian Gaming Commission, July 13, 2004, http://www.nigc.gov/nigc/documents/releases/pr_revenue_2003.jsp (accessed August 7, 2004)

2002. This revenue is broken down by region in Table 5.1 and by revenue class in Table 5.2.

As shown in Table 5.1 tribal casinos in California and northern Nevada were the most profitable, earning $4.7 billion in 2003. Because there are no tribal casinos in northern Nevada, all of this revenue is actually from California tribal casinos. Gaming tribes in California earned 28% of all tribal casino revenue. Their market share is equivalent to that reported for commercial casinos on the Las Vegas strip during 2002.

The second most profitable region of the nation for gaming tribes during 2003 was Region VI including the states of Connecticut, New York, Louisiana, Mississippi, Alabama, Florida, and North Carolina. This region was responsible for $4.3 billion in casino revenues, or 26% of total tribal revenue. Casinos operating in Connecticut are thought to be the largest source of this region's revenue.

According to the GAO, tribal gambling revenues grew from only $171 million in 1988 (when the Indian Gaming Regulatory Act was passed) to $3.8 billion in 1994. Revenues reported by the NIGC for 1995 through 2003 are shown in Figure 5.1. Over this time period tribal casino revenues increased by 207%. By contrast, revenues at commercial casinos increased by only 69%.

Tribal gaming revenues reported by the NIGC for 2003 are broken down by revenue class in Table 5.2. As shown in this table, 22% of tribal gambling operations earned revenues of less than $3 million. Forty-three operations (13% of the total number) earned $100 million or more during 2003. These forty-three facilities accounted for 64% of all tribal casino revenue. There were only twenty-eight tribal operations in this revenue class in 1999.

The Indian Gaming Regulatory Act requires that net revenues from tribal gaming be used in five specific areas:

- To fund tribal government operations or programs

- To provide for the general welfare of the tribe and its members

- To promote tribal economic development

- To donate to charitable organizations

- To help fund operations of local government agencies

According to the NIGA, only one-fourth of the gaming tribes distribute gaming revenues to individual tribe members through per capita payments. Such payments are allowed under law but must be approved by the secretary of interior. The recipients must also pay federal income tax on these payments. For example, in spring 2002 the Puyallup Tribe of Washington began issuing monthly checks of $2,000 to each member of the tribe. The funds issued to children will be held in trust by the tribe until the children reach age eighteen. The tribe operates a riverboat casino and has plans to build a large land-based casino.

The NIGA reports that tribal casinos are increasingly making money from their nongambling enterprises, such as lodging, restaurants, and entertainment. These enterprises brought in $1.8 billion in revenue during 2003, a 5.9% increase from 2002.

TRIBAL-COMMERCIAL CASINO VENTURES

Casino building is very expensive. Those tribes that have built casinos have had to borrow large sums of money and/or obtain investors to do so. In general, for

TABLE 5.2

Tribal gaming revenues by revenue class (in thousands), 1999–2003

Gaming Revenue Range	Number of operations	Revenues (in thousands)	Percentage of operations	Revenues	Mean (in thousands)	Median (in thousands)
Gaming operations with fiscal years ending in 2003						
$100 million and over	43	10,714,581	13%	64%	249,176	184,332
$50 million to $100 million	35	2,459,698	11%	15%	70,277	65,416
$25 million to $50 million	55	1,984,673	17%	12%	36,085	37,029
$10 million to $25 million	67	1,144,779	20%	7%	17,086	16,894
$3 million to $10 million	57	350,398	17%	2%	6,147	5,819
Under $3 million	73	76,019	22%	0%	1,041	833
Total	**330**	**16,730,148**				
Gaming operations with fiscal years ending in 2002						
$100 million and over	41	9,510,660	12%	65%	231,967	179,101
$50 million to $100 million	24	1,694,606	7%	12%	70,609	65,577
$25 million to $50 million	55	1,978,519	16%	13%	35,976	38,984
$10 million to $25 million	65	1,067,513	19%	7%	16,423	16,570
$3 million to $10 million	63	386,399	18%	3%	6,133	5,373
Under $3 million	100	78,359	29%	1%	784	461
Total	**348**	**14,716,056**				
Gaming operations with fiscal years ending in 2001						
$100 million and over	39	8,398,523	12%	65%	215,347	158,836
$50 million to $100 million	19	1,415,755	6%	11%	74,513	79,083
$25 million to $50 million	43	1,528,611	13%	12%	35,549	34,264
$10 million to $25 million	58	997,546	18%	8%	17,199	16,328
$3 million to $10 million	57	385,654	17%	3%	6,766	7,292
Under $3 million	114	96,257	35%	1%	844	575
Total	**330**	**12,822,346**				
Gaming operations with fiscal years ending in 2000						
$100 million and over	31	6,606,284	10%	60%	213,106	141,684
$50 million to $100 million	24	1,693,510	8%	15%	70,563	73,314
$25 million to $50 million	41	1,360,777	13%	12%	33,190	29,944
$10 million to $25 million	50	856,464	16%	8%	17,129	17,335
$3 million to $10 million	55	350,110	18%	3%	6,366	6,250
Under $3 million	110	91,545	35%	1%	832	541
Total	**311**	**10,958,690**				
Gaming operations with fiscal years ending in 1999						
$100 million and over	28	5,845,787	9%	60%	208,778	136,897
$50 million to $100 million	19	1,323,995	6%	14%	69,684	70,412
$25 million to $50 million	33	1,193,049	11%	12%	36,153	35,990
$10 million to $25 million	59	1,028,834	19%	10%	17,438	17,562
$3 million to $10 million	54	322,268	17%	3%	5,968	5,764
Under $3 million	117	86,907	38%	1%	537	395
Total	**310**	**9,800,840**				

SOURCE: National Indian Gaming Commission Tribal Gaming Revenues, in *NIGC Announces Indian Gaming Revenue for 2003,* National Indian Gaming Commission, July 13, 2004, http://www.nigc.gov/nigc/documents/releases/pr_revenue_2003.jsp (accessed August 7, 2004)

Native American casinos, the law requires that tribes partner with companies for no more than five years and limits the companies' revenue to 30% of the total revenue. Under some circumstances, the partnership can last seven years and the companies' portion can be as much as 40% of total revenue.

At the end of 2003 the NIGC reported that forty-two gaming tribes had approved management contracts in place with commercial companies. Another eighteen potential contracts were under review at that time. One-third of the existing contracts are with gaming companies based in Las Vegas. Harrah's Entertainment is a partner in five of these contracts.

Tribal casinos have faced fierce opposition from commercial casino operators, who fear the competition. This is particularly true in California, where tribal casinos could cut deeply into Nevada casino revenues, as California's residents provide a large share of Nevada's gambling revenue. However, commercial casino companies see new opportunities for revenue gain through partnerships with Native American tribes. Some tribes have welcomed the investment capital and casino management experience offered by commercial partners. This is particularly true for small tribes.

For example, the Trump 29 Casino is a $60 million venture located in the Mojave Desert 130 miles southeast of Los Angeles, California. The casino, which opened in April 2002,

FIGURE 5.1

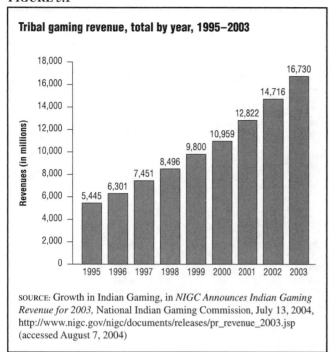

Tribal gaming revenue, total by year, 1995–2003

SOURCE: Growth in Indian Gaming, in *NIGC Announces Indian Gaming Revenue for 2003,* National Indian Gaming Commission, July 13, 2004, http://www.nigc.gov/nigc/documents/releases/pr_revenue_2003.jsp (accessed August 7, 2004)

is owned by the Twenty-Nine Palms Band of Luiseno Mission Indians, which has thirteen adult members. The casino is managed by Trump Hotels and Casino Resorts of Atlantic City, a commercial company owned by billionaire businessman Donald Trump. A tribal spokesperson said that the tribe selected the company for its name recognition appeal and for the management expertise it could bring to the casino.

In July 2002 the Augustine Band of Cahuilla Mission Indians opened a $16 million casino in southern California near the Salton Sea. The tribe has only one adult member. The tribe teamed with the company Paragon Gaming of Las Vegas to develop the casino, which has several table games and about 350 slot machines.

Casino business ventures between companies and very small tribes are particularly controversial. Critics say that small tribes are being manipulated by outside investors who only want to cash in on tribal casinos. The California Nations Indian Gaming Association insists that small tribes should not be denied the tremendous economic opportunities offered by casinos. According to a spokesperson, "The reason some of these tribes have only one or two people left is because Indians were exterminated."

THE STORY OF NATIVE AMERICAN CASINOS IN TWO STATES

Connecticut Tribal Casinos

Tribal casinos are not required by law to make their financial records public. Although exact figures are not known, various reports indicate that the tribal casinos operating in Connecticut are extremely profitable. In October 2003 the American Gaming Association (AGA)

attributed $2.0 billion in annual revenue to Connecticut's tribal casinos, making them the fourth largest casino market in the country, behind only the Las Vegas Strip, Atlantic City, and Chicagoland.

Only two tribal casinos were operating in Connecticut as of mid-2004. The Foxwoods Casino and Resort is operated by the Mashantucket Pequot in Ledyard, and the Mohegan Sun is operated by the Mohegan in nearby Uncasville. Both are located in a rural area of eastern Connecticut.

The Foxwoods is often described as the world's largest casino complex. In August 2004 the resort featured six casinos, 1,400 hotel rooms, a spa, a golf and country club, a 12,000-square-foot shopping mall, dozens of restaurants, and a 4,000-seat arena. The Foxwoods has more than 6,400 slot machines, 350 table games, and the world's largest bingo hall. It also offers keno and sports gambling. The resort receives about 40,000 visitors every day. The Mohegan Sun has just more than 1,000 hotel rooms and twenty-nine restaurants. It also includes a 10,000-seat arena, its own gas station, a showroom, extensive retail complex, and 295,000 square feet of casino floor.

The Foxwoods in particular has an interesting history. According to Kim Isaac Eisler in *Revenge of the Pequots: How a Small Native American Tribe Created the World's Most Profitable Casino* (New York: Simon and Schuster, 2001), a law was passed in Connecticut in the 1980s that allowed the wagering of "play-money" on casino games such as blackjack, roulette, craps, and poker. The law was championed by the Mothers Against Drunk Driving organization to encourage high schools to hold casino-type events following proms in order to reduce drunk driving by teenagers. Under this law, the Mashantucket Pequot Tribe was able to get a license for a "charity" gambling casino. They also procured $60 million from an Asian investor named Sol Kerzner to begin construction.

The Foxwoods Casino opened in 1992. At that time, slot machines were not permitted. In 1993 the tribe negotiated a deal with Connecticut's governor that provided the tribe with exclusive rights to operate slot machines within the state. In return, the tribe agreed to make yearly payments to the state of $100 million or 25% of their slots revenue, whichever was greater. The next year the Mohegan tribe signed its own compact with the governor to operate a casino. The Mashantucket Pequots granted the Mohegan permission to include slot machines in their new casino. In return, the state set the annual payment required from each tribe at $80 million or 25% of their slots revenue, whichever was greater. The Mohegan Sun opened in 1996 after receiving financing from Sol Kerzner, but by 1997 Foxwoods was the largest and most profitable casino in America.

The Mashantucket Pequot's standing as a tribe is not without controversy. In *Without Reservation: The Making*

TABLE 5.3

Connecticut tribal gaming payments to state general fund, 1992–2004

Fiscal year end 06/30	Casino		
	Foxwoods	Mohegan Sun	Subtotal
1992	$30,000,000		$30,000,000
1993	113,000,000		$113,000,000
1994	135,724,017		$135,724,017
1995	148,702,765		$148,702,765
1996	145,957,933	$57,643,836	$203,601,769
1997	165,067,994	91,007,858	$256,075,852
1998	173,581,104	113,450,294	$287,031,398
1990	189,235,039	129,750,030	$318,985,069
2000	190,683,773	141,734,541	$332,418,314
2001	199,038,210	169,915,956	$368,954,166
2002	196,300,526	190,953,944	$387,254,472
2003	196,300,528	190,952,944	$387,254,472
2004	196,883,096	205,850,884	$402,733,980
	$1,884,174,459	$1,100,307,343	$2,984,481,802

Notes:
[1]Revenue transferred on cash basis per fiscal year.
[2]The above transfers represent actual Casino contributions through July 15, 2004, based on reported video facsimile/slot machine revenue through June 30, 2004.

SOURCE: Adapted from "Transfers to General Fund," in *Connecticut Division of Special Revenue Transfers to General Fund, Accumulative to Date— through June 2004*, Connecticut Division of Special Revenue, July 26, 2004, http://www.dosr.state.ct.us/PDFFolder/stmt2004.pdf (accessed September 28, 2004)

FIGURE 5.2

Connecticut gaming payments to state general fund, 1972–2004

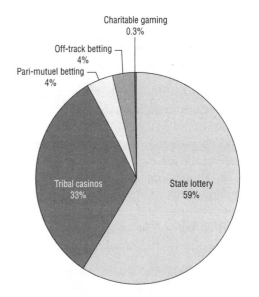

SOURCE: Adapted from "Transfers to General Fund," in *Connecticut Division of Special Revenue Transfers to General Fund, Accumulative to Date—through June 2004*, Connecticut Division of Special Revenue, July 26, 2004, http://www.dosr.state.ct.us/PDFFolder/stmt2004.pdf (accessed September 28, 2004)

of America's Most Powerful Indian Tribe and Foxwoods, the World's Largest Casino (New York: HarperCollins, 2001), Jeff Benedict claimed that the Pequots never should have been legally recognized as a tribe by the federal government in 1983 because some members were not actually descendants of the historic Pequot tribe. The tribe achieved its recognition by an act of Congress. Benedict made the allegations a major theme in his unsuccessful run for Congress during the summer of 2002. He later helped to found the Connecticut Alliance against Casino Expansion (CAACE), a nonprofit coalition that lobbied against additional casinos is Connecticut and successfully led the drive to repeal the state's "Las Vegas Night" law that provided the legal opening for the original casinos. The CAACE additionally seeks federal legislation to reform the tribal recognition process.

In Connecticut, legalized gambling is regulated by the Division of Special Revenue, which conducts licensing, permitting, monitoring, and education. It also ensures that the correct revenues are transferred to the state's general fund and to each municipality that hosts a gaming facility or charitable game. Table 5.3 shows the annual and cumulative revenues paid into the general fund by the Foxwoods and Mohegan Sun casinos. Nearly $3 billion had been collected through June 2004. This includes $1.9 billion from Foxwoods and $1.1 billion from Mohegan Sun. This revenue comprises 33% of all gambling revenue collected by the Connecticut general fund since 1972, even though the casinos have only been operating since 1992 and 1996, respectively. (See Figure 5.2.)

In June 2002 two other Connecticut tribes achieved federal recognition: the Eastern Pequots and the Paucatuck Eastern Pequots. The BIA determined that the two bands, which share a 225-acre reservation in North Stonington, are actually one tribe to be called the Historic Eastern Pequots. North Stonington is less than ten miles from the town of Ledyard, where Foxwoods is located. The Eastern Pequots and Paucatuck Eastern Pequots originally petitioned the BIA for recognition in 1978 and 1989, respectively. The recognition was fought by state and local officials, who argued that the two bands were not a legitimate tribe and that the recognition process was too political.

Tribal spokespeople said that recognition was not pursued just to be able to open casinos, but that a casino was in their plans. The Paucatuck Eastern Pequot band's recognition campaign was largely financed by Donald Trump. He has threatened to sue the tribe if it leaves him out of future casino plans. The tribe has a reservation but wants to use it for living purposes only. In order to develop a casino on other lands, the tribe would have to take land into trust and negotiate a new tribal-state compact with Connecticut. Local officials have indicated that they are opposed to any tribal efforts to take more land into trust.

California Tribal Casinos

California has forty-five gaming tribes, by far the most of any state. The state's tribal casinos earned nearly

$4.7 billion in 2003, approximately one-fourth of the nationwide tribal total. Industry analysts predict that this percentage will continue to grow as the California market matures. The state includes 108 federally recognized tribes, nearly one-fifth of the national total. Most are described as small extended family groups living on a few acres of federal trust property called rancherias. Some tribes have only a handful of members.

Prior to 2000, California tribes were largely limited to bingo halls because state law prohibited the operation of slot machines and other gambling devices, certain card games, banked games, and games where the house collects a share of the amount wagered. In 2000 California voters passed Proposition 1A, amending the state constitution to permit Native American tribes to operate lottery games, slot machines, and banking and percentage card games on tribal lands. The constitutionality of the measure was immediately challenged in court.

In January 2002 California governor Gray Davis signed sixty-two gambling compacts with California tribes. The compacts allowed each tribe to have a maximum of two thousand slot machines. The governor also announced plans to cap the number of slot machines in the state at 45,000. At the time, there were already 40,000 slot machines in operation and dozens of tribal casinos in the planning stages. The governor put a moratorium on new compacts while the constitutionality of Proposition 1A was challenged in court. In August 2002 a U.S. district court ruled that tribal casinos were entitled to operate under the provisions of the state gaming compacts and Proposition 1A.

In 2003 the State of California suffered a severe budget crisis. Governor Davis was ultimately forced out of office through a special recall election held in October 2003 in which Arnold Schwarzenegger became the new governor. In televised campaign ads Schwarzenegger promised voters to make tribal casinos "pay their fair share" arguing that "their casinos make billions, yet pay no taxes and virtually nothing to the state." The California Nations Indian Gaming Association (CNIGA) was outraged and issued a press release calling the remarks "hurtful" and accusing Schwarzenegger of having "a complete and almost frightening lack of understanding of the legal status of Indians and tribal governments." CNIGA also reminded voters that the gaming tribes paid more than $100 million per year into a special fund designated to pay for impacts of tribal gaming on local communities ("Schwarzenegger Far Off the Mark on Tribal Governments," California Nations Indian Gaming Association Press Release, September 23, 2003).

In June 2004 Governor Schwarzenegger signed new compacts with five California tribes preserving the tribes' exclusive gaming rights. The five tribes are as follows:

• Pala Band of Mission Indians

• Pauma Band of Mission Indians

• Rumsey Band of Wintun Indians

• United Auburn Indian Community

• Viejas Band of Kumeyaay Indians

The slot machine cap was also increased above two thousand machines per tribe. In exchange the tribes agreed to pay the state $1 billion up front and a licensing fee for each new slot machine added above the current limit. This is estimated to result in payments of $150–275 million per year through the compact's expiration date in 2030. The governor announced plans to negotiate similar deals with other tribes in the state. However, several tribes announced plans to fight the new compacts. The Rincon Indian Tribe sued the state, arguing that the new compacts showed favoritism to some tribes and put others at an economic disadvantage. Other tribes announced plans to push for statewide ballot initiatives that would tax tribal casinos at fixed rates, but allow expansion of casino-type gambling in the state.

CHAPTER 6

CASINOS, PART 4: THE EFFECTS OF CASINOS

NATIONAL PUBLIC OPINION

According to a 2002 poll conducted for the American Gaming Association (AGA) by Peter D. Hart Research Associates, Inc., and the Luntz Research Companies, Americans in favor of casinos in their communities outnumber those who disapprove of local casino gambling. Of those with an opinion, 49% indicated some degree of favor, while 40% indicated disfavor. A 2004 AGA poll showed that about two-thirds of people polled believe that casinos bring widespread economic benefits to other industries and businesses in their region.

Proponents of casino gambling consider it part of the leisure/entertainment sector—like amusement parks or movie theaters. In a casino, participants exchange their money for a good time. Those who support casino gambling generally do not see it as a moral issue.

Those who are opposed to casinos are less unified in their opinions. Some disapprove of gambling. Others are wary of an industry that was associated with mobsters, swindlers, and corrupt politicians throughout much of this country's history. Still others believe that casinos are a bad idea because they provide a place for those who are prone to problem gambling to act on those urges. Easy accessibility to casinos might also encourage some people to gamble who otherwise would not and should not. Many social reformers believe in protecting people from their own bad judgment.

There is also the so-called NIMBY factor, which stands for "not in my backyard." Some people support casinos in theory and may even visit them on vacation, but they do not want one in their hometown, for whatever reason. According to the AGA in *2004 State of the States,* four out of ten Americans do not want a casino in their own neighborhood, although just over five out of ten feel casino gambling is perfectly acceptable for anyone. Local residents and politicians are often opposed to casinos because they fear increased traffic and crime and may want to protect their community's image. Also, many state governments are running lotteries and do not want competition from casinos for their residents' gambling dollars.

THE EFFECTS OF NATIVE AMERICAN TRIBAL CASINOS

Native American tribes who encounter opposition to their casino plans attribute some of the opposition to the issues described above and some of it to racism. On the other hand, some critics of tribal casinos believe that they encourage a cycle of dependence. These critics claim that tribe members who were formerly dependent on the federal government are now dependent on their tribal government.

The Pros

In 2004 the National Indian Gaming Association (NIGA) published *Indian Gaming: Final Impact Analysis,* a study of the economic and social effects of tribal gaming. The report notes the following advantages that tribal gaming and associated businesses have brought to Native Americans:

- Generated revenues of nearly $18 billion in 2003

- Created nearly 500,000 jobs

- Paid wages of approximately $5 billion to employees of tribal governments and economic development enterprises

- Contributed to substantial development in Indian-owned small businesses during the late 1990s

- Provided millions of dollars to nongaming tribes through special trust funds

- Provided a means for trade and commerce between gaming and nongaming tribes, for example, through purchasing of goods and services

- Resulted in contributions of more than $100 million in 2003 from tribal governments to charities and non-profit organizations

- Funded essential tribal programs, such as schools, hospitals, water and sewer systems, roads, police and firefighting programs, infrastructure needs, and cultural and social projects

The report concludes that "gaming has given Tribal leaders the opportunity to acquire the knowledge, skills and self-confidence needed to build strong Tribal governments and, for the first time in generations, provide for the health, education, and welfare of their people."

A study published in April 2000 (Jonathan B. Taylor, Matthew B. Krepps, and Patrick Wang, *The National Evidence on the Socioeconomic Impacts of American Indian Gaming on Non-Indian Communities,* Chicago: Lexecon) found that Native American casinos had substantial economic and social benefits to surrounding communities and that these impacts were greater than those from non–Native American casinos. This was because Native American casinos were more likely to be in areas suffering from severe economic depression.

The researchers examined a hundred communities across the country including twenty-four in which commercial casinos had been introduced and sixteen in which tribal casinos had been introduced. Analysis of thirty indicators of socioeconomic health revealed no harmful impacts associated with the introduction of tribal casinos. The casinos were praised for benefits including infrastructure improvements, economic growth, higher employment, better social programs, greater indigenous language retention, and all-around community vitality.

The Cons

Critics of tribal gambling claim that tribal casinos unfairly compete against local hotels, restaurants, and pari-mutuel operators; hurt state lottery sales; place an increased burden on states to address problems resulting from pathological gambling; introduce opportunities for money laundering and organized crime; and hurt the culture and political stability of the tribes.

An editorial by the staff of the *Wall Street Journal* (April 4, 2002) made three major claims against the tribal casino industry: that it is underregulated, linked with organized crime, and rife with political scandal. The editorial cited the relatively low budget of $8 million under which the National Indian Gaming Commission (NIGC) operates as proof that the industry is underregulated. The NIGC, which is responsible for oversight of hundreds of tribal casinos, employs fewer than thirty full-time auditors and inspectors, while in contrast, the New Jersey gaming authorities employ more than two hundred auditors to oversee only twelve casinos. The editorial cited reports

from other newspapers linking tribal casinos in Minnesota, Florida, and California with known Mafia figures. Finally, the editorial accused politicians of misusing the federal recognition process to give tribal status to "groups of dubious lineage" so that these tribes could open casinos.

The journal *Indian Country Today* called the editorial "generalized fiction" and insisted that tribal gambling is more regulated than other gambling enterprises in the country. Comparison of the NIGC budget to those of state gaming commissions is inaccurate because the NIGC is not the primary regulatory authority over Class III gambling. The tribes spend more than $100 million per year on their own regulatory structures.

Furthermore, the states that enter compacts with tribes have input in how tribal gaming is conducted, and no states have complained about problems with underregulation. The magazine reports that there have been isolated incidents of organized crime figures trying to infiltrate tribal gaming operations, but that the wrongdoers have been ferreted out and caught. The article cited a statement by the chief of the Organized Crime and Racketeering Section of the U.S. Department of Justice, who in 2001 reported to a Senate committee that there had been isolated incidents but no systematic infiltration by organized crime figures.

In general, state and local authorities associate tribal casinos with increased regulatory, law enforcement, and infrastructure costs, but also with savings on welfare assistance payments. Increased costs can be offset by licensing fees collected from the tribes as dictated in state-tribal compacts.

THE LACK OF BALANCED DATA

Assessing the overall effects of casinos on society is a difficult task. There are many factors to consider. Most relate to economics, but some relate to quality of life and moral issues. The latter are difficult to gauge in quantitative terms.

In 1996 Congress created the National Gambling Impact Study Commission (NGISC) to study the economic and social impacts of legalized gambling. The commission included nine members and conducted hearings during 1998 in Las Vegas, Nevada; Atlantic City, New Jersey; Chicago, Illinois; San Diego, California; and Biloxi, Mississippi. The NGISC's final report was published in 1999.

The report's findings on the local impact of casino gambling can be summarized as follows:

- Casinos are associated with increased per capita income in the construction, hotel, lodging, recreation, and amusement industries but decreased per capita income for those working in local restaurants and bars.

- The economic benefits of casinos are particularly impressive in economically depressed communities.

- Casinos create full-time entry-level jobs that are badly needed in areas suffering from chronic unemployment and underemployment.

- Unemployment rates, welfare payments, and unemployment insurance declined by approximately one-seventh in communities close to newly opened casinos.

- In terms of income, health insurance, and pensions, casino jobs in the destination resorts of Las Vegas and Atlantic City are better than comparable jobs in the service industries.

- Small business owners located near casinos often suffer from loss of business.

- Tribal casino workers have complained about lack of job security, an absence of federal and state antidiscrimination laws, and the lack of workers' compensation benefits.

- Elected officials from casino towns expressed support for casinos because they improved the quality of life in their towns and funded community improvements.

- Problems with pathological gambling increased in seven of nine communities surveyed.

- The AGA is the largest source of funding for research on pathological gambling.

- Many casinos train management and staff to identify problem gamblers among customers or employees.

- Many tribal casinos contribute money to nonprofit groups dealing with problem gambling.

The report concluded that lack of objective research data on gambling issues was a major hurdle in determining the extent of its effects on society.

PURE ECONOMICS

American casinos took in nearly $44 billion during 2003, making the casino industry a very big business. From an economic standpoint, most casinos have been a huge success for their investors. Commercial casino investors range from middle-class stockholders in major corporations to billionaires like Donald Trump and Steve Wynn. Most tribal casinos have been economically successful as well, bringing unimagined wealth to Native Americans, many of whom were at the very bottom of America's economic ladder only a decade ago.

Also, casinos are labor-intensive businesses that employ hundreds of thousands of people. These employees support their families, pay taxes, and buy goods and services—factors that contribute to the economic health of their communities.

The economic effects of casinos on local and state governments in terms of taxes and fees are also significant. Commercial casinos pay billions of dollars every year to government agencies in the form of application fees, regulatory fees, wagering taxes, and admission taxes. These monies fund programs that improve the quality of life of people in the immediate vicinity or same state as the casinos. In turn, governments incur increased costs for more police, roads, sewers, and so forth when casinos open in their jurisdictions. Tribal casinos, though exempt from state and local taxation, pay billions of dollars each year to compensate states and municipalities for regulatory and public-service expenses.

Economic factors alone do not justify or vilify an industry. One could argue that the steel industry benefits society by providing many economic benefits (jobs, marketable goods, corporate taxes, and so forth) and harms society by creating pollution. Benefits and harms must be weighed against one another. In addition to crime, bankruptcy, and suicide rates, important issues that are affected by the presence of casinos include employment, tourism, domestic problems, compulsive and underage gambling, and politics.

DIRECT GOVERNMENT REVENUE

From Commercial Casinos

According to the AGA study *2004 State of the States*, commercial casinos generated tax revenues of $4.32 billion in 2003, up from $4 billion in 2002. Nevada generated the greatest tax revenue in 2003 ($776.5 million), followed by Illinois ($719.9 million) and Indiana ($702.7 million). Racetrack casinos generated tax revenues of $765.6 million in 2003, up from $718 million in 2002.

According to a 2003 AGA survey, 70% of Americans believe that legalized casino gambling is a good way to generate local and state revenues without having a general tax increase. However, respondents seemed uncertain as to where those gaming tax revenues go. Only 58% of those polled agreed that such revenues have helped pay for local roads, schools, hospitals, and other projects.

Gaming revenue taxes can be a substantial portion of a state's revenue. In Nevada in fiscal year 2003, gaming taxes and the casino entertainment tax accounted for 37% of the state's total budget. In July 2003 the *Las Vegas Sun* estimated that the gaming industry actually contributes 50% of the state's budget, when associated property and commercial taxes are considered ("Gaming Takes It on Chin During Session," by Jeff Gorman, July 5, 2003). Nevada legislators increased the maximum gaming tax rate from 6.25% to 6.75% during 2003, the first increase in years. The move was driven by a severe state budget crisis.

During 2002 and 2003 the state of Illinois raised gaming taxes on its casinos in an effort to ease state budget woes. The AGA complained that the increase caused the casinos to raise prices, lay off employees, and limit their capital investments, thus hurting the industry in the long term. Legislators in other casino states are increasingly considering raising gaming taxes to ease their budget problems.

According to statistics published on the Web site of the Mississippi Gaming Association (www.mississippi-gaming.org) the state's casino industry contributes about 10% of the state's total budget. In Mississippi in 2001, gaming revenue taxes were greater than the combined corporate taxes paid by all other corporations in the state.

According to statistics provided by the Mississippi Gaming Commission (www.mgc.state.ms.us), the number of people receiving food stamps in Tunica County dropped 56% between June 1992, when the first casinos opened there, and August 1997, while the assessed value of personal property rose from $16 million to $566 million. The tax rate dropped from 11.4 cents per $1,000 assessed value to 4.2 cents per $1,000. The county improved its roads and sewers and built new schools and a medical center.

From Native American Casinos

As described in Chapter 5, the Indian Gaming Regulatory Act requires that net revenues from tribal gaming be used in five general areas:

- To fund tribal government operations or programs
- To provide for the general welfare of the tribe and its members
- To promote tribal economic development
- To donate to charitable organizations
- To help fund operations of local government agencies

Figure 6.1 shows the tribal government services funded by tribal casinos during 2003. This breakdown was compiled by the NIGA based on a survey of its member tribes.

The revenues earned by tribal casinos are not taxable, because the casinos are operated by tribal governments. Just as the federal government does not tax the states for revenue earned from lottery tickets, the federal government does not tax tribal governments for revenue earned from casinos. Therefore, tribal casinos generate less tax revenue than commercial casinos. Tribe members who live on the reservation and are employed at tribal enterprises (such as casinos) are not subject to state income taxes. On the other hand, tribe members do pay federal income tax, FICA, and social security taxes on their wages, even if earned at tribal enterprises. Wages paid to tribe members living off-site and to nontribe employees are subject to state income taxes.

FIGURE 6.1

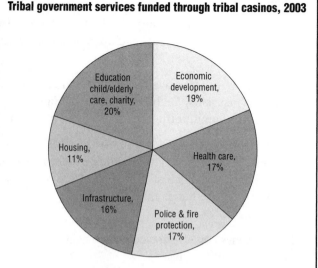

Tribal government services funded through tribal casinos, 2003

SOURCE: "2003 Indian Government Services Funded through Indian Gaming," in *Indian Gaming: Final Impact Analysis,* National Indian Gaming Association, 2004, http://www.indiangaming.org/info/Final_Impact_Analysis.pdf (accessed September 13, 2004)

The NIGA says that tribal casinos and associated business generated $4.7 billion in federal taxes during 2003. This includes employer and employee Social Security taxes, personal and corporate income taxes, and excise taxes. *Indian Gaming: Final Impact Analysis* estimates that jobs created by tribal casinos reduced federal unemployment and welfare payments by $1.2 billion during 2003.

According to the NIGA report *Indian Gaming: Final Impact Analysis,* tribal governments spent more than $200 million during 2003 on casino regulatory costs. They gave another $50 million to their home states and $9 million to the NIGC to offset oversight expenses. The report also notes that tribal casinos and associated businesses paid $1.6 billion to state governments during 2003 and $100 million to local governments.

EMPLOYMENT

At Commercial Casinos

According to the AGA in *2004 State of the States,* commercial (nonracetrack) casinos employed more than 350,000 people in 2003. Although this number is up slightly from 2002, it is down from the nearly 365,000 people employed in 2001. Nevada accounted for 192,812 of commercial casino jobs in 2003, or 55% of the total. Racetrack casinos in Delaware, Iowa, Louisiana, New Mexico, Rhode Island, and West Virginia employed nearly 13,000 people during 2003. This number is up substantially from 8,000 employed during 2001.

At Native American Casinos

The NIGA reports that tribal gambling directly employed 205,000 people during 2003. (See Figure 6.2.)

FIGURE 6.2

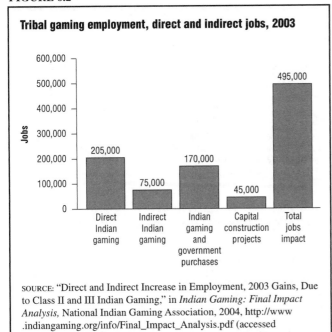

Tribal gaming employment, direct and indirect jobs, 2003

SOURCE: "Direct and Indirect Increase in Employment, 2003 Gains, Due to Class II and III Indian Gaming," in *Indian Gaming: Final Impact Analysis,* National Indian Gaming Association, 2004, http://www.indiangaming.org/info/Final_Impact_Analysis.pdf (accessed September 13, 2004)

Approximately 155,000 of these jobs were at tribal casinos. The remainder were in directly associated businesses and tribal government enterprises. Another 75,000 jobs were attributed to the indirect effects of tribal casinos, for example, businesses at which casino workers spent their wages. The NIGA estimates that tribal casinos were indirectly responsible for another 170,000 jobs by purchasing goods and services from various businesses around the country. Capital construction projects (for example, casino building) were associated with creation of another 45,000 jobs. In total the NIGA credits tribal gaming with employing 495,000 people during 2003.

In 1999 the NGISC reported that the great majority of employees in tribal casinos were not Native Americans. In 2001 the NIGA concurred, estimating that tribal casino employees were roughly 25% Native Americans and 75% non-Native Americans. This discrepancy is due at least in part to the fact that some tribes have fewer members than employees.

The applicability of federal labor laws to tribal casinos is a controversial subject. Tribes are expressly excluded from Title VII of the Civil Rights Act of 1964 and Title I of the Americans with Disabilities Act of 1990. Some court cases have held that Occupational Safety and Health Administration (OSHA) requirements, the Fair Labor Standards Act, and the Employee Retirement Income Security Act do apply to tribal businesses conducted on the reservation. The National Labor Relations Act exempts government entities from the requirement that employees be permitted to form unions and bargain collectively with their employers. The National Labor Rela-

tions Board and a federal court have both ruled that a tribe is a government and therefore exempt from the act. Because tribal governments are sovereign, they are not subject to state labor laws. Instead, tribal labor laws apply.

A May 2002 article in the *Wall Street Journal* accused tribal casinos in California of using their sovereignty to avoid federal labor laws, unions, and costly worker benefits and lawsuits. Under the Indian Gaming Regulatory Act, tribes are required to follow federal minimum wage and safety provisions. They also are prohibited from hiring felons to handle money. State compacts determine whether tribes must follow state employment laws. However, day-to-day enforcement is left up to tribal gaming agencies. Lawyers complain that tribes fire sick and injured workers to avoid paying workers' compensation and also dismiss those who advocate unionization.

The Hotel Employees and Restaurant Employees Union (HEREU) accuses tribes of abusing and firing casino employees at will. HEREU alleges that casino managers warn workers not to discuss unionization during their breaks. Tribal-state compacts negotiated in California, Wisconsin, Connecticut, and New York recognize the right of tribal casino employees to be represented by a union as their collective bargaining agent. HEREU plans to focus its organizing campaign on the 60,000 workers employed in California's tribal casinos. It complains that wages and working conditions at these casinos are "generally substandard." It also claims that HEREU has been blocked from organizing casino workers at the Foxwoods and Mohegan Sun casinos in Connecticut.

The Gaming Industry: A New Career Choice

The booming casino market has introduced a new career choice for many young people. The University of Nevada at Las Vegas (UNLV), only 1.5 miles from the Strip, has included gaming courses as part of its curriculum since it opened in 1967. Courses offered include Casino Operations and Management, Protection of Casino Table Games, and Mathematics of Casino Games. The UNLV International Gaming Institute is part of the William F. Harrah College of Hotel Administration. It includes a casino and a surveillance room.

Michigan State University's business school offers courses in casino operations and management that reportedly have waiting lists. Students are drawn to the unique nature of casino careers and the perceived excitement and fantasy aspect. Students at Central Michigan University, which is located near the Soaring Eagle Casino and Resort operated by the Saginaw Chippewa Indian Tribe of Michigan, can take upper-level courses at UNLV.

The Casino Career Institute, which includes a large mock casino, is a division of Atlantic Cape Community college in downtown Atlantic City, New Jersey. When it

TABLE 6.1

Casino occupations

Title	Responsibilities	Education/Training	Salary
Gaming Managers	Plan, organize, direct, control and coordinate gaming operations within the casino; formulate gaming policies; and select, train, and schedule activities of gaming personnel.	General education and specific occupational training. For example a Bachelor's degree in recreation or hotel management and/or casino management certificate. In-house training is also usually required.	$26,630-$96,610/year (Median $46,820/year)
Gaming Supervisors	Oversee gaming operations and personnel in an assigned area. Circulate among the tables to ensure that all stations and games are attended to each shift. Interpret the casino's operating rules for patrons. Plan and organize activities for guests staying at casino hotels. Address service complaints.	Associate or Bachelor's degree. Hands-on experience may be substituted for formal education. Most supervisors gain experience in other gaming jobs before moving into supervisory positions.	$19,620-$52,390/year (Median $34,240/year)
Gaming Surveillance Officers/Gaming Investigators	Security agents for casino managers and patrons. Monitor casino operations from a catwalk, one-way mirrors, or via audio and video equipment. Watch for and document theft and cheating.	High school diploma plus completion of a certified training program is usually required. Previous security experience is a plus.	$15,000-$30,610/year (Median $20,330/year)
Slot Key Persons (also called Slot Attendants or Slot Technicians)	Coordinate and supervise the slot department and its workers. Verify and handle payoff winning to patrons, reset slot machines after payoffs, refill slot machines with money, make minor repairs and adjustment to the machines, enforce safety rules and report hazards.	No formal education requirements, but completion of technical training is helpful. Most positions are entry-level and provide on-the-job training.	$7.02-$17.83/hour (Median $10.28/hour)
Gaming Change Persons and Booth Cashiers	Exchange coins and tokens for patron's money. Issue payoffs or obtain a patron's signature on a receipt when the winnings exceed the amount held in the slot machine. Count and audit the money in cash drawers.	Usually trained in-house. Should have experience handling cash or using calculators or adding machines. May have to pass a math test.	$6.08-$11.97/hour (Median $8.60/hour)
Gaming and Sports Book Writers and Runners	Assist in the operation of games such as bingo. Scan tickets presented by patrons and calculate and distribute winnings. May operate equipment that randomly selects the numbers, announce numbers selected, pick up tickets from patrons, collect bets, or receive, verify, and record patrons' cash wagers.	High school diploma or GED. Usually trained on-the-job.	$5.79-$10.35/hour (Median $7.53/hour)

SOURCE: Adapted from Patricia Tate, "Casino Gaming," in *Occupational Outlook Quarterly,* U.S. Department of Labor, Bureau of Labor Statistics, Summer 2001

opened in 1978 it was the first gaming school in the country affiliated with a community college.

In the summer of 2001 the Bureau of Labor Statistics, an agency within the U.S. Department of Labor, featured casino gaming in *Occupational Outlook Quarterly.* The article describes the duties, qualifications, necessary training, and earnings of casino workers. (See Table 6.1.) In general, gaming workers need excellent communication and customer service skills, personal integrity, and the ability to maintain composure when dealing with angry patrons. A high school diploma or GED is usually required for all entry-level jobs.

All employees must be at least twenty-one years old and have a license from the appropriate regulatory agency. Obtaining a license requires a background investigation. Requirements for education, training, and experience are up to individual casinos. Most casino work is physically demanding, requiring standing for long periods. Exposure to cigarette, cigar, and pipe smoke and to loud noises is common. The employment outlook for the industry is good, as increasing competition should result in more jobs for gaming workers. Prospects are best for those with a degree or certified training, previous experience, and superior interpersonal skills.

Many gaming employees must be licensed by the state in which they work, especially dealers, cashiers, and others dealing with money, slot repairmen, security personnel, and supervisors and managers. A background check is usually required to obtain a license. People can be disqualified from casino employment for a variety of reasons, including links to organized crime, the commission of felonies, and gambling-related offenses.

TOURISM

According to a poll conducted for the AGA by Peter D. Hart Research Associates, Inc., and the Luntz Research Companies, 76% of those polled in 2003 believed that casinos can play an important role in a community's entertainment and tourism options.

Las Vegas

Certainly, no destination better represents the marriage between gambling and tourism than Las Vegas, Nevada. In the early 1990s the city began a drive to make itself more family friendly. Focus shifted from an adult playground to a family destination. This change was driven by a steep decline in revenues. According to abcnews.com, the city's gambling revenues dropped by nearly $500 million in 1992 in the face of competition from legal gambling on riverboats and tribal casinos. During the 1990s the casinos spent $12 billion to refurbish almost every hotel on the Strip to include entertainment. Theme hotels became the big draw

During this shift to family entertainment, the Las Vegas Convention and Visitors' Authority focused advertising on families. Topless shows along the Strip gave way to magic shows, circus events, and carnival rides. The result was a huge increase in visitors. However, casino owners noticed that the change did not bring in more gambling revenue. Children distracted their parents from gambling or were left unattended.

During the late 1990s, the city's image began to change again. According to *USA Today*, the casinos began getting serious competition from strip clubs located off the Strip, which were bringing in millions of dollars from conventioneers. Adult entertainment along the Strip made a comeback. Casino/hotels began offering more topless and nude shows. This shift back to adult entertainment was why the MGM Grand shut down its family theme park in 2001. "We pretended to be a family destination," said the president of the MGM Grand in an interview in February 2002. He indicated that the new focus on the Strip would likely be gambling, drinking, and sex. However, casino managers insist that the nudity presented at their casinos is tasteful and artistic. They are anxious not to offend shareholders of their parent corporations or alienate women, potential gamblers who make up nearly 60% of Las Vegas visitors.

Besides its image problems, Las Vegas faces other challenges as well. The city is much more dependent on air travelers than many other gambling enterprises and was hard hit by the travel slowdown following the September 11, 2001, terrorist attacks. In addition, Las Vegas casinos rely heavily on visitors from California. With the advent of tribal gaming in California, Las Vegas casinos face stiff competition in their own backyard.

Mississippi

According to Mississippi officials, tourism contributed more than $6 billion to the state's economy in 2000. The tourist industry created more than 94,000 jobs and contributed $482 million to Mississippi's general fund tax revenues. The state's casinos are a major weekend destination, particularly for those within driving distance.

A 1999 study conducted by D.K. Shifflet & Associates found that casinos were the top activity attracting visitors to Mississippi that year. Gaming was selected by 46% of respondents, compared to other entertainment options (32%), dining (25%), shopping (21%), and sightseeing (15%).

Atlantic City, New Jersey

Tourism in Atlantic City, New Jersey, was improved by the introduction of casino gambling, but not as fast or to such a degree as people had hoped. From the 1880s to the 1940s, Atlantic City was a major tourist destination, particularly for people living in the Northeast. Visitors came for the beaches and to walk along the town's boardwalk and piers, which featured carnival-like entertainment. During the 1950s and 1960s, the town suffered a severe slump in tourism as people began traveling south to warmer beaches in Florida and the Caribbean. Because tourism had always been the town's major industry, it went into an economic depression.

Casino gambling was legalized in 1976 in the hopes that the city would recapture its former glory and rival Las Vegas as a tourist destination. Progress was slow through the 1980s and early 1990s. The casinos in Atlantic City were not as flashy or as popular as those in Las Vegas. Although visitors began to come to Atlantic City, they mostly came by bus or car and stayed only for a day or two. In 1984 the state established the Casino Reinvestment Development Authority (CRDA) to revitalize the city using the funds from a 1.25% tax on casino revenues.

The economic troubles that had ravaged the town's businesses before legalized gambling were not easily overcome. The casinos were surrounded by vacant lots, buildings in disrepair, and housing projects. The overall atmosphere was not particularly appealing to vacationers or convention-goers. A reporter for a West Paterson, New Jersey, newspaper described the city in 1993 as "trapped in a web of poverty and blight" (Mike Kelly, "Gambling with Our Future: City Poised to Hit Jackpot, or Lose Everything," *The Record*, July 1, 1993). At that time, the typical visitor was a retiree who arrived by bus and stayed only for the day. According to Kelly, Atlantic City's thirty million annual visitors actually represented about five million people making multiple trips.

In the late 1990s initiatives by CRDA and other groups began to pay off as hundreds of new homes were built and commercial businesses were established. A thirty-one-acre convention center, one of the largest in the country, opened in May 1997. The city's image began to improve, and tourism showed a moderate surge. City and casino officials cite three factors as limiting tourist growth in Atlantic City:

• Lack of a major airport

• Lack of usable land

• Cold winters

The president of the Casino Association of New Jersey was quoted in 2001 as saying, "While we can never be a worldwide destination like Las Vegas, we can become a regional destination" (William H. Sokolic, *Courier-Post,* July 15, 2001).

CRIME

Officials must realize that legal gambling will attract an unsavory element that can jeopardize the safety and well-being of the city's residents and the many visitors who come to gamble.

—*FBI Law Enforcement Bulletin,* Federal Bureau of Investigation, January 2001

The Early Link between Casino Gambling and Organized Crime

Casino gambling in its earliest years was largely run by mobsters, gangsters, and Mafia families. After gambling was legalized in Nevada in 1931, the first casinos were small, rather plain establishments operated by families and small companies. Nevada law kept corporations out of the casino business by requiring that every shareholder obtain a gaming license.

Ironically, this law, which was designed to safeguard the integrity of the casinos, gave organized crime a huge advantage. The nation was in the midst of the Great Depression, and building a flashy casino/hotel was a very expensive undertaking that required a large amount of money. Few legitimate businessmen had the cash needed for such an enterprise, and banks were reluctant to loan money for what they saw as a poor investment. Organized crime groups had made fortunes selling bootleg liquor during Prohibition and were able to make the large capital investments needed to build and operate lavish casino/hotels that attracted visitors.

The marriage between casinos and organized crime in Nevada lasted for decades but was eventually ended by gaming officials and law enforcement. Today, there is no strong evidence of organized crime activity in the casino industry, but regulatory agencies keep a watchful eye on casinos to make sure mobsters and their associates do not gain a new foothold in the industry.

Other Unsavory Elements

Casinos incorporate a number of measures into their daily operations to minimize the potential for crime by patrons and employees. The casino floor is constantly monitored by a host of security guards and cameras. Observers watch dealers and patrons at the gaming tables and all money-counting areas. Some casinos use high-tech facial recognition programs to scan incoming patrons and quickly identify any known felons or other undesirables.

Still, criminals do enter casinos. In September 2000 security guards at Harrah's casino in Las Vegas tried to arrest a man on the casino floor. The officers had identified the man from a photo of a suspected thief, but when they tried to arrest him, a gun battle erupted and an inno-

cent thirty-year-old woman from Hawaii was caught in the crossfire and killed. The woman's parents sued the casino, alleging that it had used insufficient security precautions to handle the matter. A jury denied the claim, ruling that the casino was not liable for the woman's death.

Crimes can also be committed by casino employees. Although the industry does not release data on crimes committed by casino employees, analysts estimate that employee crime accounts for millions of dollars in losses each year due to theft and embezzlement. Vice-type crimes also occur, particularly prostitution. In 2002 the Belterra Casino in Indiana was fined $2.26 million by the Indiana Gaming Commission for hiring prostitutes to entertain high-stakes gamblers at a casino-sponsored golf tournament in June 2001. The casino's license was also suspended for sixty-six hours.

In November 2000 a study called *Effects of Casino Gambling on Crime and Quality of Life in New Casino Jurisdictions* was published. The study was sponsored by the National Institute of Justice, the research and development branch of the U.S. Department of Justice. The study assessed the impact of casino gambling in eight areas that initiated casino gambling during the 1990s:

- Alton, Illinois
- Peoria, Illinois
- East Peoria, Illinois
- Sioux City, Iowa
- St. Joseph County, Missouri
- St. Louis, Missouri
- St. Louis County, Missouri
- Biloxi, Mississippi

Researchers compared official crime statistics from four years prior and four years subsequent to the initiation of casino gambling in these jurisdictions. The study concluded that results were mixed. Three of the jurisdictions—Peoria, Sioux City, and Biloxi—experienced a significant increase in certain crimes. However, crime in Alton and the city and county of St. Louis significantly decreased. Researchers decided that there was no single effect of casino initiation on crime.

The study also assessed the opinions of residents and community leaders in the eight areas on the effects of the casinos on crime and other quality-of-life issues. Attitudes about crime differed depending on who was asked. In general, residents associated casinos with increased crime, while community leaders felt that casinos improved the quality of life and economy. A majority (59%) of community leaders asked were in favor of the casinos, with 77% of leaders believing that the casinos had a positive effect on the local economy and 65% indicating that the casinos had a positive effect on the quality of life in the community. Those leaders in economic development positions were almost unanimous in their belief that casinos were a positive economic influence (95%) and that they improved the quality of life (86%). Fewer community leaders in positions concerned with providing social services (60%) felt that casinos enhanced the quality of life in their communities.

Tribal Casinos

A May 2002 article in *Indian Country Today* said that 225 criminal cases related to tribal gambling were referred to the Department of Justice between 1992 and 2000. Most of the cases involved theft from tribal casinos by patrons or employees. According to the FBI, theft and embezzlement are the most common crimes associated with casinos.

Biloxi, Mississippi

The article "When Casino Gambling Comes to Your Hometown" (*FBI Law Enforcement Bulletin,* January 2001) was written by the police chief of Biloxi and an FBI agent. Mississippi law requires that 20% of casino revenues turned over to local officials must be used to support public safety budgets. The Biloxi police department reported in the article that their department's budget more than tripled after casinos began operating. It used the money to build a new public safety building, hire more officers, and increase starting salaries.

The Biloxi police department also enacted personal-conduct rules for its employees to reduce gambling-related problems. It prohibits police officers from working at the casinos during off-duty hours. Officers in uniform are not even allowed to take meal breaks at the casinos. Officers who frequent the casinos are barred from conducting criminal investigations at them. Within a year of the casinos' opening, the number of pawnshops in Biloxi doubled. Over the next four years, the number doubled again. The police department increased monitoring to ensure that stolen property was not being pawned at these shops.

Crime statistics show that reported crimes in the Biloxi community increased after the first casino opened in 1992—mostly robberies, check and credit-card fraud, property crimes, domestic abuse, and alcohol-related violations. There were also more violations in traditional vice crimes, such as prostitution, pornography, loan-sharking, and extortion. However, the increase is attributed in part to a population increase, from 46,319 in 1990 to more than 53,400 in 2000. The city police department developed a task force with the FBI and other agencies to target organized crime groups involved in check and credit-card fraud, prostitution, money laundering, and pornography in and around the casinos.

TABLE 6.2

Charges filed as a result of arrests made by troopers assigned to the Missouri Gaming Division, July 2002–June 2003

Type of charge	Number	Type of charge	Number
Assault	32	Motor vehicle	120
Conservation	2	Obstruction of judicial process	461
Damaged property	136	Obstructing police	8
Dangerous drugs	40	Peace disturbance	6
Family offense	7	Prostitution	1
Flight/escape	18	Public order	1
Forgery	43	Robbery	2
Fraud	53	Sex offenses	1
Gambling	187	Sexual assault	1
Homicide	1	Stealing	81
Liquor laws	8	Stolen property	6
Misc. admin. charges	5	Weapons	4
Misc. fed. charges	1	**Total charges**	***1,225**

*These totals reflect the number of charges filed by agents of the Commission. The number of individuals arrested will be lower as some individuals may have multiple charges filed as a result of an individual incident. These totals also include arrests made attendant to outstanding warrants for criminal activity that did not occur on property of excursion gambling boats.

SOURCE: "Charges Filed as a Result of Arrests Made by Troopers Assigned to the Gaming Division from July 1, 2002 through June 30, 2003," in *Missouri Gaming Commission Annual Report to the General Assembly, Fiscal Year 2003,* Missouri Gaming Commission, July 2003, http://www.mgc.dps.mo .gov/annual%20reports/2003/annual2003.pdf (accessed September 28, 2004)

There were also minor problems associated with casinos, including increased traffic, nighttime construction noise, and flashing lights on business signs. However, the report describes the overall benefits of casinos as being "undeniable." The attraction and retention of more qualified police officers is noted as one of the chief benefits.

Missouri

According to the *Missouri Gaming Commission Annual Report to the General Assembly: Fiscal Year 2003,* commission agents filed more than 1,200 charges between July 1, 2002, and June 30, 2003, as shown in Table 6.2. The total includes charges for acts committed at the casinos as well as arrests made for criminal activities that did not occur on casino property.

Michigan

In July 2002 the *Detroit News* reported that at least five people had been arrested in Michigan during the previous year for robbing banks in order to get money to pay their large gambling debts or to make up gambling losses. The accused included an elementary school teacher, an electrical engineer, and even a dealer at the Greektown casino. Law enforcement officials reported that most of the people had no prior criminal records but turned to crime after charging the maximum allowed on their credit cards and exhausting other sources of credit (such as loans).

Counselors who work with compulsive gamblers say that those who turn to crime do not have the typical mindset of criminals but delude themselves into believing that the money they take is a short-term loan that they will repay. The newspaper cites a report from the University of Nevada at Reno that found that seven cities across the country experienced a sharp increase in theft, abuse, and drug crimes following the introduction of casinos. Another study from a University of Illinois economist indicated that such crimes begin to increase approximately three to five years after casinos are introduced in a community. This time frame is thought to reflect the amount of time it takes compulsive gamblers to exhaust their financial resources and resort to criminal actions.

SUICIDE

In January 2000 an off-duty police officer shot and killed himself at a high-stakes blackjack table at a Detroit casino after losing more than $15,000 in one afternoon.

The possible link between casino gambling and suicide rates has been the subject of much study over the years. A study done in 1997 at the University of California at San Diego concluded that cities with casino gambling had suicide rates that were four times those of comparably sized cities without casino gambling. However, researchers at Dalhousie University in Halifax, Nova Scotia, reported in 2000 that only 3% of the suicides that occurred in Las Vegas between 1990 and 1999 were directly related to gambling. The study concluded that mental, emotional, and physical health issues were more likely the major factors.

Nevada, a state in which gambling is widely practiced, has the highest suicide rate in the nation. According to the Centers for Disease Control and Prevention, the suicide rate in Nevada in 1999 was 22.3 suicides per 100,000 population. (See Table 6.3.) This is more than twice the national average of 10.7 per 100,000 population. However, many mental health experts attribute Nevada's high suicide rate to the huge inflow of new residents who lack a support system of family and friends. Loneliness and despair are more likely to overwhelm such people than those who have an emotional safety net in place. In general, suicide rates are higher in the western states than in any other region. Even Utah, which allows no legal gambling, was among the fifteen states with the highest suicide rates in 1999, with a rate of 13.2 suicides per 100,000 population.

A study published in July 2002 (*Suicide and Life-Threatening Behavior*) found little to no correlation between suicide rates and the presence of casino gambling in U.S. communities. The study, which was performed by epidemiologists at the University of California at Irvine, compared the 1990 suicide rates of 148 metropolitan areas in different regions of the country. The results indicated that the presence of casinos could account for only 1% of the regional differences in suicide rates. Researchers also compared "before and after" suicide rates for cities in

TABLE 6.3

Suicide rate, 1999

State	Number of Suicides	Suicide Rate
Nevada	404	22.3
Wyoming	98	20.4
Montana	162	18.4
New Mexico	318	18.3
Arizona	766	16.0
Alaska	96	15.5
Oklahoma	492	14.7
Idaho	181	14.5
Washington	816	14.2
Colorado	574	14.2
Maine	175	14.0
South Dakota	103	14.0
Florida	2029	13.4
Tennessee	726	13.2
Utah	282	13.2
National Average		10.7

Note: Suicide rate per 100,000 population in each state in 1999.

SOURCE: Adapted from Donna L. Hoyert, Elizabeth Arias, Betty L. Smith, Sherry L. Murphy, and Kenneth D. Kochanek, "1999 Suicide Rate by State," in *Deaths: Final Data for 1999,* U.S. Department of Health and Human Services, Centers for Disease Control and Prevention, National Center for Health Statistics, National Vital Statistics Report, vol. 49, no. 8, September 21, 2001

which gambling had been legalized. Although increased suicide rates were noted in Atlantic County, New Jersey, and Harrison County, Mississippi, after the advent of gambling, the increases were not considered statistically significant. In fact, suicide rates experienced a significant drop in Lawrence County, South Dakota, after casino gambling was introduced in the town of Deadwood.

BANKRUPTCY

A gambling problem and bankruptcy are like baseball and hot dogs.

—James Houston, a compulsive gambler

Establishing a definitive link between gambling habits and bankruptcy is difficult. A study published in 2001 by SMR Research Corporation of Hackettstown, New Jersey, attributed 14.2% of U.S. bankruptcy filings to gambling problems. The researchers compared bankruptcy filing rates during 2000 for more than three thousand counties. They found that the 244 counties in which casinos operated had a bankruptcy rate that was 13.5% higher than those counties without a casino. The president of the AGA disputed the report's findings, pointing out that other factors had not been considered—mainly liberal bankruptcy laws and the ease with which credit cards can be obtained.

Examination of personal bankruptcy filings for 2002 shows that the five states with the highest number of filings per 100,000 population were Missouri, Indiana, Nevada, Utah, and Oklahoma. There were no casinos operating in Utah in 2002. The other four states did have casino gambling.

According to the Council on Compulsive Gambling of New Jersey, Inc., the bankruptcy rate in Atlantic City more than doubled between 1994 and 2000, increasing from 5.28 to 11.68 per 1,000 adult population. During the same time period, the bankruptcy rate for the rest of the state rose from 3.83 to 5.99 per 1,000 adult population.

Researchers at the University of Nevada at Reno compared the bankruptcy rates in eight towns without casino gambling with those in areas that initiated casino gambling during the 1990s, namely Alton, Illinois; Peoria, Illinois; East Peoria, Illinois; Sioux City, Iowa; St. Joseph County, Missouri; St. Louis, Missouri; St. Louis County, Missouri; and Biloxi, Mississippi.

The study, sponsored by the National Institute of Justice, chose the control communities to mirror the casino communities as closely as possible in terms of demographics and social and economic factors. Results indicated that there was a statistically significant increase in the bankruptcy rate in five of the eight communities with casino gambling. The communities in which casinos had operated the longest tended to show the largest increase. However, the bankruptcy rate in one of the communities—Biloxi, Mississippi—actually decreased significantly. The decrease was attributed to the unique nature of the casino industry in that town—namely, that casinos had greatly enhanced tourism there. This positive effect had economic benefits that outweighed any financial problems that local residents might have incurred due to overindulgence at the casinos.

DOMESTIC PROBLEMS

In its final report the NGISC briefly addresses the relationship between casino gambling and domestic problems, such as abuse and neglect. The NGISC relied on the report *Gambling Impact and Behavior Study: Report to the National Gambling Impact Study Commission,* conducted by the National Opinion Research Center (NORC) at the University of Chicago. NORC examined the rates of domestic problems in ten casino communities and found that six of the communities reported an increase in domestic violence after the introduction of casinos.

The NGISC also heard testimony from domestic violence counselors and law enforcement officials regarding specific problems in casino communities. A domestic violence shelter in Harrison County, Mississippi, reported a 300% increase in the number of requests for help after casinos opened in the county. A large majority of the women seeking refuge at the shelter stated that gambling by their spouses had contributed to the abuse. The attorney general of Rhode Island reported a "significant increase" in the number of domestic assaults that occurred in the town of Westerly, Rhode Island, after the Foxwoods Casino opened in nearby Connecticut.

The NGISC's report also mentions numerous cases in which children were locked in cars or were unsupervised for long periods of time while their parents or babysitters gambled at casinos. In a 1997 case, a seven-year-old girl was raped and murdered in a bathroom stall at a Las Vegas casino while her father gambled during the early-morning hours.

One NGISC member was Dr. James Dobson, founder and president of the nonprofit organization Focus on the Family. The group's mission is to spread the Christian gospel and help preserve traditional values, and it opposes gambling for moral, religious, and ethical reasons. On its Web site (www.family.org), Focus on the Family describes some of the detrimental effects of casino gambling on families.

Both the NGISC and Focus on the Family cite statistics showing that children and spouses of compulsive gamblers are more prone to suffer abuse and neglect. The NORC study found casino communities that reported increased cases of child neglect attributed the increase at least in part to parents leaving their children unsupervised at home, in casinos, or in casino parking lots while they gambled. However, these communities did not report any noticeable increases in cases of child abuse or infant mortality after casino gambling was introduced.

Casino officials insist they do all they can to discourage people from leaving children unattended on casino grounds. According to the NGISC, the Foxwoods casino posted signs in its parking lot warning that children left alone in cars would be reported to the police. Industry spokespeople also point out that similar cases of child neglect occur at places unrelated to gambling, such as at shopping malls, and should be blamed on irresponsible parents, not on casinos.

COMPULSIVE GAMBLING

In the AGA's 2003 *State of the States: The AGA Survey of Casino Entertainment* survey, participants were asked to indicate who they thought bore the most responsibility for addressing the problem of compulsive gambling in the United States. The majority of respondents (63%) said that gamblers themselves should be held most responsible. Another 15% thought that society at large should take the most responsibility, and 10% put the burden on the owners of gambling facilities.

Self-Exclusion Programs

Many states that allow commercial casino gaming operate self-exclusion programs in which people can voluntarily ban themselves from the casinos. For example, Missouri's voluntary exclusion program was created in 1996 after a citizen requested that he be banned from the riverboats because he was unable to control his gambling. As of August 2003 more then 5,800 people were on the exclusion list. The Missouri Gaming Commission requires that the casinos remove self-excluded persons from their direct marketing lists, deny them check-cashing privileges and membership in player's clubs, and cross-check for their names on the list before paying out any jackpots of $1,200 or more. The casinos are not responsible for barring listed people from the casinos, but anyone listed is to be arrested for trespassing if he or she violates the ban and is discovered in a casino. Excluded people can enter the casino for employment purposes, however.

Programs in other states are similar. A self-excluded person discovered in an Illinois casino is to have any chips and tokens in his or her possession taken away and their value donated to charity. The Illinois self-exclusion program runs for five years. After that time, people can be removed from the program if they provide written documentation from a licensed mental health professional that they are no longer problem gamblers.

Self-exclusion in Michigan is permanent; a person who chooses to be in the program is banned for life from Detroit casinos.

The New Jersey Casino Control Commission also offers a program in which people can voluntarily suspend their credit privileges at all Atlantic City casinos. The commission maintains a list of those who have joined the program and shares the list with the casinos.

Hotlines

All of the states operate gambling hotlines that either refer callers to other groups for help or provide counselors over the phone. According to the Mississippi Council on Problem and Compulsive Gambling, 54% of the callers to their hotline obtained the number through a casino.

Hotlines, Treatment, and Loss Limits in Missouri

Missouri operates a twenty-four-hour gambling hotline (1-888-BETS-OFF) that received an average of 335 calls per month during the first half of 2004. Since its inception, the hotline has received more than six thousand calls.

Missouri also offers free treatment to residents suffering from problem gambling and to their families. The program is administered by the Department of Mental Health through a network of private mental health providers that have been certified as compulsive gambling counselors. Until July 2001 the program was funded by communities hosting gambling activities. Passage of Senate Bill 902 means that the state can allocate to the program up to one cent of each $1 admission fee paid to the state.

Iowa's Problem Gamblers Prefer Slot Machines

Iowa's Department of Public Health tracks statistics on clients admitted to its gambling treatment program. Table 6.4 shows the types of gambling that clients had pri-

TABLE 6.4

Primary type of wagering reported by clients admitted to Iowa Gambling Treatment Program, 1998–2003

| | Fiscal year | | | | | |
	1998	1999	2000	2001	2002	2003
Slots	59%	62%	63%	59%	64%	69%
Table games	16%	12%	14%	11%	12%	9%
Video	10%	9%	11%	12%	11%	6%
Lottery/scratch tickets	4%	4%	4%	4%	3%	3%
Sports	2%	2%	2%	4%	4%	4%
Other	9%	11%	6%	10%	6%	6%

SOURCE: "Iowa Gambling Treatment Program: A Profile of Gamblers Admitted to Treatment in Fiscal Years 1998 through 2003," in *Iowa Gambling Treatment Program: A Profile of Gamblers Admitted to Treatment in Fiscal Years 1998 through 2003*, Iowa Department of Public Health, Iowa Gambling Treatment Program, 2004, http://www.1800betsoff.org/stats4.html (accessed September 2, 2004)

marily engaged in for the six months prior to their admittance to the program. Data for fiscal years 1998 through 2003 show that slot machines were the game of choice for a majority of the gamblers, accounting for 69% of those admitted to gambling treatment in 2003. Table games were the second most often played games by problem gamblers.

Recent AGA Educational Efforts

In 2004 the AGA published the *American Gaming Association Code of Conduct for Responsible Gaming*. The booklet describes the actions that AGA members pledge to take to ensure that responsible gambling is conducted and encouraged at casinos. These actions include proper training of employees and promotion of responsible gambling at company Web sites and through brochures and signs posted at the casinos. AGA members also agree to provide opportunities for patrons to self-exclude themselves from casino play.

UNDERAGE GAMBLING

The legal gambling age in all commercial casinos in the United States is twenty-one, and in tribal casinos it varies from eighteen to twenty-one.

AGA's 2003 *State of the States* survey asked participants about who they thought bore the most responsibility for addressing the problem of underage gambling in the United States. Survey respondents indicated that the owners of gambling facilities should be held most responsible (39%), followed by gamblers themselves (24%) and society at large (22%). When asked to rate the job that the casino gaming industry was doing in preventing underage gambling, a majority (65%) rated the casino industry as doing a fairly good or very good job. The reputation of the casino industry in doing a good job in preventing "underage use of their product" was superior to that of the tobacco (30%), alcohol (38%), and gun (42%) industries.

TABLE 6.5

Minors and casinos in Detroit, Michigan, 2003

	MGM Grand 1/1/03– 12/31/03	MotorCity 1/1/03– 12/31/03	Greektown 1/1/03– 12/31/03
1. The number of minors who were denied entry into the casino.	796	4,822	1073
2. The number of minors who were physically escorted from the casino premises.	13	3	13
3. The number of minors who were detected participating in gambling games other than slot machines.	4	2	2
4. The number of minors who were detected using slot machines.	1	0	2
5. The number of minors who were taken into custody by a law enforcement agency on the casino premises.	13	3	0
6. The number of minors who were detected illegally consuming alcohol on the casino premises.	0	0	1

SOURCE: "Casino Licensees' Reported Contacts with Minors on Licensed Casino Premises during Calendar Year 2003," in *Michigan Gaming Control Board Annual Report to the Governor, Calendar Year 2003,* Michigan Gaming Commission, April 15, 2004, http://www.michigan.gov/documents/annrep03_88990_7.pdf (accessed September 28, 2004)

In 2000 the Nevada Gaming Commission banned slot machines with themes that were "derived from or based on a product currently and primarily intended or marketed for use by persons under twenty-one years of age." The so-called "slots for tots" regulation is supposed to prevent the introduction of slot machines displaying cartoon characters that might appeal to children. The issue receives particular attention in Nevada because the state's casinos allow escorted children to walk through the casino. Most states prohibit the passage of minors through the gambling area.

The Michigan Gaming Control & Revenue Act of 1997 requires the Michigan Gaming Control Board to compile information regarding casino contacts with minors. Table 6.5 shows this information as reported by the three Detroit casinos for calendar year 2003. In total, 6,691 minors tried to enter the casinos, but were denied entry. Twenty-nine minors were caught on casino premises and escorted off the premises by casino personnel. Another sixteen minors were taken into custody by law enforcement agencies.

POLITICS

Casino gambling and politics have always been linked. Concerns about influence peddling and bribery are major issues to many people. Some states prohibit casino applicants from making political contributions to state and local candidates. For example, the Michigan Gaming Control & Revenue Act of 1997 prohibits political contributions to state and local candidates and committees from "certain persons with interests in casino and supplier license applicants and licensees."

State Political Influence

In May 2000 Governor Edwin Edwards of Louisiana was convicted of racketeering, extortion, and fraud for extorting $3 million from people seeking riverboat casinos licenses. The number of licenses available for riverboats in Louisiana is set at fifteen, so there are a very limited number of casino opportunities available in that state. Mississippi has not set a limit on the number of casinos that can be built. That state's politicians claim this will prevent the bribery, extortion, and favoritism that plagued Louisiana's licensing process.

Local Political Influence

Political issues can be local as well. The city of Hammond, Indiana, inserted a clause into its contract with the Horseshoe Casino that allows the city to borrow money from the casino at extremely low interest rates. In 2001 the city borrowed $3 million to fund an environmental reclamation project. The loan was repaid, but in June 2002 the city decided to borrow nearly $3 million more from the casino at 5% interest to be paid back over six years. The money is to be used to develop golf courses near George Lake. Critics complain that the financial relationship is improper and gives the casino excessive influence in city politics.

Tribal Casinos and Politics

Politics is even more of a concern when it comes to tribal casinos. Critics say that financial backers of tribal casinos use their political pull to push recognition petitions.

A three-member tribe called the Buena Vista Rancheria of Me-Wuk Indians in California received national attention in 2002 as the center of alleged influence peddling in Washington, D.C. Articles published in the *New York Times* and *Washington Post* during the spring and summer of 2002 describe the tribe, which was thought to have disappeared 150 years ago. In 1958 the tribe was disbanded by the federal government and its land turned over to the two remaining members—Annie and Louie Oliver. In 1983 the tribe achieved federal recognition again following a federal lawsuit filed by numerous small tribes.

The tribe's rancheria occupies sixty-seven acres near Sacramento. As of late 2002, two women were fighting over leadership of the tribe. The first, Donnamarie Potts, lives on the rancheria and was willed the land by the Olivers' daughter, to whom she was related by marriage. Potts also claims to be the illegitimate daughter of an Oliver descendent. In 1998 Potts signed an agreement with Cascade Entertainment to build a $150 million casino on the land. The company had already invested $10 million in the project when a second woman, Rhonda Pope, filed suit to stop the project, presenting documents proving that she was a lineal descendant of the Olivers. A federal court halted the casino project while the BIA investigated. In May 2002 the BIA ruled that Pope was entitled to organize the tribal government. Potts then appealed both the BIA decision and the court decision. As of 2004 the two women remained locked in a legal battle for control of the rancheria, though Potts was recognized as the tribe's spokesperson.

During the heated legal wrangling in 2002, a top official at the BIA, Wayne Smith, was fired amid allegations that his prior partner, Philip Bersinger, was using Smith's name to solicit business from Native American tribes. *Time* magazine reported that Bersinger had been offering to help tribes in California (including the Buena Vista Rancheria) gain access to Smith in exchange for large consulting fees. Smith, on the other hand, claims that he was fired for complaining to his superiors that an unnamed source at the White House was pressuring him to push pro-casino interests.

CHAPTER 7
LOTTERIES

A lottery is a game of chance in which people pay for the opportunity to win prizes. All money taken in by a lottery is pooled and used to award the winners and to pay the costs of administering the lottery. The money left over is profit. Lotteries are extremely popular around the world and are legal in more than a hundred countries.

In the United States all lotteries are operated by state governments that have granted themselves the sole right to do so. In other words, they are monopolies that do not allow any commercial lotteries to compete against them. The profits from U.S. lotteries are used solely to fund government programs. As of August 2004, lotteries operated in forty states and the District of Columbia. (See Figure 7.1.) This means that at that time, 90% of the U.S. population lived in a state with an operating lottery. In addition, lottery tickets can be legally purchased by any adult physically present in a lottery state, even if that adult does not reside in the state.

As shown in Figure 7.2, Americans wagered more than $44 billion in lotteries during fiscal year 2003 (July 2002–June 2003). U.S. lottery sales were up 6.6% from fiscal year 2002 and increased steadily between 1998 and 2003.

LOTTERY HISTORY

Early History

The drawing of lots to determine ownership or other rights is recorded in many ancient documents, including the Bible. The practice became common in Europe in the late fifteenth and the sixteenth centuries. Lotteries were first tied directly to the United States in 1612 when King James I of England created a lottery to provide funds to the Jamestown, Virginia, settlement, the first permanent British settlement in America. Lotteries were used by public and private organizations after that time to raise money for towns, wars, colleges, and public-works projects.

An early American lottery, conducted by George Washington in the 1760s, was designed to finance con-struction of the Mountain Road in Virginia. Benjamin Franklin was also a lottery advocate and supported their use to pay for cannons during the Revolutionary War. John Hancock ran a lottery to finance the rebuilding of Faneuil Hall in Boston. Although many lotteries are mentioned in early American documents, the 1999 report of the National Gambling Impact Study Commission (NGISC) describes most colonial-era lotteries as "unsuccessful." Amid concerns about the public harm of lotteries, in the 1820s New York became the first state to pass a constitutional prohibition against lotteries.

The Rise and Fall of Lotteries in the United States

The southern states relied on lotteries after the Civil War (1861–65) to finance Reconstruction. The Louisiana lottery, in particular, became widely popular. In 1868 the Louisiana Lottery Company was granted permission by the state legislature to operate as the state's only lottery provider. In exchange, the company agreed to pay $40,000 per year for twenty-five years to the Charity Hospital of New Orleans. The company was allowed to keep all other lottery revenues and to pay no taxes upon those revenues. The Louisiana lottery was very popular nationwide and brought in more than 90% of its revenue from out of state. It was also extremely profitable, returning a 48% profit to its operators.

In 1890 the U.S. Congress banned the mailing of lottery materials. The Louisiana lottery was abolished in 1895 after Congress passed a law against the transport of lottery tickets across state lines. Following its closure, the public learned that the lottery had been operated by a northern crime syndicate that regularly bribed legislators and committed widespread fraud and deception in its operations. The resulting scandal was huge and widely publicized. Public opinion turned against lotteries, and by the end of the nineteenth century, they were outlawed across the country.

FIGURE 7.1

States with lotteries, 2004

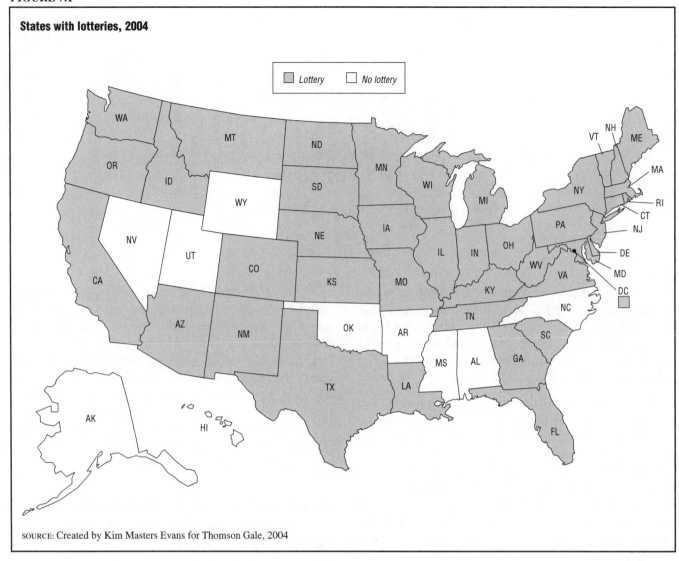

SOURCE: Created by Kim Masters Evans for Thomson Gale, 2004

Negative attitudes about gambling began to soften during the early twentieth century, particularly after the failure of Prohibition. The state of Nevada legalized casino gambling in the 1930s, and gambling for charitable purposes became more commonplace across the country. Still, lingering fears about fraud kept lotteries out of the picture for another two decades.

Rebirth in the 1960s

In the early 1960s the New Hampshire legislature began considering a state-run lottery as a means to raise revenue. The state had no sales or state income tax at that time and desperately needed money for education programs. A lottery bill was passed in 1963, and the lottery (called the New Hampshire Sweepstakes) began in 1964. The game was patterned after the Irish Sweepstakes, which was very popular at that time, and was much different from the lotteries of today. Drawings were held infrequently, and the largest prize was $100,000. Tickets sold for $3 each. The biggest prizes were tied to the outcomes of particular

horse races at the Rockingham Park racetrack. Nearly $5.7 million was wagered during the lottery's first year.

The state of New York followed quickly, introducing its own lottery in 1967. This lottery was particularly successful, grossing $53.6 million during its first year alone. It also enticed residents from neighboring states to cross state lines and buy tickets. Twelve other states established lotteries during the 1970s (Connecticut, Delaware, Illinois, Maine, Maryland, Massachusetts, Michigan, New Jersey, Ohio, Pennsylvania, Rhode Island, and Vermont). The lottery was firmly entrenched throughout the Northeast by the end of the decade. The reasons for this growth pattern are threefold. First, there was a desperate need to raise money for public projects without increasing taxes. Second, these states had large Catholic populations that were generally tolerant of gambling activities. Third, history has shown that states are most likely to start a lottery if one is already offered in a nearby state.

During the 1980s, lottery fever spread south and west with incredible swiftness. Seventeen states (Arizona, Cal-

FIGURE 7.2

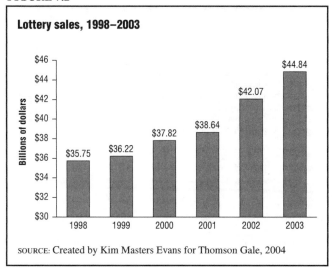

Lottery sales, 1998–2003

SOURCE: Created by Kim Masters Evans for Thomson Gale, 2004

ifornia, Colorado, Florida, Idaho, Indiana, Iowa, Kansas, Kentucky, Missouri, Montana, Oregon, South Dakota, Virginia, Washington, West Virginia, and Wisconsin) plus the District of Columbia started lotteries. Six more states started lotteries during the 1990s (Georgia, Louisiana, Minnesota, Nebraska, New Mexico, and Texas). They were joined in the early 2000s by South Carolina, Tennessee, and North Dakota.

LOTTERY GAMES

Early lottery games were simple raffles in which a person purchased a ticket preprinted with a number. The player might have had to wait for weeks for a drawing to determine if the ticket was a winner. These types of games were called passive drawing games. Passive drawing games were the dominant type of lottery game in 1973 but were nonexistent by 1997. Over time, consumers have demanded more exciting games that provide quicker payoffs and more betting options. Table 7.1 describes the common types of lottery games staged today.

La Fleur's 2004 World Lottery Almanac lists the types of lottery games offered by various states as of mid-2003. (La Fleur's is a Maryland-based research firm that publishes statistics on the world's lotteries.) Nearly all states operating lotteries offered cash lotto and instant games. Most offer other numbers games, such as three-digit and four-digit games. Pull tabs, spiel, keno, and video lottery games are much less common. In general, keno and video lottery games are considered casino-type games. This makes them more controversial and generally less acceptable to the public than traditional lottery games, like lotto.

Most lotto tickets sell for $1 each. Each dollar buys a chance to choose a small set of numbers out of a larger set of numbers. Drawings are held once or twice per week to determine the winning numbers. In 2002 Connecticut,

Georgia, and Michigan launched new lottery games that can be played for pocket change, anywhere from 25 cents to 99 cents.

Today many lottery games are online, using a computer network. Retail outlets have computer terminals that are linked by phone lines to a central computer at the lottery commission. The central computer records the wagers as they are made. Retailers can sell tickets for online games and validate winning tickets. The computer network is a private dedicated network accessible only by lottery officials and retailers. Thus, online lottery games differ from the Internet, which anyone can access. Lotto, keno, and numbers games are all conducted as online games. Players can either choose their numbers themselves or allow the computer to select numbers randomly, an option known as "Quick Pick."

Most lotto drawings are televised live. In addition, some states air lottery game shows in which contestants compete for money and prizes. The California lottery's game show, *The Big Spin,* has aired since 1985. Contestants are chosen through lottery drawings or special promotions. During the thirty-minute show, contestants spin a big wheel in an attempt to win cash prizes while family and friends cheer from the audience.

Lottery winners generally have six months to one year to collect their prizes, depending on state rules. The top prize in a lotto game is called the jackpot. In most lotto games a jackpot that is not won rolls over to the next drawing, increasing the jackpot each time. The most popular lotteries are often those in which a jackpot has rolled over several times and therefor has grown to an unusually large amount.

Most states allow players to choose in advance how a jackpot will be paid to them—either all at once or in installments. Either way, taxes are subtracted from the prize. Jackpots paid all at once are called cash lump-sum prizes. Annuities are jackpots paid out over many years—usually twenty or twenty-five. Even those who choose annuities can pursue ways to receive most of their money all at once. Businesses engaged in cash-flow financing often purchase the rights to annuities from lottery winners and pay them a discounted lump sum in exchange. For example, a $1 million jackpot winner might choose to collect the winnings in installments of $36,000 per year for twenty years. This totals $720,000. A broker would probably offer the winner about $500,000 in immediate cash in exchange for the future rights to the monthly installments.

Scratch Games

In 1974 Massachusetts became the first state to offer an instant lottery game based on scratch-off tickets. Today, games involving scratch tickets (or "scratchers," as they are called in some states) are extremely popular. Lot-

TABLE 7.1

Modern lottery games

Type	Description	Administration
Lotto	A game where players select a group of numbers from a large set and are awarded prizes based on how many match a second set chosen by a random drawing. In a typical lotto game, a player might be asked to select six numbers from a set of 49. At a predetermined time six numbers are randomly selected by the lottery. The player wins a major prize if all six of their numbers match those chosen in the random drawing. The player wins smaller prizes for matching three, four, or five of the drawn numbers.	Drawings are held anywhere from once a day to once a week. Requires computers and communication networks
Cash lotto	Cash Lotto is a lotto where the prize is awarded as a lump-sum cash payment. Unwon jackpots do not roll over. Cash lotto games typically have a smaller top prize than large jackpot games, more favorable odds of winning that top prize, and require players to select fewer numbers out of a smaller field.	
Spiel	An add-on feature to a lotto game. For an additional fee an extra set of numbers (typically four to six numbers) is printed on the bottom of a ticket. Players win by matching one or more of these numbers to those selected in a random drawing.	
Scratch-off instant games	Players purchase preprinted paper tickets on which spaces have been coated with a latex substance that can be scratched off to reveal numbers or text underneath. They must match posted sequences to win.	Do not require computerized terminals. Can be sold out of vending machines.
Pull tabs (also called Breakopens)	Players purchase two-ply laminated paper tickets that have perforated tear-away tabs that can be pulled back to reveal symbols or numbers underneath. A winning ticket must match the posted symbol combinations either across, down, or diagonally (similar to tic-tac-toe).	
Daily numbers games	Players select three or four digits (0 to 9) and match them with a similar set selected at random by the lottery. The player can select several different types of wagers with payoffs varying accordingly. For example, players making a "straight" bet win if their three digits match the three digits selected by the lottery in the same order.	Requires computers and communication networks.
Keno	A lotto game in which a set of numbers (typically 20) is selected from a large field of numbers (typically 80). Players select a smaller set of numbers (up to 10) and are awarded prizes based on how many of their numbers match those in the drawn set. Players have discretion over how many numbers to select, and can choose to play for a small prize with good odds (by selecting a small set of numbers such as three), a large prize with much greater odds (by selecting a large set of numbers such as 10) or combinations in between. In "fast keno" drawings may be held every few minutes. Fast keno is typically hosted by bars, lounges, and other establishments.	Requires computers and communication networks.
Video lottery terminals (VLTs)	Electronic games of chance played on a video screen. They often simulate popular casino games such as blackjack, poker, or spinning-reel slot machines. Unlike slot machines, video lottery terminals do not dispense money. Rather, a winning player is provided a ticket that is redeemed by the retailer for prizes.	Limited to only a few states
Sports lottery	Games where outcomes are determined by the results of sports events. Sports lotteries are the most popular lottery games in much of the world (where they are frequently called "toto" or "football pools").	Available only in Oregon

SOURCE: Adapted from "Modern Lottery Games," from *Glossary of Lottery Terms,* North American Association of State & Provincial Lotteries, 2001, http://www.naspl.org/terms.html (accessed September 14, 2004)

tery organizations offer many different scratch games with various themes. For example, during the summer of 2004 the Connecticut lottery had more than one hundred scratch games ongoing.

Scratch games run for a specified period of time, usually for several months to up to a year. The top prize amounts are often hundreds of thousands of dollars. However, a wide variety of prizes are offered in these games besides money, including merchandise, trips, vehicles, and tickets to sporting events and concerts. In 2004 the Texas lottery offered scratch players a chance to instantly win a Corvette convertible. A Missouri lottery scratch game gave away sixty trips to Las Vegas, plus $500 in spending money. The winning tickets included payment by the lottery commission of federal and state income taxes on the value of the prizes.

Many lotteries have teamed with sports franchises and other companies to provide popular products as prizes. Lotteries in several states during the early 2000s offered scratch games featuring Harley-Davidson motorcycles as the top prizes. The use of licensed brand names in lottery games has become very popular. Most brand-name promotions feature famous celebrities, sports figures/teams, or cartoon characters. Lottery officials seek out joint merchandising deals in which companies provide prizes for scratch games. The companies benefit through product exposure and advertising. The lotteries benefit when companies share in advertising costs.

The latest trend in instant games is the sale of high profit point (HPP) tickets. Traditional scratch tickets sell for $1 each. HPP tickets are priced as high as $20 each and are usually part of a holiday or themed promotion. Most states offer several $5 and $10 ticket games, particularly around Christmas and other gift-giving holidays. In 2002 the Connecticut lottery was the first in the United States to offer a $30 instant ticket. The HPP tickets appeal to many scratch players because they offer more valuable prizes and payouts than regular-priced tickets. Lottery officials hope they will attract more affluent players to the games.

In 2001 the California lottery was sued for continuing to sell scratch-game tickets after the top prizes had been awarded. In other words, people bought scratch-game tickets not knowing that there was no chance for them to win the most valuable prizes. In January 2002 California lottery officials apologized for their actions and promised to stop selling instant-win tickets in the future after the top prizes were awarded. The state also set up a second-chance drawing for people holding losing scratch tickets from the earlier promotion.

A similar problem occurred in Colorado in 1997 after a Colorado Springs newspaper reported that more than $2 million in tickets were sold after the grand prizes had already been awarded. A lawsuit was filed against the state in 2000 by a woman with losing scratch tickets from the Luck of the Zodiac game. A judge dismissed the case because the plaintiff had not pursued her complaint through lottery administrative channels first. The ruling was appealed, and in August 2002 the state appeals court reinstated the lawsuit. The woman's lawyers hope to have the suit certified as a class-action suit on behalf of all scratch players who played the game. Similar lawsuits have been filed in Arizona and the state of Washington.

Most lotteries operate a toll-free number or Web site that provides information on scratch game prize claims. Patrons can find out which prizes have already been awarded and which prizes remain to be claimed.

Second-Chance Games

Sometimes even nonwinning lottery tickets have value. Most state lotteries run occasional second-chance drawings, and even third-chance drawings, in which holders of nonwinning tickets for particular games can still try for cash or prizes. The Colorado lottery held a second-chance drawing during the summer of 2004 in which holders of nonwinning Lucky Dog scratch tickets could win money for animal-related nonprofit organizations and themselves. Other state lotteries offer new vehicles, concert tickets, and a variety of other prizes.

Video Lottery Games

Video lottery games are computer games played on video lottery terminals (VLTs). VLTs are essentially slot machines (video gaming devices) that are monitored and controlled by a central computer system that is overseen by a state's lottery agency. Thus, VLT profits (all or in part) benefit state lotteries.

According to *La Fleur's 2004 World Lottery Almanac,* VLTs were operated in only eight states in 2003—Delaware, Louisiana, Montana, New York, Oregon, Rhode Island, South Dakota, and West Virginia. Video lottery games are highly profitable. During fiscal year 2003, nearly 42,000 VLTs were in operation with a net income of $2.4 billion.

VLTs in Louisiana, Montana, and South Dakota are owned by private entities. Those in Rhode Island are leased by the state to private operators. VLTs in the other states are owned by state lottery commissions. VLTs in Delaware, New Mexico, New York, and Rhode Island are only allowed at racetracks. Profits from these VLTs are split between the racetracks and the state lotteries.

In 2001 the state of New York passed legislation allowing the installation of video lottery games at racetracks in the state. Although the VLTs finally began operating in early 2004, they have been fought in lawsuits. In July 2004 a state appeals court ruled that the legislation authorizing VLTs at racetracks was unconstitutional. New York's constitution requires lottery proceeds to benefit education programs. Some VLT revenue was going to the racetrack owners and operators and to the racing industry. This diversion of lottery revenue was considered unconstitutional by the court. As of August 2004 the state's VLTs were still operating while the ruling is appealed to a higher court.

In general, video lottery games are controversial because many people consider them "hard-core" gambling. They allow continuous gambling for large sums of money, as opposed to lotto play, which features drawings only once or twice a week. Opponents of video lottery games contend that they are much more addictive than traditional lottery games because of their availability and instant payoffs. They also have special appeal to children and adolescents, who are already accustomed to playing video games.

Multistate Games

During the 1980s, lottery officials realized that multistate lotteries could offer higher payoffs than sole-state lotteries because the costs of running one game could be shared by numerous states. Table 7.2 lists the states that operate lotteries and participate in multistate lotteries.

POWERBALL. The Multi-State Lottery Association (MUSL) was formed in 1988 as a nonprofit association of states offering lotteries. It is entirely owned and operated by the member-state lotteries. The MUSL administers various games, the best known of which is called Powerball. Powerball is a lotto game in which five numbers are selected out of fifty-three numbers, and then a separate number is selected out of forty-two numbers, for a total of six numbers. The first Powerball drawing was held on April 22, 1992. Drawings are held twice weekly. In December 2002 Powerball paid out the largest jackpot ever awarded to a single winner—$314.9 million. It was won by a West Virginia contractor who reported that he only played the lottery when the jackpot exceeded $100 million.

TABLE 7.2

State lottery games, 2004

State	State lottery	Powerball	Mega Millions[a]	Hot Lotto[b]	Wild Card	Mega Bucks	Lotto South	2 By 2
Alabama	None							
Alaska	None							
Arizona	X	X						
Arkansas	None							
California	X							
Colorado	X	X						
Connecticut	X	X						
Delaware	X	X						
District of Columbia	X	X		X				
Florida	X							
Georgia	X		X				X	
Hawaii	None							
Idaho	X	X			X			
Illinois	X		X					
Indiana	X	X						
Iowa	X	X		X				
Kansas	X	X						X
Kentucky	X	X					X	
Louisiana	X	X						
Maine	X	X				X		
Maryland	X		X					
Massachusetts	X		X					
Michigan	X		X					
Minnesota	X	X		X				
Mississippi	None							
Missouri	X	X						
Montana	X	X		X	X			
Nebraska	X	X						X
Nevada	None							
New Hampshire	X	X		X		X		
New Jersey	X		X					
New Mexico	X	X						
New York	X		X					
North Carolina	None							
North Dakota	X	X		X				
Ohio	X		X					
Oklahoma	None							
Oregon	X	X						
Pennsylvania	X	X						
Rhode Island	X	X						
South Carolina	X	X						
South Dakota	X	X		X	X			
Tennessee	X	X						
Texas	X		X					
Utah	None							
Vermont	X	X				X		
Virginia	X		X				X	
Washington	X		X					
West Virginia	X	X		X				
Wisconsin	X	X						
Wyoming	None							

[a] Formerly called "The Big Game"
[b] Formerly called "The Multi-State Rolldown"

SOURCE: Created by Kim Masters Evans for Thomson Gale, 2004

As of August 2004 MUSL had thirty members. Each member state offers at least one MUSL game, and twenty-eight of them offer the Powerball game. (See Table 7.2.) Each member state keeps 50% of its own Powerball ticket sales. The rest is paid out in prizes. The profits from all MUSL games are retained by the individual states.

MEGA MILLIONS. Another popular multistate game is called Mega Millions. It is played by eleven states, as shown in Table 7.2. Players choose six numbers from two separate number pools: five numbers from 1 to 52, and one number from 1 to 52. All six numbers must match to win the jackpot. Drawings are held twice weekly.

Mega Millions was formerly known as the Big Game. The first Big Game ticket was sold on August 31, 1996, and the first drawing took place on September 6, 1996. The Big Game became very popular and soon offered jackpots in excess of $50 million. As of late 2002, it held the record for the largest jackpot ever offered in a North American lottery—$363 million in May 2000. That jackpot was split by two winners, one in Michigan and one in

Illinois. Overall, the Big Game had an average jackpot of $47 million during its run.

The Big Game was plagued by lagging sales during fiscal year 2001. Average sales had dropped by 34% from the year before. At that time, the Big Game accounted for approximately 6% of total lottery sales in the states in which it was offered. The game operators wanted to capture a bigger market and so renamed the game Mega Millions and increased the initial jackpot to $10 million, twice what it was for the Big Game. The lure of higher jackpots proved to be a strong sales incentive. Ticket sales increased dramatically.

CONSTITUTIONAL QUESTIONS. In January 2002 church groups and other lottery opponents sued the state of Ohio over a bill passed the month before allowing the state to join the Mega Millions lottery. The lawsuit claimed that the state's constitution required Ohio to run its own lottery and that the bill would transfer this authority to other states. Ohio officially joined Mega Millions in May 2002 in hopes of raising $41 million annually to overcome a $1.5 billion budget gap.

In July 2002 a judge ruled that Ohio's participation in Mega Millions was not unconstitutional because the state would retain sufficient control over the lottery to satisfy the constitution. However, he did overturn a part of the bill that would have allowed the state to divert the money raised away from the Department of Education into the general budget. The Ohio Constitution specifies that lottery revenues must go toward education programs. The bill writers had tried to circumvent this requirement with an accounting maneuver that would have initially assigned the revenues to the Department of Education but then allowed them to be taken out for other purposes. The judge ruled that this practice did violate the state's constitution.

New York's decision to join Mega Millions in May 2002 was also challenged in court on constitutional grounds. The plaintiffs claimed that participation in the multistate lottery diverted lottery profits away from education programs. In July 2004 a state appeals court ruled that the administrative costs of participating in the lottery were insignificant and did not constitute a diversion of funds.

INTERNATIONAL LOTTERY GAMES

Lotteries operate in more than one hundred countries around the world. According to *La Fleur's,* worldwide lottery sales were $160 billion during 2003. The North American Association for State and Provincial Lotteries (NASPL) reports on its Web site (www.naspl.org) that U.S. lotteries accounted for $45.3 billion (or 28% of this total). Canadian lotteries had sales of $8.1 billion (Canadian), meaning that North America accounted for about one-third of worldwide lottery sales during 2003. North

American sales were up 7% from $50.7 billion reported for 2002.

More than seventy-five government and private lotteries operated in Europe during 2003. The European market generally accounts for 40–45% of world lottery sales. According to Scientific Games Corporation the top five lotteries in terms of sales during 2003 were in Spain, Japan, France, Italy, and the United Kingdom. In 2004 Spain, France, and the United Kingdom teamed together to start the Euro Millions lottery.

One of the most popular lotteries in the world is the Spanish lotto, El Gordo ("the fat one"). El Gordo has been conducted in Spain since 1812. Drawings are held four times a year, and the December drawing, called the Navidad (or Christmas) Lottery, is the largest single gambling event in the world. The lottery is operated by Organismo Nacional de Loterías y Apuestas del Estado (ONLAE). The number of tickets printed is limited to 66,000, meaning that the odds of winning a prize are about one in six. Winnings are paid out in a lump sum and are not taxed by the Spanish government. The Christmas Lottery has a 70% payout rate, much higher than most European and North American lotteries. In December 2003 the total prize for the El Gordo lottery reached $1.3 billion. The jackpot was only $470 million, but more than 10,000 prizes were awarded in all.

Beginning in the late 1990s several U.S. lottery agencies began talks with foreign countries regarding development of an international lottery. The International Lottery Alliance was led by Edward J. Stanek, director of the Iowa lottery. By April 2003 at least thirty states and dozens of foreign countries were negotiating terms for an international lottery (tentatively called Super Pool). It was expected to offer jackpots of up to $500 million. There were many logistical problems to overcome including setting a location for drawings and dealing with time zone and currency differences.

In April 2004 the *Indianapolis Star* reported that the deal had fallen apart after several European nations backed out in protest over the U.S. invasion of Iraq ("War Dampens Indiana's Hopes of International Lottery," April 3, 2004). The remaining foreign countries also backed out amid fears that U.S. residents would dominate ticket sales and prizes without more international participation.

LOTTERY ADMINISTRATION

States differ in how they administer lotteries within their governments. In 1998 the Council of State Governments (CSG) found that all but four lotteries operating at that time were directly administered by a state lottery board or commission. The lotteries in Connecticut, Georgia, Kentucky, and Louisiana were operated by quasi-governmental or privatized lottery corporations. The CSG reported that lottery oversight is most frequently performed by the lottery board or commission or by an executive branch agency. Enforcement authority regarding fraud and abuse rested with the attorney general's office, state police, or the lottery commission in most states. The amount of oversight and control that each state legislature has over its lottery agency differs from state to state.

Although lotteries are a multimillion-dollar business, lottery commissions employ only a few thousand people nationwide. Lottery commissions set up, monitor, and run the games offered in their states, but the vast majority of lottery sales are at retail outlets, such as stores, gas stations, bars, and so forth. These retailers contract with state lottery commissions to sell their games. In exchange, the retailers receive sales commissions on all tickets sold and cash bonuses for selling winning tickets.

Retailers

According to the NASPL Web site, nearly 186,000 retailers were selling lottery tickets around the country in 2003. California had the most retailers (19,000), followed by Texas (16,395) and New York (15,300). Approximately three-fourths of all lottery retailers offer online services. Approximately half of all lottery retailers are convenience stores. Other outlets include various kinds of stores, non-profit organizations (churches and fraternal organizations), service stations, restaurants and bars, bowling alleys, and newsstands.

Retailers are attracted to lottery sales because they increase traffic and earn commissions for the operators. Outlets that sell winning jackpot tickets receive cash bonuses from the lottery, are often featured in media stories, and receive other public attention. Those that become known "lucky" places to purchase lottery tickets can greatly enhance their business.

Because lottery tickets are often an impulse purchase, they are usually sold at the front of the store near the checkout area. This also allows store operators to keep an eye on ticket vending machines to prevent play by underage customers. Increasingly, convenience stores offer pay-at-the-pump gasoline sales. This is likely to decrease in-store traffic and have a negative impact on lottery ticket sales. Lottery officials in Indiana want to develop a method for selling and printing tickets at the gas pumps to overcome this problem. Lottery officials in South Dakota have expressed interest in selling lottery tickets in mass-merchandise stores like Wal-Mart and Kmart.

Lottery personnel and retailers work together to ensure that merchandising and advertising are effective for both. The New Jersey lottery launched an Internet site during 2001 just for its lottery retailers. On the site, retailers can read about game promotions, ask questions of lottery officials online, and access individual sales data.

During 2001 Louisiana implemented a lottery retailer optimization program, in which lottery officials supply retailers with demographic data to help them increase sales and improve marketing techniques. Although most states do not limit the number of retailers that can sell lottery tickets, they usually try to space them out to ensure that each obtains a good market share.

According to the Web site of the National Association of Convenience Stores (NACS; www.nacsonline.com), roughly half of all lottery sales during 2001 were in convenience stores. NACS says that nearly 80% of U.S. convenience stores sell lottery tickets. The typical commission paid to their retailers is 5 to 8%.

The NACS reported in its *1997 NACS Lottery Study* that frequent lottery customers spend more than twice as much per visit as nonlottery customers ($7.07 as opposed to $3.47). Even infrequent lottery customers spend $4.80 per visit. The study found that lottery customers purchased at least one other nonlottery item in 95% of their store visits. Lottery customers also shop more times per week at convenience stores than do nonlottery customers. More than half of the customers surveyed (55%) felt that lottery ticket availability was important in their choice of store. Lottery tickets ranked fifth among store items in generating other impulse sales (behind household items, beer, cigarettes, and magazines/newspapers).

However, NACS also noted that the average cost of handling a lottery transaction is 39 cents higher than that of a nonlottery transaction. Lottery tickets actually have a lower margin than most other convenience store items, particularly those pushed at the front counter. Store managers report complaints from lottery officials about merchandise such as batteries and candy hiding lottery advertising from customer view.

Advertising

Just like any other business, lotteries aggressively market their products. Some of their best advertisements are provided free through media coverage of jackpot winners. The lotteries also allot a portion of their operating budget to advertising.

According to the NASPL, lottery states spend hundreds of millions of dollars on advertising. A 1998 study of lottery marketing plans found that the most commonly used themes relate to the size of the prize or the jackpot and the fun and excitement of playing the lottery. (See Table 7.3.)

Lottery advertising is sometimes controversial, particularly when ads focus on winning and neglect to mention the odds against the players. The NGISC's final report from 1999 criticizes lottery advertising, saying "much of it is misleading, even deceptive." The report complains that lottery advertisements rarely explain the poor odds of winning big prizes and that most imply the chances of

TABLE 7.3

Advertising themes identified in marketing plans of lottery agencies, 1998

	Percent of plans using theme
Size of the prize or the jackpot	56
Fun and excitement of playing the lottery	56
Winner Awareness	46
Benefits to state of lottery dollars	28
Sports themes	28
Product Awareness	24
How to Play	20
Playing responsibly	16
Odds of winning	16
Tie-in with fairs and festivals	12
Play more often	12
Emotions of Winning	12
Answer to your Dream	12
Benefits of Winning	8
Instant gratification	8
Social interaction of playing	4
Low Price	4

SOURCE: Charles T. Clotfelter, Philip J. Cook, Julie A. Edell, and Marian Moore. "Table 13: Advertising Themes Identified in Marketing Plans of Lottery Agencies, 1998," in *State Lotteries at the Turn of the Century: Report to the National Gambling Impact Study Commission,* U.S. Government Printing Office and University of North Texas Libraries, April 23, 1999

FIGURE 7.3

Percentage of Americans who have purchased a lottery ticket within the previous 12 months, March 2004

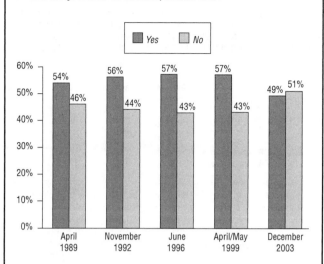

SOURCE: Adapted from Jeffrey M. Jones, "Please tell me whether or not you have done any of the following things in the past 12 months. Bought a state lottery ticket?" in Gambling a Common Activity for Americans, The Gallup Organization, March 24, 2004 http://www .gallup.com/content/default.aspx?ci=11098 (accessed August 14, 2004). Copyright © 2004 by The Gallup Organization. Reproduced by permission of The Gallup Organization.

winning are quite good. The NGISC report is also critical of lottery advertisements that focus attention on the jackpot amount but list the odds of winning any prize, including far smaller ones.

La Fleur's 2004 World Lottery Almanac reports the advertising restrictions on various state lotteries. Twenty-one states and the District of Columbia have no restrictions on the types of advertising that can be done, while fifteen have various restrictions, including no minors in lottery ads (Kansas), no ads for VLTs (Oregon), and inclusion of the odds of winning (Vermont, Oregon, Connecticut, and Colorado).

In February 2004 economist Edwin Rubenstein with the Oklahoma Council of Public Affairs complained that lottery states spend more on lottery advertising than any other message geared toward the public, such as "Just Say No" or "Stay in School" ("A Closer Look at the Lottery," February 1, 2004). Rubenstein estimates that lottery advertising takes up 1–2% of lottery sales.

LOTTERY PLAYER DEMOGRAPHICS

A national poll conducted by the Gallup Organization in December 2003 found that 49% of adults had purchased a lottery ticket within the previous year. (See Figure 7.3.) The percentage is the lowest recorded since 1989. In 1999 a Gallup poll found that 15% of teenagers aged thirteen to seventeen had purchased a lottery ticket within the previous year.

In general, public opinion polls consistently show high approval ratings for lotteries as a means of raising public funds. The results of a lottery question from the most recent national gambling poll conducted in 1999 by the Gallup Organization are summarized in Table 7.4 and compared to previous years. Approval of state lotteries for cash prizes has remained strong since the late 1980s, with 75% of adults and 82% of teenagers expressing favorable opinions in 1999.

Lottery demographics were reported in the October/ November 2001 issue of *Lottery Insights,* the official publication of the NASPL. The article uses data from the NGISC and the National Opinion Research Center (NORC). The study found that just more than half of the U.S. adult population purchased at least one lottery ticket during 1998. Those aged thirty to sixty-four were most likely to purchase lottery tickets. However, the amount spent on lottery tickets varied by age. People aged fifty to sixty-four spent the most—an average of $6.72 the last time they purchased lottery tickets. The youngest (eighteen to twenty-nine) and oldest (sixty-five and up) adults spent the least amount.

In 1998 NORC interviewed nearly 3,000 people as part of a survey on lottery participation and spending in the United States. The final results represent data on 2,867 people. The respondents were characterized by demographics and asked about their lottery play during the previous year, month, and week. The survey indicated that approximately half of the respondents had played the lottery during the previous year. However, researchers dis-

TABLE 7.4

Public opinion on states' use of lotteries to raise revenue, selected years 1989–99

QUESTION: AS YOU MAY KNOW, SOME STATES LEGALIZE BETTING SO THAT THE STATE CAN RAISE REVENUES. PLEASE TELL ME WHETHER YOU APPROVE OR DISAPPROVE OF EACH OF THE FOLLOWING TYPES OF BETTING AS A WAY TO HELP YOUR STATE RAISE REVENUE. FIRST, DO YOU APPROVE OR DISAPPROVE OF LOTTERIES FOR CASH PRIZES?

		Approve %	Disapprove %	No Opinion %	Sample size
Adults (18+)	99 Apr 30–May 23	75	24	1	1,523
	96 Jun 27–30	77	22	1	1,004
	92 Nov 20–22	75	24	1	1,007
	89 Apr 4–9	78	21	1	1,208
Teens (13–17)	99 Apr 30–May 23	82	18	-	501

SOURCE: Adapted from "Question 2C. Please tell me whether you approve or disapprove of each of the following types of betting as a way to help your state raise revenue. Lotteries for cash prizes?" in *Gambling in America*, The Gallup Organization, June 22,1999, http://www.gallup.com/poll/content/default.aspx?ci=9889&pg=2 (accessed September 26, 2004) Copyright © 1999 by The Gallup Organization. Reproduced by permission of The Gallup Organization.

TABLE 7.5

Characteristics of the top 20% of lottery purchasers, 1999

Demographic group	Percentage of heaviest players	Percentage of US adults
Male	61.4%	48.5%
Black	25.4%	12.2%
High school dropouts	20.3%	12.3%
Household income under $10,000	9.7%	5.0%
Median age	47.5	43.0

Note: Heaviest lottery players defined as those in the top 20% of lottery purchasers.

SOURCE: Charles T. Clotfelter, Philip J. Cook, Julie A. Edell, and Marian Moore. "Table 12: Characteristics of Heaviest Lottery Players," in *State Lotteries at the Turn of the Century: Report to the National Gambling Impact Study Commission,* U.S. Government Printing Office and University of North Texas Libraries, April 23, 1999

covered that only 5% of the players accounted for 54% of the group's total lottery spending. The vast majority of the group's lottery spending (82%) was due to the play of only 20% of the respondents. The survey concluded that a relatively small group of "heavy" players are responsible for most lottery sales.

Some characteristics of the heaviest lottery players are listed in Table 7.5. The NORC survey found that:

- Men are slightly more likely to play lottery games than women.

- Participation is lowest for those aged sixty-four and up.

- Single people spend less on lottery tickets than married or divorced people.

- Per capita lottery spending is highest for those aged forty-five to sixty-four years.

- Participation rates do not differ significantly by race or ethnicity. However, per capita spending by African-Americans is higher than for any other group.

- Per capita spending is higher for those respondents who did not complete high school and for low-income households.

NORC respondents did not have overly rosy views about payout and win rates. Most (63%) thought that lotteries paid out less than 25% of total sales as prizes. (The actual payout percentage is around 50%.) The vast majority (86%) of those who had played the lottery during the previous year indicated that they had lost more money than they had won. Only 8% of respondents believed that they had made money playing the lottery.

GTECH Corporation is a major supplier of equipment to the gambling industry. The company conducted its most recent national survey on gaming during July 2000. According to the survey of 1,200 adults nationwide, lotteries were considered an acceptable form of entertainment by 65% of respondents. As Figure 7.4 shows, nearly three-quarters of those surveyed were in favor of states operating lotteries. Favor was highest among those under thirty-five years old, who had an 83% favorability rating. Approval decreased with age, as 72% of those aged thirty-five to fifty-four favored state lotteries, as opposed to 63% of those aged fifty-five and up.

Seventy percent of survey respondents in lottery states in 2000 indicated that they would vote in favor of continuing their lottery. Support at the ballot box is slightly higher among Democrats (70%) than among Republicans (61%). In nonlottery states, the survey shows that 66% of respondents would vote in favor of a state lottery if given the chance.

Fifty-four percent of those asked believed that lotteries keep taxes lower. (See Figure 7.5.) As shown in Figure 7.6, lotteries are favored over higher taxes as a means of raising revenue by more than a three-to-one margin. Survey respondents provided the following as the main benefits of lotteries:

- Provide funding for education and other programs (42%)

- Entertainment/fun/can win money (15%)

- Keep taxes lower (15%)

- Jobs/economy/revenue (8%)

Education was deemed the most appropriate use of lottery proceeds by 54% of respondents, compared with roads/public transportation (17%), long-term care for the elderly (8%), and protecting the environment (7%). Support for education as the most appropriate use of lottery revenue declined with age. Seventy percent of those asked

FIGURE 7.4

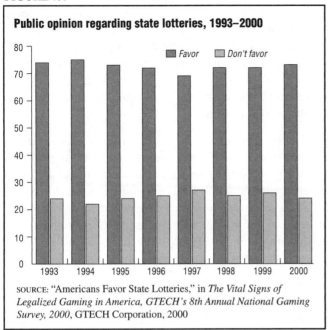

Public opinion regarding state lotteries, 1993–2000

SOURCE: "Americans Favor State Lotteries," in *The Vital Signs of Legalized Gaming in America, GTECH's 8th Annual National Gaming Survey, 2000*, GTECH Corporation, 2000

FIGURE 7.5

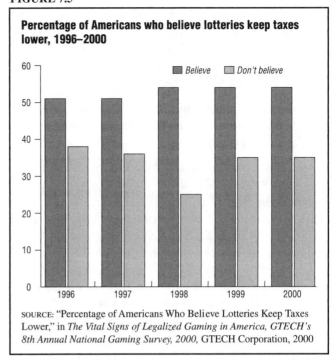

Percentage of Americans who believe lotteries keep taxes lower, 1996–2000

SOURCE: "Percentage of Americans Who Believe Lotteries Keep Taxes Lower," in *The Vital Signs of Legalized Gaming in America, GTECH's 8th Annual National Gaming Survey, 2000*, GTECH Corporation, 2000

FIGURE 7.6

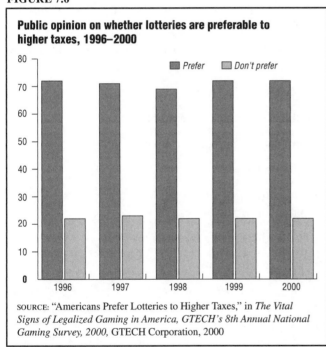

Public opinion on whether lotteries are preferable to higher taxes, 1996–2000

SOURCE: "Americans Prefer Lotteries to Higher Taxes," in *The Vital Signs of Legalized Gaming in America, GTECH's 8th Annual National Gaming Survey, 2000*, GTECH Corporation, 2000

believed that some lottery proceeds should fund research into understanding and helping problem gamblers.

Survey respondents were more likely to play the lottery if proceeds go to specific causes. Sixty-five percent of those asked would be more likely to play the lottery if funds were set aside for a specific cause rather than going into a state's general fund. When asked about problems facing the lottery industry, 27% of respondents indicated that insufficient prize money is the most important problem. Improper use of lottery proceeds was selected by 24% of respondents. Other problems included underage

gambling (12%), lack of funding for research into problem gambling (11%), and too much advertising (5%).

The disadvantages or weaknesses of state-sponsored lotteries that survey respondents named are as follows:

• People wasting money who cannot afford to do so (33%)

• Misuse of lottery money (24%)

• Compulsive gambling (17%)

• Players not winning enough money (13%)

• Promotion of gambling (10%)

GROUP PLAY

It has become quite common for groups of people to pool their money and buy lottery tickets, particularly for very large jackpots. According to California lottery officials, 30% of that state's jackpots are won by multiple winners on one ticket. Group wins are beneficial to the lotteries from a public relations standpoint. They generate more media coverage than solo wins and expose a wider group of friends, relatives, and coworkers to the idea that lotteries are winnable.

In 2001 the California lottery started the Lotto Captain program to help so-called group leaders manage lotto pools. Lotto captains have access to a special Web site that gives them tips on organizing and running group play. They can download and print forms that help them track players, games, dates, and jackpots. As an incentive, Lotto Captains can participate in special drawings for cash and prizes. Lottery officials are extremely pleased with the program's success, as far more people enrolled to be captains than was expected. These are hard-core players who promote lottery games, recruit new players, and provide valuable feedback about lottery promotions. In January 2004 the Missouri Lottery started is own Lottery Captain program for group-play organizers.

Still, pooling arrangements, even if between only two people, can lead to all kinds of legal headaches if a group actually wins a jackpot.

In May 2001 a group of twenty-three cabdrivers working at Atlanta's Hartsfield Airport won a $49 million jackpot in the Big Game. Before the money could be paid out, it was frozen by lottery officials when seven other cabbies filed a lawsuit contending that they were also part of the winning lottery pool. The man heading the pool was accused of sloppy record keeping in regards to who was participating in each lottery. In addition, the plaintiffs contend that they regularly participated in the pool, and it was understood that small amounts won would be pooled together to buy more tickets in the next lottery. They believe that even though they did not directly contribute to the pool that purchased the big jackpot ticket, they are still entitled to a share of the money.

Also in 2001, a New York judge awarded $1.6 million to a Brooklyn woman who sued her former live-in boyfriend for breach of oral contract after he secretly collected a $7 million jackpot from a lottery ticket they had purchased while together in 1999. Although the defendant denied ever agreeing to split lottery winnings with the plaintiff, a clerk at the store where the ticket was purchased testified to the contrary. The plaintiff was awarded half of the after-tax amount of the jackpot. The defendant also had to pay $200,000 in punitive damages and attorney fees.

A California woman lost all of her $1.3 million jackpot in 2001 after a court found that she had fraudulently concealed the award from her husband. After winning, the woman sought advice from lottery officials about how to conceal the award from her husband. They advised her to get divorced before her first annuity check arrived. The woman did so and never declared the money as an asset during the divorce proceedings. This lack of disclosure was ultimately discovered by the ex-husband. Under California law, a court can award 100% of an undisclosed asset, plus attorneys' fees, to one spouse if the other spouse commits oppression, fraud, or malice during divorce proceedings.

WHY DO PEOPLE PLAY LOTTERIES?

A lottery is a unique gambling event because it costs only a small amount of money to get a chance to win a very large jackpot, albeit at very long odds. The huge jackpot is the main selling feature of the lottery. Rollover jackpots spur ticket sales. As more people buy tickets, the jackpot grows, while the odds of winning decrease. However, this does not deter ticket sales—sales actually increase under these circumstances. Lottery players often go against the statistical odds, playing in games with large rewards but small probabilities of winning rather than games with small rewards and better probabilities of winning. The lottery lure seems to be that winning a multimillion-dollar jackpot would be life-changing.

Lotteries are successful because people are ignorant of or choose to ignore the laws of probability. For example, the odds of choosing six numbers correctly out of forty-nine are approximately fourteen million to one. Ian Stewart, professor of mathematics at the University of Warwick in Coventry, England, once said that lotto games "are a tribute to public innumeracy" ("It Probably Won't Be You," *Times Higher Education Supplement,* April 12, 1996).

A 1998 study performed on behalf of European lotteries (Mark D. Griffiths and Richard T. A. Wood, *Lottery Gambling and Addiction: An Overview of European Research,* European State Lottery and Toto Association, Lausanne, Switzerland, 1999) looked at why people continue to play the lottery despite the long odds. The following reasons were given:

• The lure of a very large jackpot in exchange for a very small investment

• Successful advertising

• Publicity about jackpot winners

• Ignorance of probability theory

• Televised drawings

• Overestimating of positive outcomes and underestimating of negative ones

• The credibility of government backing

• Belief in players' own luck

One of the most interesting theories of the study concerns the role of entrapment in lottery play. Many people select the same numbers week after week. For example, a United Kingdom newspaper reported that 67% of people surveyed chose the same lottery numbers each week, mostly based on birthdates, address numbers, and lucky numbers. As time goes by and their numbers are not selected, these people do not become discouraged. Instead, they think their chances of winning are getting better. This mind-set is called "the gambler's fallacy." It is a common myth that the probability of winning increases the longer a losing streak lasts. Often players experience near-misses, in which two or more of their numbers are drawn during the jackpot drawing. This only convinces them that they are getting closer to the big win. They become increasingly entrapped in playing their numbers and fear skipping even one drawing.

The study also reports on a 1996 survey that found that 22% of respondents believe they will win a lottery jackpot at some point. The lotteries themselves feed the illusion that winning is commonplace by encouraging widespread media coverage of winners and their stories.

THE EFFECTS OF LOTTERIES

Economic Effects

Proponents of lotteries mostly use economic arguments to justify their positions. Lotteries provide state governments with a relatively easy way to enhance their revenues without imposing more taxes. Lotteries are also financially beneficial to the many small businesses that sell lottery tickets and to larger companies that participate in merchandising campaigns or provide advertising or computer services. Finally, lotteries provide cheap entertainment to people who want to play, while raising money for the betterment of all.

Lottery opponents also have economic arguments. They contend that the role of lotteries in funding state programs is actually quite small. Lotteries contribute only a small percentage of total state revenues. In addition, they cost money to advertise and operate. Lotteries lure people into parting with their money under false hopes. Opponents contend that those targeted come particularly from lower income brackets and may not be able to afford to gamble.

THE DIVISION OF LOTTERY MONEY. Lottery money can be categorized as sales, prizes, administrative costs, retailer commissions, and state profits. The sales amount is the total amount taken in by the lottery. In general, 50–60% of U.S. lottery sales are paid out as prizes to winners. Administrative costs for advertising, employee salaries, and other operating expenses usually account for 1–10% of sales. On average, retailers collect 5–7% of sales in the form of commissions and approximately 2% as bonuses for selling winning tickets. The remaining 30–40% of sales is profit turned over to the state.

U.S. state lotteries had approximately $45 billion in sales for fiscal year 2003. A fiscal year is defined differently from state to state, but in most states it runs from July 1 to June 30. Thus, fiscal year 2003 is the twelve-month period from June 30, 2002, to July 1, 2003. According to the NASPL national sales were up 6.8% in fiscal year 2003 from the previous year's sales of $42.4 billion. By comparison sales increased by 9% from 2001 to 2002.

According to sales figures reported by the NASPL for fiscal years 2001 through 2003 for each state, the District of Columbia, and Puerto Rico, nine states reported declining sales for 2003 compared to 2002. These states were California, Colorado, Connecticut, Delaware, Illinois, Louisiana, Massachusetts, Minnesota, and Vermont. Delaware had the sharpest decline (6.8%). By contrast four jurisdictions that were operating lotteries in 2002 and 2003 had sales increases in excess of 20%. These were West Virginia (up 27.5%), Puerto Rico (up 26.4%), Florida (up 23.1%), and Missouri (up 21.1%).

According to the NASPL during fiscal year 2003 New York had the highest lottery sales ($5.4 billion), followed by Massachusetts ($4.2 billion) and Texas ($3.1 billion). These three states accounted for 28% of national lottery sales. In total fifteen states had lottery sales in excess of $1 billion during 2003.

According to *La Fleur's,* total U.S. sales for all lotteries from the time of their inception through fiscal year 2003 add up to $556 billion. About $296 billion was paid in prizes over the same period, and $191 billion was collected by state governments.

The New York lottery has the largest cumulative sales, $57.6 billion since its inception in 1967. It has also achieved the highest profits of any state government (nearly $23 billion). New Jersey had the highest percentage return to any state government from a lottery (41%). Massachusetts has paid out the most in cumulative prizes (nearly $31 billion).

The states allocate their lottery profits in different ways. Table 7.6 describes each state's cumulative allocation of profits from each lottery's inception to June 2002. The list does not include lotteries that began during or after 2002 (South Carolina, Tennessee, and North Dakota).

RETAILER PAYMENTS. According to *La Fleur's,* the average prize payout from each state lottery's inception to fiscal year 2003 is 53% of cumulative sales. The average state profit is 34%. Thus, administrative costs and retailer payments account for an average of 13% of cumulative lottery sales.

The primary means of retailer compensation is a commission on each ticket sold. In other words, a lottery retailer keeps a certain percentage of the money taken in from lottery sales. Most states also have incentive-based programs for retailers that meet particular sales criteria. For example, the Wisconsin lottery pays retailers a bonus for increasing ticket sales by particular amounts. The state implemented the program in January 2000 in response to declining sales and a drop in the number of lottery retailers. Lottery officials believe that the incentive program is more effective than an increase in retailer commission at increasing sales. The incentive program encourages retailers to ask customers if they would like to buy lottery tickets. Retailers that sell a winning ticket in Wisconsin receive 2% of the value of the ticket (up to $100,000).

UNCLAIMED LOTTERY WINNINGS. It is estimated that unclaimed lottery winnings add up to hundreds of millions of dollars each year. In early 2004 the California lot-

TABLE 7.6

Cumulative distribution of state lottery proceeds as of June 30, 2003

(in millions of dollars)

Arizona (1982)

Education	$375.95
Health and welfare	$148.44
Protection and safety	$69.90
Economic Development Fund	$40.52
General government	$41.10
Inspection and regulation	$7.11
Natural resources	$5.86
Local Transportation Assistance Fund	$489.00
County Assistance Fund	$129.68
Heritage Fund	$238.53
Mass transit	$25.74
Clean Air Fund	$0.50
Court Appointed Special Advocate Fund (unclaimed prizes)	$21.34
State General Fund	$1.50
	$1,595.17

California (1985)

Education	**$14,000.00**

Colorado (1983)

Capital Construction Fund	$439.80
Division of Parks and Outdoor Recreation	$128.10
Conservation Trust Fund	$512.90
Great Outdoors Colorado Trust Fund	$311.60
General Fund	$1.30
School Fund	$12.20
	$1,405.90

Connecticut (1972)

General Fund (to benefit education, roads, health and hospitals, public safety, etc.)	**$5,060.00**

D.C. (1982)

General Fund	**$1,200.00**

Delaware (1975)

General Fund	**$1,600.00**

Florida (1987)

Education Enhancement Trust Fund	**$13,030.00**

Georgia (1993)

HOPE scholarships	$2,500.00
Pre-kindergarten program	$2,100.00
Capital outlay and technology for primary and secondary schools	$1,800.00
	$6,400.00

Idaho (1989)

Public schools (K-12)	$124.80
Public buildings	$124.80
	$249.60

Illinois (1974)

Illinois Common School Fund (K-12)	**$11,600.00**

Indiana (1989)

Education	$370.30
Build Indiana Capital Projects Fund	$317.10
Teachers' Retirement Fund	$402.60
Police & fire Pension Relief Fund	$214.70
License Plate Taxes	$592.80
Property Tax Fund	$55.20
General Fund	$288.40
Job creation/economic development	$30.00
	$2,271.10
	$8,309.38

Iowa (1985)

Iowa Plan (economic development)	$170.31
CLEAN Fund (environment and agriculture)	$35.89
Gambler's Treatment Program	$8.68
Special appropriations	$20.82
Sales tax	$136.03
General fund	$456.23
	$827.96

Kansas (1987)

Economic Development Initiatives Fund	$519.70
Correctional Institutions Building Fund	$61.30
County Reappraisal Project (FY 88–90)	$17.20
Juvenile Detention Facilities Fund	$17.70
State General Fund (FY 1995–2003)	$76.50
Problem Gambling Grant Fund	$0.24
	$692.64

Kentucky (1989)

Education	$214.00
Vietnam veterans	$32.00
General fund	$1,300.00
Post-secondary & college scholarships	$316.00
Affordable Housing Trust Fund	$20.80
Literacy programs & early childhood reading	$12.00
	$1,894.8

Louisiana (1991)

General Fund	$1,380.00
Problem gambling	$3.00
	$1,383.00

Maine (1974)

General Fund	$641.90
Outdoor Heritage Fund	$10.30
	$652.20

Maryland (1973)

General Fund	$7,909.00
Subdivisions (for one year only, FY 1984–85)	$20.90
Stadium Authority	$379.48

Massachusetts (1972)

Cities and towns	$10,180.00
Arts Council	$173.65
General Fund	$2,660.00
Compulsive gamblers	$9.80
	$13,023.45

Michigan (1972)

Education (K-12)	**$11,000.00**

Minnesota (1989)

General Fund	$670.90
Environmental and Natural Resources Trust Fund	$311.80
Game & Fish Fund	$32.10
Natural Resources Fund	$32.10
Other state programs	$36.70
Compulsive gambling	$16.50
	$1,100.10

Missouri (1986)

Public education	$1,500.00
General Revenue Fund (1986–1993)	$542.54
	$2,042.54

Montana (1987)

Education	$49.40
Juvenile detention	$2.50
General Fund	$54.60
Study of socioeconomic impact of gambling	$0.10
	$106.60

Nebraska (1993)

Compulsive gambling	$3.90
Education	$92.50
Environment	$74.00
Solid Waste Landfill Closure Fund	$18.50
	$188.90

New Hampshire (1964)

Education	**$857.00**

New Jersey (1970)

Education and institutions	**$13,150.00**

New Mexico (1996)

Public school capital outlay	$66.55
Lottery Tuition Fund	$111.46
	$178.01

TABLE 7.6

Cumulative distribution of state lottery proceeds as of June 30, 2003 [CONTINUED]

(in millions of dollars)

New York (1967)		**Virginia (1988)**	
Education	$23,030.00	General Fund (FY 1989–98)	$2,800.00
Ohio (1974)		Direct aid to public education K-12 (FY 1999–present)	$1,720.00
Education	$12,400.00	Literary Fund (primarily for school construction additions	
Oregon (1985)		and renovations)	$119.23
Economic development	$1,300.00	Debt set-off collection	$10.45
Public education	$1,670.00		**$4,649.68**
Natural resource programs	$186.00		
	$3,156.00	**Washington (1982)**	
		General Fund	$1,800.00
Pennsylvania (1972)		Education Funds	$170.20
Older Pennsylvanians	$13,800.00	Seattle Mariners Stadium	$25.70
Rhode Island (1974)		King County Stadium and Exhibition Center	$32.50
General Fund	$1,690.00	Literacy programs: 27,000 new children's books	
South Carolina (2002)		Local food banks: 27,000 new children's books	
Education Lottery Fund	$301.00		**$2,028.40**
South Dakota (1989)		**West Virginia (1986)**	
General Fund	$358.70	Education	$524.80
Capital Construction Fund	$11.50	Senior citizens	$251.50
Property Tax Reduction Fund	$718.90	Tourism	$246.70
	$1,089.10	Bonds covering profit areas	$270.60
Texas (1992)		General Fund	$259.60
General Fund	$4,960.00	Other	$99.60
Foundation School Fund	$5,610.00		**$1,652.80**
	$10,570.00	**Wisconsin (1988)**	
Vermont (1978)		• Public benefit such as property tax relief	**$2,110.00**
General Fund	$212.80		
Education Fund	$88.40	**Total – US**	**$190,596.53**
	$301.20		

SOURCE: Adapted from "NASPL: Where the Money Goes," in *NASPL: Where the Money Goes,* North American Association of State & Provincial Lotteries, 2004, http://www.naspl.org/benefits.html

---

tery turned over more than $15 million from an unclaimed lotto jackpot to educational programs in the state. According to the California lottery more than $530 million in unclaimed prizes have been forwarded to public schools since 1985.

Unclaimed winnings are allocated differently by each state. Some states require by law that unclaimed winnings be returned to the prize pool. This is the case with the New York lottery. Other states allocate such funds to lottery administrative costs or to specific state programs. For example, the Texas lottery turns over unclaimed prizes to funds that benefit hospital research and payment of indigent health care.

STATE BUDGETS. Lottery revenues make up a very small portion of state budgets. One study (Charles T. Clotfelter et al., *State Lotteries at the Turn of the Century: Report to the National Gambling Impact Study Commission,* 1999) found that lottery revenues comprise anywhere from 0.67% to 4.07% of their states' general revenue. The average portion was approximately 2.2%. This compares with an average of 25% each for general sales taxes and income taxes.

TAXES AND OTHER WITHHOLDING FROM LOTTERY WINNINGS. Lottery winnings over a certain value are taxable as personal income. All prizes awarded greater than $600 are reported by the lotteries to the Internal Revenue Service. In general, the lottery agencies subtract taxes

prior to awarding large prizes. For example, the New York lottery withholds federal, state, and local income taxes on prizes greater than $5,000. The lottery withholds 25% for federal taxes and 7.7% for state taxes from prizes greater than $5,000 won by U.S. residents. An additional 4.45% is withheld if the winner is a New York City resident. Non-U.S. residents face even higher tax withholding rates.

In addition, the New York lottery is required by law to subtract past-due child support payments and collect repayment of public assistance from prizes of $600 or more.

In June 2002 the South Carolina lottery launched a new online game called Carolina 5. The game was unique because the $100,000 jackpot featured prepaid taxes. This was the first online game to offer a tax-free jackpot.

Education

Lottery proponents often advocate lotteries for their economic benefits to education. Some lotteries dedicate a portion of their profits toward K–12 or higher education. Concerns have been raised, however, that these profits are not additional dollars for education but simply replace general fund dollars that would have been spent on education anyway.

In April 2004 mathematics professor Donald Miller of Saint Mary's College in Indiana argued in a *USA Today* article that educational spending per student gradually decreases once a state starts a lottery ("Schools Lose Out in Lotteries," April 15, 2004). The finding is based on examination of data from 1965 to 1990 for twelve states that enacted lotteries for education during this time. According to Miller, average pre-lottery spending increased each year by approximately $12 per student in these states. Post-lottery spending showed a huge increase in the immediate years following lottery initiation. On average the states increased their education spending by nearly $50 per student. However, the increase fell sharply in following years and eventually lagged behind states without lottery-generated education funds. Miller blames the problem on legislators using lottery funds "to replace rather than add to existing sources of education funding."

A 1999 study conducted by researchers at Duke University for NGISC calls earmarking lottery proceeds for education "an excellent device for engendering political support for a lottery." However, the study noted that it was doubtful that earmarked lottery revenues actually increase the funds available for specific programs. Some lottery funds earmarked for education just replace other funding sources. This is not true of programs initiated solely with lottery money, like Georgia's HOPE scholarship program.

THE HOPE SCHOLARSHIP. Begun in 1993, the Georgia lottery funds three educational programs:

- The HOPE scholarship program

- A voluntary pre-kindergarten program

- Grants to train teachers in advanced technologies and capital outlay projects for educational facilities

HOPE stands for Helping Outstanding Pupils Educationally. HOPE scholarships and grants are available to Georgia residents who enroll in certain programs at public and private institutions in the state. Students must have at least a B grade average to qualify for HOPE money in the first place and to maintain their eligibility in subsequent years. Most recipients are recent high school graduates who pursue college degrees.

At public colleges, the HOPE Scholarship pays for tuition and fees and provides a $300 book allowance per academic year. Room and board expenses are not covered. At private colleges, the HOPE Scholarship provides $3,000 per academic year to full-time students, plus students can qualify for the Georgia Tuition Equalization Grant (GTEG) of $900 per academic year. Part-time students attending private colleges are eligible for $1,500 per academic year, but do not qualify for the GTEG.

During its first ten years of operation the lottery provided approximately $2.5 billion to the HOPE scholarship program, $2.1 billion to the pre-kindergarten program, and $1.8 billion to the remaining programs.

As of August 2004 more than 800,000 students have received HOPE scholarships. HOPE is the country's largest state-financed merit-based aid program and is credited with significantly increasing the attendance of in-state residents at Georgia colleges. Similar programs include Kentucky's Educational Excellence Scholarship and New Mexico's Lottery Success Scholarship.

Social Effects

Think of lottery winnings just like other income—except you don't have to work for it.

—Charles T. Clotfelter et al., *State Lotteries at the Turn of the Century: Report to the National Gambling Impact Study Commission,* April 23, 1999

Lotteries are undeniably a cultural and social phenomenon. They are operated on every continent around the world with the exception of Antarctica. In the United States, lotteries enjoy unprecedented popularity in the gambling realm. They are legal in forty states and generally considered a benign form of entertainment with two enormous selling points. First, they seem to offer a shortcut to the "American Dream" of wealth and prosperity. Second, they are a voluntary activity that raises money for the public good in lieu of increased taxes. Lottery opponents generally base their objections on religious or moral reasons. Some people consider all forms of gambling to be wrong, and state-sponsored lotteries may be particularly abhorrent to them.

The NGISC final report of 1999 complained about the appropriateness of state governments pushing luck, instant gratification, and entertainment as alternatives to hard work, prudent investment, and savings. Such a message might be particularly troubling if it is directed to lower-income people.

Because online lottery tickets are so widely circulated, lottery officials in several states have decided to use them as a means to spread critical information. The Amber Alert message system is used around the country to notify the public via television, radio, and electronic billboards about abducted children. Lotteries in several states have all agreed to use the message system to alert ticket buyers about abducted children.

UNDERAGE PLAY. The legal minimum age to play the lottery varies by state from eighteen to twenty-one. However, numerous studies have shown that children and adolescents are buying lottery tickets. A 1999 Gallup poll on gambling found that 15% of adolescents age thirteen to seventeen had purchased a lottery ticket in the previous year.

Similar findings are reiterated in other surveys. Dr. Martin Lazoritz and his colleagues interviewed 1,051 Florida teens over the phone about their gambling habits. (Parental permission for the interviews was obtained first.) The Florida researchers reported at the October

2002 meeting of the American Academy of Child and Adolescent Psychiatry that 18.5% of Florida adolescents (age thirteen to seventeen) surveyed had purchased a lottery ticket at some time in their lives. In addition, 12.5% of the respondents had purchased a lottery ticket during the previous year. (The results also appear in the study *Teen Gambling: Evidence from the University of Florida's Statewide Epidemiological Study.*)

The NGISC reported in 1999 that 47% of seventh-graders in Massachusetts had played the lottery. The commission developed seven advertising recommendations for lottery officials to discourage underage play:

- The legal minimum age should be posted at lottery points of sale.

- Lottery advertising should not be directed primarily toward minors.

- Lottery advertising should not contain symbols or language primarily intended to appeal to those under the legal minimum age.

- Animated characters used in lottery advertising should not have any association with television programs and movies geared toward children.

- Celebrities who would primarily appeal to minors should not be used in lottery advertising.

- Lottery advertisements should not picture people that are or appear to be minors.

POVERTY AND RACE/ETHNICITY. One of the most common criticisms leveled against state lotteries is that they unfairly burden the poor—they are mostly funded by low-income people who buy tickets, but benefit higher-income people for the most part. In economics terminology, a tax that places a higher burden on lower-income groups than higher-income groups (in terms of percentage of their income) is called a "regressive" tax. Although the lottery is not really a tax, many people consider it to be a form of voluntary taxation because the proceeds fund government programs. In 1999 Dr. Philip Cook testified to NGISC that "the tax that is built into the lottery is the most regressive tax we know."

Cook and his colleague Dr. Charles Clotfelter examined this issue at length in their book *Selling Hope: State Lotteries in America* (Cambridge, MA: Harvard University Press, 1989). The researchers found that lottery players with annual incomes of less than $10,000 spend more on lottery tickets ($597 per year) than any other income group. They also found that high school dropouts spend four times as much as college graduates, and that African-Americans spend five times as much as Caucasians. The NGISC final report expressed serious concern about the heavy reliance of lotteries upon less-educated, lower-income people. It

also mentions that an unusually large number of lottery outlets are concentrated in poor neighborhoods.

In response to these claims, the president of the NASPL made the following points at a presentation in July 1999 to the National Conference of State Legislatures:

- The NGISC report does not provide any evidence that lotteries target their marketing to poor people.

- Marketing to poor people would be unwise on the part of lotteries from a business and political standpoint.

- People often buy lottery tickets outside of the neighborhoods in which they live.

- Many areas associated with low-income residents (for example, inner cities) are visited or passed through by higher-income shoppers and workers.

- High-income residential neighborhoods have relatively few stores and gas stations, making them less likely to have lottery outlets.

In 2001 researchers at the Vinson Institute of Government Studies at the University of Georgia reviewed a number of nationwide and state studies on the relationship between income and lottery participation and found that "the regressivity finding remains largely consistent throughout the literature" (Joseph McCrary and Thomas J. Pavlak, *Who Plays the Georgia Lottery?*, 2002). Researchers cite a common belief among lower-income people that playing the lottery is their only chance to escape poverty.

In October 2002 the *Chicago Reporter* published a report on its analysis of lottery sales in Illinois since 1997. The story "Illinois Lottery: The Poor Play More" compared lottery sales figures around the state with income and demographic data from the 2000 census. The ten zip codes with the highest lottery sales for the past six fiscal years were all in the city of Chicago. The residents of all ten zip codes had average incomes of less than $20,000 per year, compared to the city average of $24,000 per year. Eight of the zip code areas had unemployment rates in excess of the city average of 10%. Residents of half of the zip code areas were populated by at least 70% African-Americans. The newspaper found that average lottery sales per capita in the city's mostly African-American zip codes were 29% to 33% higher than in mostly white or Latino zip code areas.

The zip code with the highest lottery sales in the state, 60609, coincides with predominantly African-American and Latino low-income communities on the city's south side. Residents of that zip code spent nearly $23 million on lottery tickets during fiscal year 2002. The newspaper also found that residents in poorer communities spent a larger portion of their incomes on lottery tickets than did people in more affluent neighborhoods. Lottery spending during fiscal year 2002 was $224 per person (or $1.57 for every $100 of income) in zip codes that were at least 70% African-American and $173 per person (or $0.46 for every $100 of income) in zip codes that were at least 70% Caucasian.

In Georgia the Vinson Institute reported that African-Americans and less-educated people are more likely to be active lottery players than Caucasians and more-educated people. Proceeds from the Georgia lottery fund only education programs. If these programs provide more benefits to the poor than to the wealthy, it could be argued that this compensates for the regressive nature of the state lottery.

Studies performed by Ross Rubenstein and Benjamin Scafidi ("Who Pays and Who Benefits?" *National Tax Journal,* June 1, 2002) and by Christopher Cornwell and David Mustard (*The Distributional Impacts of Lottery Funded Merit-Based Aid,* Athens, GA: University of Georgia, August 2001) have criticized Georgia's lottery for providing more lottery benefits to white households than to minority households. Cornwell and Mustard claim that counties with the highest incomes and white populations receive significantly more HOPE college scholarships.

Researchers at the Vinson Institute argue that a county-by-county comparison of HOPE scholarship recipients is not appropriate because there are other factors that affect these statistics—for example, whether a particular county contains a college or university. However, they did conclude that minorities in Georgia are "slightly less likely" than whites to get a HOPE scholarship while in college.

In late 2003 the latest findings of the Vinson Institute regarding the lottery were published in "The Georgia Lottery: Assessing Its Administrative, Economic, and Political Effects" (*Review of Policy Research,* Winter 2003). The researchers examined census data, polls, and other statistics from lottery inception through 1999. They found that lottery play was inversely related to education level. In other words, people with fewer years of education played the lottery more often than those with more years of education. The study also noted that lottery spending per person was highest in counties with larger percentages of African-American populations.

Regarding the HOPE scholarship program, the researchers found that white students received a disproportionately high amount of the funds compared to African-American students. In 1999 white students comprised 66% of the freshman class in Georgia, but accounted for 74% of all HOPE scholars. By contrast, African-Americans comprised 26% of all freshmen, but accounted for only 21% of HOPE scholars. The authors note that this disproportionate relationship was true for every year examined, back to 1994. However, they noted that the gap narrowed substantially over that time.

Analysis of Georgia's lottery-funded prekindergarten program provided completely different results. The Vinson Institute found that the rate of enrollment in the prekindergarten program is higher in lower-income areas of the state than in affluent areas. The researchers conclude that this particular lottery program is more beneficial to poorer people, African-Americans, and those who regularly play the lottery than to other groups in the state.

In another study published in the January 2004 issue of *Journal of Hispanic Higher Education* a researcher from Saint Leo University in Florida found that minority and low-income students did not have proportionate access to higher education in lottery states ("State Lotteries: Their Effect on Equal Access to Higher Education").

COMPULSIVE GAMBLING AND "COGNITIVE DISTORTION." All state lotteries have programs in place that encourage responsible play. Messages are included in promotional materials, advertisements, public service announcements, and even on lottery tickets. Some states publicize toll-free numbers or Web sites that offer help to problem gamblers.

Still, some people and organizations believe any type of gambling can be harmful, even lottery play. The Naples, Florida, office of the Salvation Army, an evangelical Christian charity, refused a $100,000 donation from Florida Lotto winner David L. Rush in December 2002. A spokesperson for the head of the office, Major Cleo Damon, explained that "there are times when Major Damon is counseling families who are about to become homeless because of gambling." Major Damon expressed concern that taking lottery winnings would constitute "talking out of both sides of his mouth." Two other charities, Habitat for Humanity and the Rotary Club of Marco Island, accepted large donations from Rush's lottery winnings in the same time period.

The vast majority of states operate lotteries, meaning they are easily accessible to large numbers of people. Surveys, including one conducted by the Gallup Organization in December 2003, have shown that lottery play is the most popular and widely practiced form of gambling in the United States. But does the combination of easy and widespread access and general public acceptance mean that lottery players are more likely to develop serious gambling problems?

The *Gambling Impact and Behavior Study: Report to the National Gambling Impact Study Commission* was conducted by NORC of the University of Chicago in 1999. The NORC study concluded that there is a significant association between lottery availability and the prevalence of at-risk gambling within a state. At-risk gamblers are defined as those who gamble regularly and may be prone to a gambling problem. However, the study found that multivisit lottery patrons had the lowest prevalence of pathological and problem gambling among the gambling types examined.

These researchers also warned that the patron database used in this analysis was small, meaning that the findings may not apply universally. They note that lottery players who do have a problem may be less able to recognize it because lottery players tend to undercount their losses. Lottery players generally lose small amounts at a time, even though these small amounts may eventually total a very large amount. In other words, a casino gambler who loses thousands of dollars in a day may be more likely to admit to having a gambling problem than a lottery player who loses the same amount over a longer period of time.

In July 2001 *The Wager,* a report of the Harvard Medical School and the Massachusetts Council on Compulsive Gambling, described a study published by Canadian researchers on the cognitive misconceptions of problem lottery gamblers. Sixty-three college students at McGill University in Montreal were screened to determine their participation in gambling activities. Those with some gambling experience were given the South Oaks Gambling Screen, or SOGS test. This is a common series of questions used to determine the probability that a person has a gambling problem. Those with a SOGS score of 0–2 are considered not to have a gambling problem. A SOGS score of 3–4 indicates a probable problem gambler, and a SOGS score of 5 or more indicates a probable pathological gambler.

All of the students were shown sixteen lotto tickets, each marked with a different sequence of six numbers out of forty-nine numbers total. All sequences followed one of these configurations:

• Random (for example: 1, 13, 19, 34, 40, 47)

• Pattern (for example: 5, 10, 15, 20, 25, 30)

• Long sequence (for example: 1, 2, 3, 4, 5, 6)

• Nonequilibrated or unbalanced (a series not covering the whole range of possible numbers, usually limited to either high or low numbers—for example: 3, 5, 9, 12, 15, 17)

The students were asked to choose the twelve tickets they would most like to play in the lottery and to rank these tickets from best to worst. Results indicated that random sequences were by far the most popular. More than half of the tickets selected by the students as their first, second, third, or fourth favorite choices contained random sequences. When choosing a favorite lottery ticket, the second most popular choice was the pattern sequence, followed by the nonequilibrated sequence and the long sequence.

The students were also asked to explain the reasoning behind their selections. Randomness was the reason given 78% of the time. The presence of significant numbers (for example, a birthdate) was the second most popular reason, named 69.5% of the time.

The researchers point out that all of the students' choices were irrational because every ticket has an equal chance of winning. However, those students who regularly play the lottery or participate in other gambling activities were more likely to display bias when choosing their favorite tickets. In other words, they had stronger opinions about what was "winnable" than did infrequent players and those who did not gamble. The probable pathological gamblers were found to have more illusions about control than all other participants. The authors concluded that there was "some level of cognitive distortion" demonstrated by all of the gamblers in the study.

THE FUTURE OF U.S. LOTTERIES

New State Lotteries?

As of August 2004, only ten states had no lotteries: Alabama, Alaska, Arkansas, Hawaii, Mississippi, Nevada, North Carolina, Oklahoma, Utah, and Wyoming. Hawaii and Utah permit no types of gambling at all. Alaskan politicians have shown no interest in a lottery. Wyoming politicians have stated publicly that they do not want to expand gambling options in their state. Lotteries are also long shots in Nevada and Mississippi because of the tremendous growth of casino gambling in these states.

However, polls conducted during the early twenty-first century in Alabama, Arkansas, North Carolina, and Oklahoma show strong support for lotteries that would benefit education in those states:

• A June 2002 poll performed by the *Mobile Register* and the University of South Alabama found 52% approval for a statewide lottery. Approval rose to 75% for a lottery dedicated only to educational programs.

• A poll conducted by the *Arkansas Democrat-Gazette* in August 2002 showed a 51.9% approval rating for a lottery conducted to fund government programs. Support was slightly higher (58% approval) for a lottery with funding dedicated only to educational programs.

• Likewise, a poll conducted during March 2002 by *The Oklahoman* newspaper and the University of Oklahoma found 68% approval for a lottery in general and 76% approval for a lottery to benefit education.

• The North Carolina House of Representatives voted in September 2002 to prevent a statewide lottery referendum from appearing on the ballot in November 2002, despite a survey by Mason-Dixon Polling & Research showing that 58% of respondents supported a lottery in the state.

As of August 2004 North Carolina shows potential for adding a state lottery in the near future. North Carolina

Governor Mike Easley is a strong proponent of a state lottery to fund education programs. However, the state's Republican party and other opponents have fought measures to introduce a lottery. With the advent of lottery play in Tennessee during early 2004, North Carolina is completely surrounded by lottery states.

Oklahoma voters overwhelming approved a lottery to fund education in November 2004. The measure was supported by Governor Brad Henry who made the lottery a key component of his successful campaign for the governorship. Following the election, Governor Henry wrote on his Web site (www.governor.state.ok.us) that he was reviewing applications for positions on the state's new Lottery Commission, and concluded that "the sooner the lottery is up and running, the sooner our children—and our state—will reap the benefits."

Attempts at a National Indian Lottery

The Coeur d'Alene Indians of Idaho have been trying to start a national lottery since 1995. The National Indian Lottery would allow residents of all lottery states to dial a toll-free number at the reservation and register numbers to be played in each drawing. Players would pay using a credit card. The plan was approved by the National Indian Gaming Commission (NIGC), and the Coeur d'Alenes had already contracted with AT&T to set up the phone lines when state attorneys general from ten lottery states challenged the plan. They warned AT&T that the company's participation in the lottery program would be illegal. The company pulled out of the deal and was sued by the Coeur d'Alene Indians. AT&T countersued and was backed up by U.S. District Judge Edward Lodge, who ruled that the national lottery would violate federal law.

In March 2002 the Ninth U.S. Circuit Court of Appeals overturned the ruling. The court ruled that the states had to take their grievances about the lottery to the NIGC instead of pressuring AT&T to not participate. As of August 2004, the Coeur d'Alene Tribal Council has not decided if it will pursue the phone lottery further. The tribe tried to run the lottery over the Internet during the late 1990s but gave up after the attorneys general of several lottery states filed suit.

COPING WITH "JACKPOT FATIGUE." A huge problem facing the lottery industry is called "jackpot fatigue." Lottery consumers demand higher and higher jackpot prizes to get excited about lotto games. However, individual states cannot increase jackpot sizes without either greatly increasing sales or decreasing the portion going to public funds. The first option is very difficult to achieve and the second is politically dangerous. Jackpot fatigue has driven increasing membership in multistate lotteries, such as Mega Millions and Powerball.

PRESSURE FOR INCREASED REVENUE. Even as they cope with jackpot fatigue, many lotteries also face pressure to increase the amount of profit going to government programs. Several states are considering decreasing their lottery payout in order to raise much needed funds. Opponents argue that cutting prize payouts will reduce sales, making it nearly impossible to increase state revenues.

CHAPTER 8
SPORTS GAMBLING

Wagering on sporting events is one of the oldest and most popular forms of gambling in the world. The ancient Romans gambled on chariot races, animal fights, and contests between gladiators. The Romans brought sports and gambling to Britain, where they have flourished for hundreds of years. Cockfighting, bear- and bullbaiting, wrestling, and footraces were popular sporting events for gambling throughout Europe during the sixteenth and seventeenth centuries. Horse races and boxing matches became popular spectator and betting sports during the eighteenth century. During the nineteenth and twentieth centuries, sporting events became more team-oriented and organized as rugby, soccer, and cricket grew in popularity.

Many early colonists in America brought their love of sports and gambling with them. Horse racing, in particular, became a part of American culture. However, the morals of the late eighteenth and early nineteenth centuries squelched popular support for legalized sports gambling. By 1910 almost all forms of gambling were illegal in the United States. This did not stop people from gambling on sports, however. The practice continued to flourish, and horse racing, in particular, managed to maintain some legal respectability as a betting sport.

Nevada legalized gambling again in 1931 and permitted sports wagering for a couple of decades. The influence of organized crime and sports gambling scandals led to a crackdown during the 1950s. Legal sports gambling did not return to Nevada until 1975, when it was tightly licensed and regulated.

Today sports gambling in the United States can be broken down into three primary categories. The first is pari-mutuel betting on horse and greyhound races and jai alai games. This form of gambling is legal in forty-three states. Although once quite popular, pari-mutuel betting has suffered a decline in recent years. The second form of sports gambling, permitted only in Nevada, is legal betting using a bookmaker. The third and most widespread form of sports gambling is illegal betting.

SOCIAL ATTITUDES TOWARD SPORTS GAMBLING

The popularity of sports gambling is attributed to several factors—a growing acceptance of gambling in general, intense media coverage of sporting events, and emerging technologies that make wagering easier. Sporting events are increasingly broadcast through an array of media sources. There are entire television networks dedicated solely to sports. Americans can pick up a wide variety of sporting events from around the world via local and cable television stations, satellite services, and even the Internet. Cellular phone users can have the latest scores sent right to their wireless phones. Sports bars and restaurants are also popular. These establishments feature multiple television sets tuned into various sporting events.

In December 2003 the Gallup Organization conducted its annual lifestyle poll. Participants were asked if they had participated within the previous twelve months in various forms of gambling. As shown in Figure 2.1 in Chapter 2, nearly half of those asked (49%) had purchased a state lottery ticket, while 30% had visited a casino, 15% had played bingo for money, and 14% had played video poker. The percentages for sports gambling were much lower. Only 10% had bet on a professional sporting event, and 6% had bet on college sports. Another 4% said they had bet on a horse race, and 2% had bet on a boxing match. Table 8.1 shows trends over time reported by Gallup for these sports gambling activities. In 2003 participation was historically low in every category.

The most recent national poll conducted to determine American attitudes about gambling was performed during April and May 1999 by the Gallup Organization. The poll was conducted among 1,523 adults (aged eighteen and up) and 501 teenagers (aged thirteen to seventeen). At that time, 64% of the adults and 52% of the teenagers approved of legalized gambling in general. The participants were asked several questions about their participation in and attitudes about sports gambling. It is not clear how much of the adult

TABLE 8.1

Participation in sports gambling within the previous 12 months, March 2004

Bet on a professional sports event such as baseball, basketball, or football

	Yes %	No %	No opinion %
2003 Dec 11–14	10	90	*
1999 Apr 30–May 23	13	87	—
1996 Jun 27–30	10	90	—
1992 Nov 20–22	12	88	—
1990 Feb 15–18	21	79	—
1989 Apr 4–9	22	78	—

Bet on a college sports event such as basketball or football

	Yes %	No %	No opinion %
2003 Dec 11–14	6	94	*
1999 Apr 30–May 23	9	91	—
1996 Jun 27–30	7	93	—
1992 Nov 20–22	6	94	—
1990 Feb 15–18	11	89	—
1989 Apr 4–9	14	86	—

Bet on a boxing match

	Yes %	No %	No opinion %
2003 Dec 11–14	2	98	*
1996 Jun 27–30	3	97	*
1992 Nov 20–22	6	94	—
1990 Feb 15–18	5	95	—
1989 Apr 4–9	8	92	—

Participated in an office pool on the World Series, Superbowl, or other game

	Yes %	No %	No opinion %
2003 Dec 11–14	15	85	*
1999 Apr 30–May 23	25	75	—
1996 Jun 27–30	23	77	—
1992 Nov 20–22	22	78	—

*Less than 0.5%

SOURCE: Jeffrey M. Jones, "Gambling Activity in the United States," in *Gambling a Common Activity for Americans*, The Gallup Organization, March 24, 2004, http://www.gallup.com/content/default.aspx?ci=11098 (accessed September 26, 2004). Copyright © 2004 by The Gallup Organization. Reproduced by permission of The Gallup Organization.

gambling discussed in the poll is legal and how much is illegal. However, most (if not all) gambling conducted by the teenaged respondents must be illegal because they are younger than eighteen, the lowest legal gambling age in most states for any type of sports gambling.

Only 9% of adults said they had bet on a horse or dog race during the previous year. Surprisingly, 5% of the teenagers had also done so. When asked about college sporting events, 9% of adults and 18% of teenagers admitted having bet on them. The percentages were somewhat higher for professional sports: 13% of adults and 27% of teenagers had placed wagers during the previous year. One-quarter of adults and 15% of teenagers had bet on a major sporting event, such as the Super Bowl or World Series, through an office pool. A large majority of adults (68%) and teenagers (67%) indicated that they believed "legalized betting on sporting events leads to cheating or fixing games."

A slight majority of adults (53%) and teenagers (55%) thought that off-track betting on horse races should be legalized as a means of raising state revenues. The legalization of gambling on professional sporting events for the same purpose was approved by 41% of adults and 60% of teenagers.

PARI-MUTUEL GAMBLING

"Pari-mutuel" is a French term meaning "mutual stake." In pari-mutuel betting, all wagers on a particular event or race are combined together into a pool that is split between the winning bettors and the management. The larger the pool, the bigger the payoff. In pari-mutuel gambling, patrons bet against each other, not against the house. The principles of the pari-mutuel system were developed in France during the late nineteenth century by Pierre Oller.

The pari-mutuel system has been used on horse races in the United States since around 1875, but it did not really catch on until the 1920s and 1930s, when an automatic odds calculator called a totalizator came into use. The totalizator was a machine that took money, printed betting tickets, and continuously calculated odds based on betting volume.

Prior to this time, horse betting was conducted mostly by bookmakers who were notoriously corrupt. In 1933 California, Michigan, Ohio, and New Hampshire legalized pari-mutuel gambling on horse racing as a means of regulating the industry and gaining some revenue. Dozens of states followed suit over the next decade. Pari-mutuel gambling was also adopted for greyhound racing and matches of jai alai (a game similar to handball). Table 8.2 lists the states that currently allow pari-mutuel gambling in some form. A handful of these states permit pari-mutuel gambling by law, but do not have facilities or systems in place to conduct it. For example, pari-mutuel gambling on horses is permitted in Shelby County, Tennessee, but the state does not have a racing commission. Therefore, no pari-mutuel gambling takes place in Tennessee.

In pari-mutuel gambling the entire amount wagered is called the betting pool, the gross wager, or the handle. The system ensures that event managers receive a share of the betting pool, regardless of who wins a particular race or match. The management's share is called the takeout. The takeout percentage is set by state law and is usually around 20%.

Another important term is "breakage," which refers to the odd cents not paid out to winning bettors because payoffs are rounded. In other words, a winning ticket is not paid down to the penny. The payout on a $2 bet is typically rounded off in $.20 increments. The cents left over are the breakage. Although breakage amounts to only pennies per bet, it adds up quickly with high betting volume. For example, California horse racetracks accumulated more

TABLE 8.2

Pari-mutuel gambling, 2004

	Horse racing	Greyhound racing	Jai Alai	Additional features
Alabama		X		
Arizona	X	X		
Arkansas	X	X		
California	X			
Colorado	X	X		
Connecticut		X	X	
Delaware	X			Slot machines
Florida	X	X	X	Card rooms
Idaho	X			
Illinois	X			
Indiana	X			
Iowa	X	X		Slot machines
Kansas	X	X		
Kentucky	X			
Louisiana	X			Slot machines
Maine	X			
Maryland	X			
Massachusetts	X	X		
Michigan	X			
Minnesota	X			Card rooms
Missouri	X			
Montana	X			
Nebraska	X			
Nevada	X			
New Mexico	X			Slot machines
New Hampshire	X	X		
New Jersey	X			
New York	X			Slot machines
North Dakota	X			
Ohio	X			
Oklahoma	X			
Oregon	X	X		
Pennsylvania	X			
Rhode Island		X	X	Slot machines & video lottery terminals
South Dakota	X			
Tennessee	X			
Texas	X	X		
Vermont	X			
Virginia	X			
Washington		X		
West Virginia	X	X		Slot machines
Wisconsin		X		
Wyoming		X		

SOURCE: Created by Kim Masters Evans for Thomson Gale, 2004

A race book is an establishment (usually a room at a casino) in which ITW takes place on pari-mutuel betting events, such as horse and greyhound races. A race book typically features many television monitors that show races as they occur. Some racetracks also have ITW rooms that they call race books. Race books are included in many Nevada and Atlantic City, New Jersey, casinos, as well as some tribal casinos. Figure 8.1 shows race book wagering statistics for Nevada casinos from 1996 to 2003. Just over $516 million was wagered in Nevada race books during 2003.

According to statistics available at the Web site of industry analyst Christiansen Capital Advisors, LLC (www.cca-i.com), the total gross revenue (handle minus payout) on pari-mutuel gambling in the United States was $3.8 billion in 2003. Most of this amount ($3.4 billion) came from horse racing, followed by greyhound racing ($398 million) and jai alai games ($25 million).

Horse Racing

Horse racing has been a popular sport for thousands of years and was enjoyed by the ancient Greeks and Romans. It was popularized in western Europe when knights returning from the Crusades brought back fast Arabian stallions. These horses were bred with sturdy English mares to produce a new line of horses now known as Thoroughbreds. Thoroughbreds are tall lean horses with long slender legs. They are renowned for their speed and grace while running.

Thoroughbred racing became very popular among the aristocrats and royalty of British society, earning it the nickname the "Sport of Kings." The sport was transplanted to America during colonial times. According to the Jockey Club, Thoroughbred horse racing was taking place on Long Island, New York, as far back as 1665. However, the advent of organized Thoroughbred racing is attributed to Governor Samuel Ogle of Maryland, who staged a race "between pedigreed horses in the English style" in Annapolis, Maryland, in 1745. The Annapolis Jockey Club, which sponsored the race, later became the Maryland Jockey Club. Among its initial members were George Washington and Thomas Jefferson.

Thoroughbred breeding was prominent in Maryland and Virginia up until the Civil War (1861–65), when many operations were moved to Kentucky. Thoroughbred racing had already grown popular throughout the agricultural South at that time. In 1863 the Saratoga racecourse opened in northern New York. It is considered the oldest Thoroughbred flat track in the country. (A flat track is one with no hurdles or other obstacles for a racing horse to jump over.) The Jockey Club, the governing body of Thoroughbred horse racing, was established in 1894.

Horse racing remained popular in the United States until the 1940s, when it was severely curtailed during

than $10 million in breakage in fiscal year 2003. The funds were split between the state, the track operators, and the horse owners. The disposition of breakage is handled differently by each state. Takeout and breakage are subtracted from the betting pool before payouts are made.

Pari-mutuel wagering can be performed in person at the event or, increasingly, at off-track betting (OTB) facilities. The New York legislature approved the first OTB operation in 1970. Some states also allow betting by telephone or Internet when an account is set up prior to bet placement. Many races are broadcast as they occur by televised transmission to in-state and out-of-state locations (including OTB sites). This process, known as simulcasting, allows intertrack wagering (ITW) to take place. In other words, bettors at one racetrack can place bets there on races taking place at another racetrack.

FIGURE 8.1

Nevada race book gambling, 1996–2003

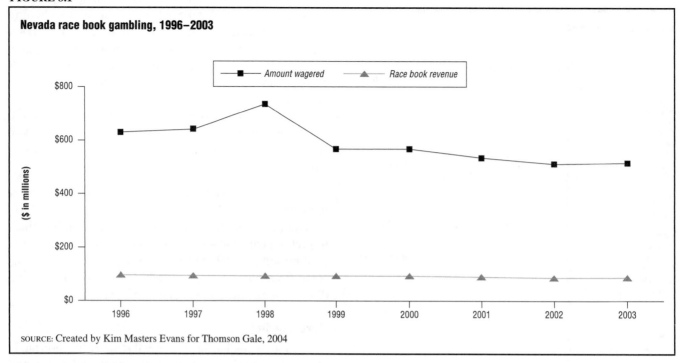

SOURCE: Created by Kim Masters Evans for Thomson Gale, 2004

World War II (1939–45). The decades following the war saw a sharp decline in the popularity of horse racing. Three reasons are commonly mentioned:

- Competition from other entertainment venues and leisure activities, such as theme parks, shopping malls, and television, increased.

- The horse-racing industry avoided television coverage of races during the 1960s for fear it would keep people away from the tracks. (This is now seen as a failure to take advantage of a major marketing tool.)

- Competition for gambling dollars from state lotteries and casinos came into being as those venues were legalized.

Despite the decline in attendance, the amount of money gambled on horse races has actually increased over the past decade. As shown in Figure 8.2, the pari-mutuel handle from thoroughbred horse racing was $15.2 billion in 2003, up from $9.4 billion in 1990. Just over 87% of the amount bet during 2003 was at OTB facilities. The OTB percentage has increased dramatically since 1996. Analysts believe that attendance at live racing will continue to decline in popularity as there are more and more OTB opportunities, including the Internet.

THE RACETRACKS AND THE RACES. There are about ninety Thoroughbred racetracks around the country. Some racetracks are only open seasonally, while those in warm climates are open year-round. Racetracks vary in size and in ownership; some are government owned and some are owned by private and public companies. *Fortune* magazine reported in October 2001 that most of the betting business associated with Thoroughbred horse racing in

FIGURE 8.2

Pari-mutuel handle from horse racing, 1993–2003

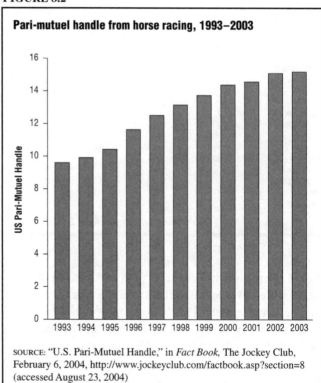

SOURCE: "U.S. Pari-Mutuel Handle," in *Fact Book,* The Jockey Club, February 6, 2004, http://www.jockeyclub.com/factbook.asp?section=8 (accessed August 23, 2004)

the United States is controlled by a relatively small group of players. Two publicly traded companies, Churchill Downs and Magna Entertainment, account for approximately 50% of the business, while another 22% is attributed to the New York Racing Association and the New York City Off-Track Betting Corporation (NYCOTB). The New York Racing Association is a not-for-profit group that controls the Belmont, Saratoga, and Aqueduct racetracks. Analysts predict that the industry will continue to undergo consolidation, with corporations taking over most of the business. In May 2004 the chairman of Magna Entertainment announced at a shareholders' meeting that the company hopes to purchase Churchill Downs, Inc., before the end of the decade.

The three most prestigious Thoroughbred races in the United States are the Kentucky Derby at the Churchill Downs track in Kentucky, the Preakness Stakes at Pimlico in Maryland, and the Belmont Stakes at Belmont Park in New York. The races are held over a five-week period during May and June of each year. A horse that wins all three races in one year is said to have won the "Triple Crown." Only eleven horses have ever captured the Triple Crown—most recently, a horse named Affirmed in 1978.

According to the Jockey Club, there were 53,503 Thoroughbred horse races in a total of thirty-seven states during 2003. (See Table 8.3.) California hosted the most events, with 5,126 races, followed by West Virginia (4,520), Pennsylvania (3,851), Florida (3,806), and New York (3,704). The total gross purses amounted to just over $1 billion. The gross purse is the amount awarded to the owners of the winning race horses. California racetracks had the highest gross purse of nearly $189 million. New York ($131 million), Florida ($85 million), Kentucky ($80 million), and Illinois ($75 million) complete the top five highest purse states. As shown in Figure 8.3, the number of Thoroughbred races held each year has generally steadily declined since the early 1990s.

NON-THOROUGHBRED HORSE RACING. Although Thoroughbred horse racing is the most popular type of horse racing in the United States, other types of horse racing are involved in pari-mutuel wagering, chiefly harness racing and the racing of quarter horses and Arabian horses.

In harness racing, horses trot or pace rather than gallop. They have to be specially trained to run races in this manner. Typically, the horse pulls behind it a two-wheeled cart known as a sulky, carrying a jockey who controls the reins. Sometimes the jockey is seated on the horse rather than in a sulky. Harness racing is performed by a type of horse called a standardbred, which is shorter, more muscled, and longer in body than the Thoroughbred. In 1879 the National Association of Trotting Horse Breeders in America established the official registry for standardbred horses. While Thoroughbred horses were the favorite of high society, standardbred racing became popular among the common folk. Today, there are approximately thirty licensed harness racetracks around the country at which pari-mutuel betting takes place. Harness racing is also conducted at county fairs and exhibitions.

A third type of horse known for racing is the quarter horse, so named because of its high speed over distances

TABLE 8.3

Thoroughbred horse races by state or Canadian province, 2003

State/province	Number of races	Gross purses*
Arizona	2,103	$14,907,871
Arkansas	505	$11,482,600
California	5,126	$188,866,549
Colorado	285	$2,572,565
Delaware	1,271	$33,037,425
Florida	3,806	$85,220,610
Georgia	11	$345,000
Idaho	293	$992,559
Illinois	3,024	$75,014,401
Indiana	1,001	$11,286,042
Iowa	770	$14,179,378
Kansas	283	$2,173,896
Kentucky	2,560	$80,292,971
Louisiana	3,426	$58,967,227
Maryland	1,964	$43,868,600
Massachusetts	1,374	$15,871,300
Michigan	1,054	$9,154,094
Minnesota	547	$8,808,271
Montana	145	$333,855
Nebraska	863	$5,246,405
Nevada	23	$62,850
New Jersey	1,194	$36,184,164
New Mexico	1,376	$21,966,206
New York	3,704	$131,413,851
North Carolina	18	$277,500
North Dakota	77	$287,264
Ohio	3,262	$26,116,132
Oklahoma	872	$6,720,250
Oregon	869	$2,985,126
Pennsylvania	3,851	$45,735,528
South Carolina	24	$590,000
Tennessee	7	$290,000
Texas	2,031	$29,644,944
Virginia	348	$8,410,300
Washington	880	$8,294,700
West Virginia	4,520	$73,826,390
Wyoming	36	$70,025
Total	**53,503**	**$1,055,496,849**
Canada		
Alberta	1,236	$14,830,244
British Columbia	744	$12,055,226
Manitoba	589	$5,984,183
Ontario	2,667	$116,858,252
Saskatchewan	262	$662,025
Total	**5,498**	**$150,389,930**

*Purses include monies not won and returned to state breeder or other funds.

SOURCE: Adapted from "2003 Analysis of Races by State or Province," in *Fact Book,* The Jockey Club, February 6, 2004, http://www.jockeyclub.com/factbook/compare%2003.html (accessed August 23, 2004)

of less than a quarter of a mile. They were originally bred by American colonists to be both hardworking and athletic. There are nearly forty quarter horse racetracks around the country.

Arabian horses are considered the only true purebred horses on the race circuit, as they have not been mixed with other breeds. Arabian horse racing is conducted at about fifteen tracks in the United States.

THE BETTING. The betting pool for a particular horse race depends on how much is wagered by bettors on that race. Each wager affects the odds. The more money bet on a horse, the lower that horse's odds and the potential pay-

FIGURE 8.3

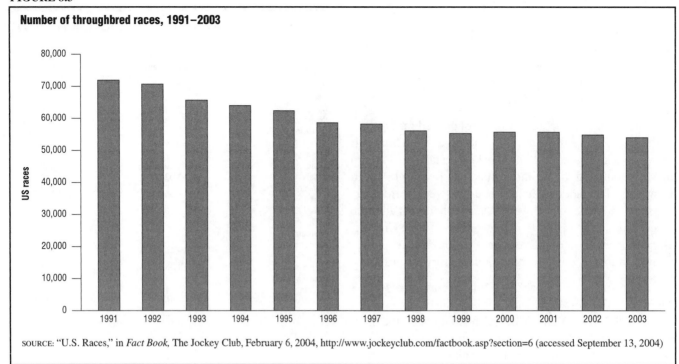

Number of throughbred races, 1991–2003

SOURCE: "U.S. Races," in *Fact Book,* The Jockey Club, February 6, 2004, http://www.jockeyclub.com/factbook.asp?section=6 (accessed September 13, 2004)

off becomes. The payout for winning tickets is determined by the amount of money bet on the winner in relation to that bet on all the other horses in that particular race.

First, the takeout is subtracted from the betting pool. This money goes toward track expenses, taxes, and the purse. Most states also require that a portion of the take-out goes into Breeder Funds to encourage horse breeding and health in the state. For example, Figure 8.4 shows the breakdown of each takeout dollar in California. (Note: In this graphic, "other states' takeout" refers to money used to pay interstate wagering fees to betting facilities outside of California that take bets on California races.) After the takeout and the breakage are subtracted from the betting pool, the remaining money is divided by the number of bettors to determine the payoff, or return, on each wager.

The odds on a particular horse winning first, second, or third place are estimated on the morning of a race and then constantly recalculated by computer during the pre-race betting period. The odds are posted on a display called the tote board and on television screens throughout the betting area. The tote board also tallies the total amount paid into each pool. Bettors can wager that a par-ticular horse will win (come in first), place (come in first or second), or show (come in first, second, or third). The payoff for a win is higher than payoffs for place or show, because the latter two pools have to be split more ways. For example, the show pool must be split between all bet-tors who selected win, place, or show. The approximate payoffs for a $2 winning ticket on horses of various odds are shown in Table 8.4.

Betting on horse racing is considered more a game of skill than a game of chance. Professional racing bettors spend a great deal of time on the observation and study of individual horses and consider previous race experience when they make their picks. This gives them some advan-tage over bettors who pick a horse based on whim—because they like its name, for example. Although bettors do not play directly against each other, an individual bettor's skill level does affect other bettors. This is because the payout odds in horse racing are adjusted based on the bets of the gamblers.

The Centre for Addiction and Mental Health (CAMH) in Toronto, Canada, publishes an electronic journal on gambling issues called *eJournal*. In October 2001 the jour-nal analyzed important aspects of playing games of skill in an article titled "The Effect of Skilled Gamblers on the Success of Less-Skilled Gamblers." The article noted that the house edge at the racetrack is at least 17%, and even higher for bets such as exactas, in which the bettor must pick the two top finishing horses in a race in the correct place order to win.

However, previous research has shown that there are some expert bettors who make money on their bets on a consistent basis. Assuming that 10% of bettors achieve a positive return of 1% means that the average among the remaining players has to be around -19%, a substantial loss, to account for that 1% profit. Considering a house edge of 17%, the researchers concluded that a "fair amount of skill" would be required to achieve a return of −10%, and that even very skilled horse bettors could end up losing money. The article's final estimate is that only 1–2% of horse race bettors actually make money.

FIGURE 8.4

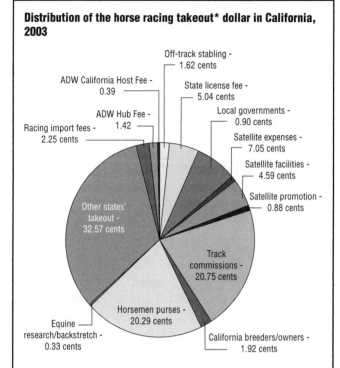

Distribution of the horse racing takeout* dollar in California, 2003

- Off-track stabling - 1.62 cents
- ADW California Host Fee - 0.39
- State license fee - 5.04 cents
- ADW Hub Fee - 1.42
- Local governments - 0.90 cents
- Racing import fees - 2.25 cents
- Satellite expenses - 7.05 cents
- Satellite facilities - 4.59 cents
- Satellite promotion - 0.88 cents
- Other states' takeout - 32.57 cents
- Track commissions - 20.75 cents
- Horsemen purses - 20.29 cents
- Equine research/backstretch - 0.33 cents
- California breeders/owners - 1.92 cents

*Money wagered but not paid out: withheld by the state for purposes of supporting the industry.

SOURCE: "The Takeout Dollar in California: Where It Goes and How It's Used," in *Thirty-Third Annual Report of the California Horse Racing Board: A Summary of Fiscal Year 2002–2003 Racing in California,* California Horse Racing Board, 2004, http://www.chrb.ca.gov/annual_reports/2003_annual_report.pdf (accessed September 13, 2004)

TABLE 8.4

Money paid out on a successful $2 pari-mutuel bet

Odds	$2 Bet returns	Odds	$2 Bet returns
1–10	$2.20	3–1	$8.00
1–5	$2.40	7–2	$9.00
2–5	$2.80	4–1	$10.00
1–2	$3.00	9–2	$11.00
3–5	$3.20	5–1	$12.00
4–5	$3.60	6–1	$14.00
1–1	$4.00	7–1	$16.00
6–5	$4.40	8–1	$18.00
7–5	$4.80	9–1	$20.00
3–2	$5.00	10–1	$22.00
8–5	$5.20	12–1	$26.00
2–1	$6.00	15–1	$32.00
5–2	$7.00	20–1	$42.00

SOURCE: "How Much Do I Win?," in *Winning Techniques,* Daily Racing Form, Spring 2004, http://www.drf.com/row/fan_ed/winning-techniques-2004.pdf (accessed September 26, 2004)

betting pool, or $3.4 billion. The state received revenues of $41.4 million.

In August 2001 California governor Gray Davis legalized a new betting method called Advanced Deposit Wagering (ADW), that permits betting over the telephone and Internet. Gamblers must put money into an account prior to making their wagers. The idea was heartily endorsed by the state's horse-racing industry. The manager of California operations for Magna Entertainment said racing would only flourish again "by bringing races to people, not bringing people to the races."

The new system began operating in January 2002. Approximately $4 million per month was bet via ADW soon after its introduction. Although analysts had predicted it would be a windfall for the racing industry, results were modest. During fiscal year 2003 ADW accounted for only 6% of all wagers.

THE ECONOMIC EFFECTS OF HORSE RACING. The horse-racing industry has a number of economic impacts on society, both within the industry and without. Examination of annual reports from the states' racing commissions shows that the industry accounts for payments in excess of $250 million in state taxes and fees each year. The largest single recipient during 2003 was the state of California, which received $41.4 million. Racetracks pay millions more to local governments.

The industry provides direct income to horse owners, trainers, and jockeys/drivers through purses. Figure 8.6 shows the purses paid out at Thoroughbred racetracks in the fifteen top racing states during 2003. California tracks paid out the highest gross purse for the year ($189 million), and the highest average purse per race ($37,000). The largest portion of a Thoroughbred race purse (typically 60%) goes to the owner of the first-place horse. The owner is responsible for paying the horse's trainer and

HORSE RACING IN CALIFORNIA. California led the nation in 2003 in terms of the number of races held and the purses paid to winning horses. The state has allowed pari-mutuel gambling on horse races since 1933, when a constitutional amendment was passed by the voters. California has six privately owned racetracks and nine racing fairs. Racing fairs are county and state fairs held at facilities including racetracks so that wagering on horse races can be conducted as one of many fair events. The fairs usually last only a week or two and are conducted at various times throughout the year. In addition to actually attending racetracks or racing fairs, gamblers can bet on horse races at twenty simulcast facilities around the state.

Thirty-Third Annual Report of the California Horse Racing Board: A Summary of Fiscal Year 2002–2003 Racing in California reports that the industry grossed $4.2 billion during 2003, the highest of any state in the country. This represented the seventh straight year that the total handle had increased (from just under $3.5 billion in fiscal year 1997). Figure 8.5 shows the handle amount broken down by on-track, off-track, and out-of-state wagers. Only 18.3% of all wagers occurred at the track during 2003. The vast majority of wagers were placed at off-track locations. Winning bettors received 80.5% of the

FIGURE 8.5

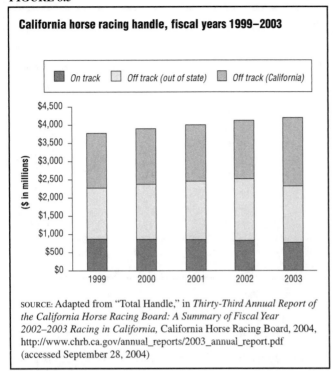

California horse racing handle, fiscal years 1999–2003

SOURCE: Adapted from "Total Handle," in *Thirty-Third Annual Report of the California Horse Racing Board: A Summary of Fiscal Year 2002–2003 Racing in California,* California Horse Racing Board, 2004, http://www.chrb.ca.gov/annual_reports/2003_annual_report.pdf (accessed September 28, 2004)

jockey. The owners of the horses finishing second and third typically receive around 20% and 12%, respectively, of a race purse. Harness track purses paid out during 2003 are shown in Figure 8.7. They totaled approximately $300 million. New Jersey was by far the state with the highest gross purse ($68 million), while Delaware had the highest average purse per race ($10,500).

The racing industry also supports a large business in horse breeding. In 1962 Maryland was the first state to establish a program to encourage breeders within the state through direct money payments. The practice spread quickly to other states involved in horse racing.

Figure 8.8 shows a flow chart developed by researchers at the University of Maryland in 1999 as part of a report titled *Economic Impact of Horse Racing in Maryland.* The report noted that the cash flows—between the wagering public; the racetracks and OTBs; the horse owners, jockeys/drivers, breeders, and trainers; and the regulatory government agencies—are cash transfers that do not create economic impacts. True economic impacts occur outside of the industry from expenditures on goods and services.

In these expenditures, racetrack/OTB operators spend money on land, labor, and other goods and services from various business sectors. Horse owners/breeders/trainers spend money on land, labor, veterinary care, and horse feed and supplies. All of these pump money into the general economy. The report concluded that the Maryland racehorse/racetrack industry was responsible for a total economic impact of nearly $600 million in the state, with roughly two-thirds of this amount attributable to the race-

horse industry and one-third to the racetrack industry. The racehorse industry was also credited with creating just over six thousand full-time positions, while the racetrack industry created nearly three thousand positions.

Unlike the casino industry, the horse-racing industry has only a minor impact on tourism. Most racetracks are not typical tourist destinations that attract overnight visitors, who would spend money on lodging, food, and other entertainment. The exceptions are the races held as part of the Triple Crown. These racing events attract visitors from all over the world and bring a significant number of tourist dollars to local businesses.

HORSE FATALITIES AND INJURIES. Horse racing does have a price in terms of horse fatalities and injuries. There were 207 racehorse fatalities in California alone between November 2002 and November 2003. Nearly half (102) of the deaths occurred during races. Another eighty-one deaths occurred during training and the remainder during other activities. In addition, 411 racing-related injuries to horses were reported in the state. The New York State Racing and Wagering Board reports that 120 racehorses died in that state during 2003.

The horse racing industry has invested millions of dollars in veterinary research on injuries and illnesses that affect racehorses. The Grayson-Jockey Club Research Foundation is the leading private source of funding for research into horse health issues. The foundation dates back to 1940. For 2004 it allocated $850,888 toward twenty research projects at twelve universities conducting equine research projects. It has contributed more than $11 million since 1983. The foundation receives financial support from donations and from special racing events staged by horse racetracks.

Two horse health issues of major concern are mare reproductive loss syndrome (MRLS) and exercise-induced pulmonary hemorrhage (EIPH). MRLS is a mysterious illness that killed more than five thousand Kentucky foals (or horses less than one year old) during 2001. Analysts estimate that the MRLS tragedy had an economic impact of $336 million. EIPH is a common condition in racehorses associated with bleeding from the lungs during strenuous exercise. Horses that experience EIPH are called "bleeders" and can be temporarily or permanently barred from racing depending on state regulations and the severity of the problem.

COMPULSIVE HORSE-RACING GAMBLERS. In terms of the human cost of horse racing, studies have shown a greater concentration of compulsive gamblers involved in pari-mutuel gambling than in other gambling activities. Results from the *Gambling Impact and Behavior Study,* published by the National Opinion Research Center at the University of Chicago in April 1999, support this. Of horse and dog racetrack patrons, 15% were considered

FIGURE 8.6

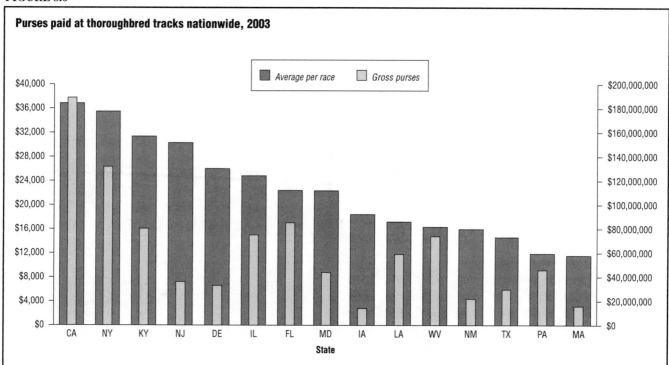

Purses paid at thoroughbred tracks nationwide, 2003

SOURCE: "Purses Paid at Thoroughbred Tracks Nationwide," in *New York State Racing and Wagering Board Annual Report and Simulcast Report: Calendar Year 2003*, New York State Racing and Wagering Board, July 20, 2004, http://www.racing.state.ny.us/pdf/2003%20Annual%20Report%20web.pdf (accessed September 28, 2004)

FIGURE 8.7

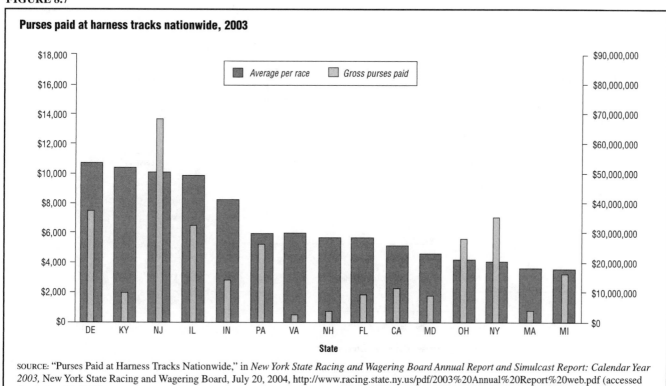

Purses paid at harness tracks nationwide, 2003

SOURCE: "Purses Paid at Harness Tracks Nationwide," in *New York State Racing and Wagering Board Annual Report and Simulcast Report: Calendar Year 2003*, New York State Racing and Wagering Board, July 20, 2004, http://www.racing.state.ny.us/pdf/2003%20Annual%20Report%20web.pdf (accessed September 28, 2004)

"problem" or "pathological" gamblers, compared to 10% of riverboat gamblers, 9% of those who visited casinos in Nevada or Atlantic City, New Jersey, and 6% of those in tribal casinos. These findings were based on the analysis of hundreds of gamblers who admitted multiple gambling visits during the previous year.

FIGURE 8.8

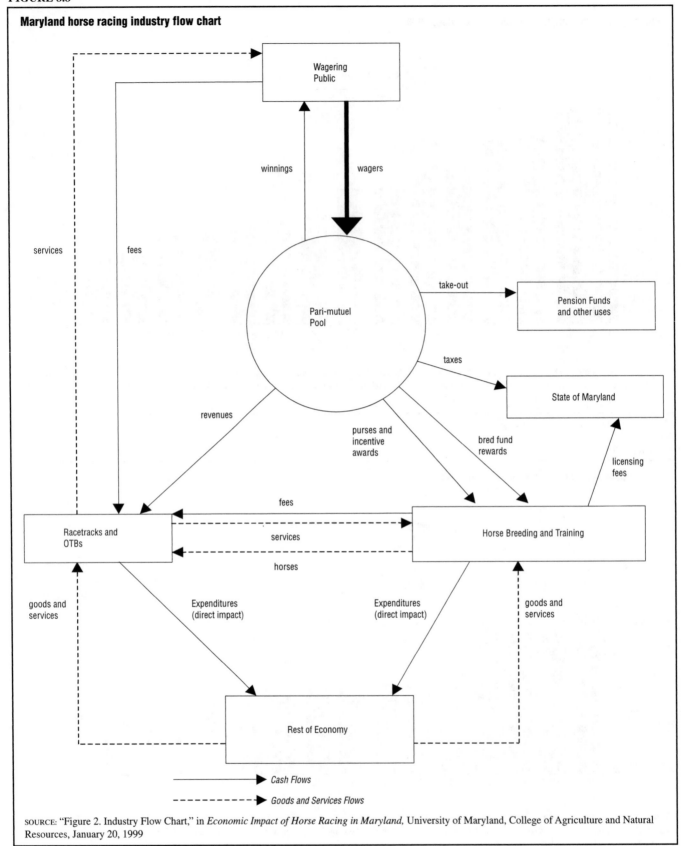

Maryland horse racing industry flow chart

SOURCE: "Figure 2. Industry Flow Chart," in *Economic Impact of Horse Racing in Maryland,* University of Maryland, College of Agriculture and Natural Resources, January 20, 1999

Greyhound Racing

Greyhounds are mentioned in many ancient documents. English noblemen used greyhounds to hunt rabbits, a sport known as "coursing." Greyhound racing is called the "Sport of Queens" because it was Queen Elizabeth I of England who established the first formal rules for greyhound coursing during the 1500s. Greyhounds were brought to America during the late 1800s to help control the jackrabbit population on farms in the Midwest, and soon local farmers began holding races. Early races were held using a live rabbit to lure the dogs to race. In the early 1900s Owen Patrick Smith invented a mechanical lure for this purpose. The first circular greyhound track opened in Emeryville, California, in 1919.

Three major organizations manage greyhound racing in the United States: the National Greyhound Association (NGA), the American Greyhound Track Operators Association (AGTOA), and the American Greyhound Council (AGC), a joint effort of the NGA and AGTOA. The NGA represents greyhound owners and is the official registry for racing greyhounds. All greyhounds that race on U.S. tracks must first be registered with the NGA. The AGTOA represents greyhound track operators. The AGC manages the industry's animal welfare programs, including farm inspections and adoptions.

Wagering on greyhounds is similar to wagering on horse races. However, greyhound racing is not nearly as popular as horse racing, and its popularity has declined dramatically in the past few decades. According to the Humane Society of the United States (HSUS), the handle from greyhound racing declined by 45% during the 1990s, leading to the closure or cessation of live racing at sixteen tracks around the country. In addition, seven states specifically banned live greyhound racing: Idaho, Maine, North Carolina, Nevada, Vermont, Virginia, and Washington.

In 2003 approximately four dozen greyhound racetracks were operating in fifteen states: Alabama, Arizona, Arkansas, Colorado, Connecticut, Florida, Iowa, Kansas, Massachusetts, New Hampshire, Oregon, Rhode Island, Texas, West Virginia, and Wisconsin. (See Table 8.2.) Greyhound racing is also legal in South Dakota, but the state has no operating racetracks. Greyhound racing is most prevalent in Florida.

FLORIDA'S GREYHOUND RACING INDUSTRY. Florida has sixteen greyhound racetracks, by far the most of any state. Greyhound races are the most attended pari-mutuel event in the state, attracting 1.7 million visitors during fiscal year 2002–03. Paid attendance was up by 9% from the previous year. The greyhound racing handle in fiscal year 2003 was $533 million, down 7% from 2002.

The handle from greyhound racing in the state experienced a steady decline over the past decade from $850 million in 1994 to $533 million in 2003. (See Figure 8.9.) This occurred even as horse racing in Florida increased its handle. Greyhound racing accounted for 35% of the state's total pari-mutuel handle during 2003.

Greyhound racetracks paid $17 million to the state during fiscal year 2002–03, accounting for 64% of the

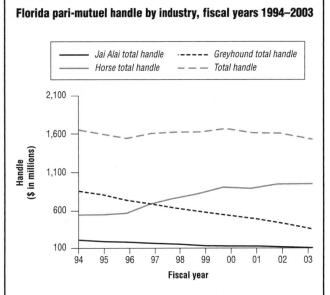

FIGURE 8.9

Florida pari-mutuel handle by industry, fiscal years 1994–2003

SOURCE: "Pari-Mutuel Handle by Industry, Fiscal Years 1993/1994–2002/2003," in *Florida Division of Pari-Mutuel Wagering 72nd Annual Report, July 1, 2002–June 30, 2003,* Department of Business and Professional Regulation, Division of Pari-Mutuel Wagering, December 2003, http://sun6.dms.state.fl.us/dbpr/pmw/annual_reports/ar0203.pdf (accessed September 28, 2004)

state's total revenue from pari-mutuel gambling. The taxes paid to the state declined by 12% from the previous year.

Florida's greyhound racing industry paid out purses totaling $32 million during 2002–03. According to the Florida Department of Business and Professional Regulation, Division of Pari-Mutuel Wagering, almost all of the state's greyhound tracks actively sponsor greyhound adoption programs, and many have on-site adoption booths. The industry is required to pay 10% of the credit it receives for uncashed winning tickets to organizations that promote or encourage greyhound adoptions. These mandatory contributions amounted to $256,150 during fiscal year 2002–03.

THE ECONOMIC EFFECTS OF GREYHOUND RACING. According to undated statistics accessed in December 2004 on the AGC Web site (www.agcouncil.com), greyhound breeding farms and racing kennels represent an investment of more than $150 million and pump another $96 million per year into local economies. The AGC valued the nation's racing greyhounds at more than $200 million. The AGC says that greyhound tracks around the country employ more than 100,000 people and raise nearly $200 million per year in state tax revenues. The tracks are credited with donating more than $10 million per year to charities and community causes. This includes donations of approximately $1 million per year to greyhound adoption efforts.

CONCERNS ABOUT DRUGGING. In May 2004 the *Tampa Tribune* reported that forty-four racing greyhounds

TABLE 8.5

Racing greyhound breeding statistics and estimated number of dogs killed, 1986–2003

Year	Number of litters born (NGA)	Estimated number born	Dogs individually to race (NGA)	Farm puppies culled before racing	Estimated greyhonds adopted[b]	Estimated dogs retained for breeding	Racing dogs killed	Total killed (farm puppies and racing dogs)
2003	5,171	33,714	26,277	7,437	14,500	1,800	9,977	17,414
2002	5,205	33,936	27,142	6,794	14,000	1,800	13,142	19,936
2001	5,015	32,698	26,797	5,901	13,000	1,800	11,997	17,898
2000	5,234	34,126	26,464	7,662	13,000	2,000	11,464	19,126
1999	5,266	34,334	27,059	7,275	13,000	2,000	12,059	19,334
1998	5,034	32,822	26,036	6,786	13,000	2,000	11,036	17,822
1997	5,192	33,852	28,025	5,827	12,500	2,000	13,525	19,352
1996	5,438	35,456	28,877	6,579	12,000	2,000	13,977	21,456
1995	5,749	37,483	31,688	5,795	10,000	2,100	19,588	25,383
1994	6,232	40,633	34,746	5,887	8,500	2,200	24,046	29,933
1993	6,805	44,369	39,139	5,230	6,000	2,500	30,639	35,869
1992	7,690	50,139	38,023	12,116	3,000	2,500	32,523	44,639
1991	8,049	52,479	38,430	14,049	1,000	3,500	33,930	47,979
1990	9,473	61,764	38,615	23,149	650	3,200	34,765	57,914
1989	7,690	50,139	38,443	11,696	450[c]	3,000	34,993	46,689
1988	7,979	52,023	37,784	14,239	300	2,750	34,734	48,973
1987	7,638	49,800	33,021	16,779	200	2,500	30,321	47,100
1986	6,688	43,606	30,219	13,387	75	2,000	28,144	41,531
Total[a]	115,548	753,373	576,785	176,588	135,175	41,650	400,860	578,348

Notes:

Litters: As reported by the National Greyhound Association (NGA), the U.S. registry organization.

Total born: Derived by multiplying the total number of litters by an average of 6.52 pups per litter (this is the conservative average that industry sources report).

Individuals registered to race: As reported by the NGA in the *Greyhound Review*, the official industry publication. Each owner must pay an additional fee to the NGA to have a greyhound individually registered.

Culled: This column shows the total number of dogs who disappear annually between birth and individual registration by 18 months of age. Very few greyhound puppies or young dogs are ever delivered to greyhound rescue groups.

[a]To arrive at an estimated eighteen-year total of greyhounds killed, one must also subtract the number of dogs still in the racing system (approximately 40,000), the number of puppies/youngsters currently at farms (approximately 28,500) and the breeding stock required to produce thousands of litters a year (about 500 males and 3,000 females).

[b]A liberal estimate of figures from those in the adoption community.

[c]Organized, large scale adoption efforts did not take place until the mid-1990s. During the late 1980s it is estimated that only a few hundred dogs made it into adoptive homes nationwide. For over 50 years all greyhounds were routinely destroyed.

SOURCE: Adapted from "U.S. Racing Greyhound Breeding Statistics and Analysis of the Annual Numbers of Dogs Killed from 1986–2003," in *Know the Facts about Greyhound Racing*, Greyhound Protection League, October 13, 2004, http://www.greyhounds.org/gpl/contents/PDFs/fact_sheet_advocate_vers.pdf (accessed October 13, 2004)

in Florida tested positive for cocaine following their races during fiscal year 2003 (Alan Snel, "Drugs Taint Integrity of Greyhound Races," May 3, 2004). In total, the newspaper found that 119 greyhounds had tested positive for cocaine since 2001. Owners of greyhounds testing positive were forced to forfeit their winnings. However, there was no recourse for bettors who had wagered on greyhounds that might have won if the positive-testing dogs had been disqualified. Drug test results are not obtained until several weeks after a race has run. Rapid-screening tests that could provide results at the race track are considered too expensive by the greyhound racing industry.

The newspaper article questioned why state officials did not investigate how the drugs got into the dogs' systems. The president of the National Greyhound Association suggested that the cause could be trace amounts of cocaine on the hands of trainers or other people touching the dogs. State officials denied that trainers were purposely drugging greyhounds to influence race outcomes.

CONCERNS ABOUT GREYHOUND WELFARE. The National Coalition against Legalized Gambling claims that there were more than seventy-five well-documented cases of cruelty and abuse in the greyhound industry during the 1990s involving thousands of dogs that were shot, starved, abandoned, or sold to research laboratories. The HSUS reports that up to 20,000 adult greyhounds are destroyed each year because they are too slow. The organization claims that the racing industry severely overbreeds greyhounds in the hopes of producing winners, leading to the destruction of thousands of unwanted puppies each year. The HSUS also says that a racing greyhound's career is typically over at the age of four years, well below its average lifespan of twelve years, meaning that thousands of adult dogs are also destroyed each year when they are no longer useful.

The Greyhound Protection League (www.greyhounds.org) compiles statistics on what it says are the number of greyhounds bred, adopted, and killed each year. (See Table 8.5. Note that these are not exact figures—many are compiled by estimate.) The league claims that more than half a million greyhound puppies and adult dogs were killed by the industry from 1986 to 2001. During the same time period about 107,000 greyhounds were adopted.

In May 2002 a sixty-eight-year-old Alabama man named Robert Leroy Rhodes was arrested and charged with felony animal cruelty after the remains of two- to three thousand greyhounds were found on his property in Baldwin County, Alabama. The man, who worked as a security guard at the Pensacola Greyhound Park in neighboring Florida, claimed that the track paid him $10 apiece to shoot the dogs and dispose of their carcasses on his eighteen-acre farm. He admitted to performing the service for forty years at the request of race dog owners. Authorities report that autopsies indicate some of the dogs were not killed instantly and therefore suffered before they died. It is a felony in Alabama to torture an animal. Racetrack officials denied involvement in the case and fired Rhodes along with several other security guards and a kennel operator.

Alabama authorities eventually charged four greyhound owners and trainers under the state's animal cruelty law based on statements from Rhodes and Clarence Ray Patterson, a kennel owner at the Pensacola Greyhound Track. At an April 2004 hearing the Baldwin County sheriff testified that Rhodes, who died in 2003, had admitted killing two- to three thousand greyhounds that were too sick or old to race. Florida investigators testified that Florida kennel owners and trainers paid Rhodes to shoot unwanted greyhounds, because it was cheaper than having the animals humanely euthanized by a veterinarian. The defendants' lawyers asked for the case to be dropped because the key witnesses could not be cross-examined. Rhodes had died, and Patterson could not be located by authorities. The judge had not yet ruled on that motion when Patterson was found.

In June 2004 the *Mobile Register* reported that Patterson had been located in an Alabama jail where he had been incarcerated since March 2004 on unrelated charges (Brendan Kirby, "Key Figure in Greyhound Case in Custody," June 30, 2004). Prosecutors in the animal cruelty case said that locating Patterson should help their case against the other defendants.

Jai Alai

Jai alai is a court game similar to handball in which players bounce a ball against the wall and catch it using a long curved basket called a cesta, which is strapped to the wrist. The term jai alai (pronounced hi-uh-lie) comes from the Spanish Basque phrase for "merry festival." The first permanent jai alai arena (called a fronton) was built in Florida in 1924.

The game's scoring system has been adjusted over the years to make it more attractive to gamblers. Typical games include eight players with only two players competing for a point at one time. The game continues until one player obtains seven points. Win, place, and show positions are winning bets, just as in horse racing.

Jai alai peaked in popularity during the early 1980s, when more than $600 million was wagered on the sport. By 1996 the total handle was down to around $240 million.

In 2004 pari-mutuel gambling on jai alai was conducted in only two states: Florida at five frontons and Rhode Island at one fronton. (See Table 8.2.) Although formerly also conducted in Connecticut, the last jai alai fronton in that state closed in 2002.

Paid attendance in Florida was 377,105 in fiscal year 2002–03, and the handle was $102 million. Attendance was down by 21%, and handle was down by 8% from the year before. The state received just over $600,000 from the jai alai industry.

The Future of Pari-Mutuel Gambling

DECREASING POPULARITY AND DECREASING INCOME. Pari-mutuel gambling is decreasing in popularity as it faces more and more competition from other gambling options, particularly casinos. The horse-racing industry, which comprises the bulk of the pari-mutuel business, experienced a 40% decline in attendance during the 1990s. Even though the handle increased over this time period, the increase is not statistically significant. The total pari-mutuel handle in 2000 was $18 billion; in 1987, it was $17 billion. Although this seems like an increase, it is actually a decrease when the effects of inflation are considered—the 1987 figure of $17 billion is equivalent to $26 billion in 2000 dollars. It has become increasingly difficult for racetracks to attract a large enough betting pool to afford to run races.

Statistics available from the Florida Department of Business and Professional Regulation, Division of Pari-Mutuel Wagering, are presented in its *72nd Annual Report* (December 2003). Pari-mutuel attendance steadily decreased from fourteen million in 1990–91 to 2.7 million in 2002–03.

ATTEMPTS TO ATTRACT MORE AND DIFFERENT GAMBLERS. Gambling industry analysts say that there is a relatively small hard-core group of horse-racing attendees, most of whom are older people. The horse-racing industry is trying to attract a larger and younger fan base (twenty-five to forty-five years old) with more disposable income. Some racetracks have tried to become entertainment venues by offering food courts, malls, and music concerts. Although these gimmicks attract visitors, those visitors do not necessarily gamble. Devoted race fans complain that such promotions are too distracting and draw attention away from the racing.

Increasingly, pari-mutuel facilities are offering other gambling choices to patrons. Seven states allowed slot machines and/or video lottery terminals at their racetracks during 2004: Delaware, Iowa, Louisiana, New Mexico, New York, Rhode Island, and West Virginia. The addition of video gaming devices has saved some racetracks. The

Dover Downs racetrack in Delaware increased its revenue from $14 million to $141 million following the addition of slot machines in 1994. The number of slot machines at racetracks is expected to triple during the first decade of the twenty-first century.

Most of Florida's racetracks and jai alai frontons have card rooms in which gamblers wager on card games, mainly poker. According to the *72nd Annual Report* of the Florida Department of Business and Professional Regulation, Division of Pari-Mutuel Wagering, the state's card room gross revenue was $2.8 million in fiscal year 2002–03. The card rooms contributed more than $363,000 to state revenues in the form of taxes and fees.

LEGAL SPORTS GAMBLING

Besides the sports involved in pari-mutuel gambling, legal sports gambling is extremely limited in the United States. Only one state, Nevada, allows high-stakes gambling on sporting events like football, basketball, and baseball games.

In 1992 Congress passed the Professional and Amateur Sports Protection Act. This act banned sports betting in all states except those that already allowed it in some form (Nevada, Oregon, Delaware, Montana, Washington, and New Mexico).

Limited Options Outside Nevada

There are a handful of states in which limited forms of sports betting are legal.

OREGON. As of August 2004 Oregon operates two sports betting games as part of its lottery. The Sports Action game began in 1989. Proceeds from the game go to the state's Intercollegiate Athletic and Academic Scholarship Fund. The game has earned more than $25 million for the fund since it was started, averaging about $2 million per year. The betting is conducted only during the football season on selected professional football games. Lottery officials avoid legal restrictions that professional football leagues have on the use of trademark names by referring to teams by location only (for example, Denver vs. Miami). A second lottery game is called Scorecard. In this game bettors win money if they correctly pick a number that matches the last digit of the scores from selected professional football games.

DELAWARE. Delaware tried a sports lottery in 1976 based on games of the National Football League (NFL). The NFL sued for trademark violations but eventually lost the case. The sports lottery, which was called Scorecard, proved to be unpopular with bettors and unprofitable for the state. It was abandoned after only one football season. A task force was formed during the summer of 2002 to investigate the feasibility of reinstating a sports lottery game in Delaware. The group's final report was issued to the Delaware General Assembly in 2003. It estimated that a legal sports lottery could raise approximately $13 million in state revenue. However, Governor Ruth Ann Minner is opposed to expanding gambling in Delaware, making it unlikely that a sports lottery will be initiated while she remains in office. The expansion of sports betting is also opposed by the National Football League, National Basketball Association, National Hockey League, Major League Baseball, and National Collegiate Athletic Association (NCAA).

MONTANA. The State of Montana allows five types of sports gambling: sports pools, Calcutta pools, fantasy sports leagues, sports tab games, and fishing derbies.

Calcutta pools are operated similarly to pari-mutuel wagering in that all money wagered on a sporting event is pooled together. In a Calcutta pool, an auction is held before a sporting event, and bettors bid for the opportunity to bet on a particular player. For example, before a golf tournament, the pool participants bid against each other for the right to bet on a particular golfer. The highest bidder for each player wins that right. Calcutta pools are sometimes called auction pools for this reason. The money collected during the auction becomes the wagering pool. It is divided among the "owners" of the best finishing players and the pool sponsor. Calcutta pools are most often associated with rodeos and golf tournaments.

Fantasy sports leagues are games in which the participants create fictitious teams assumed to be composed of actual professional athletes. Each team wins points based on its performance against other teams in the league over a designated time period. Team performance is measured based on the actual performance of the selected athletes during real sporting events. The points collected by each participant in the league can be exchanged for cash or merchandise paid for by membership fees collected from each participant.

A sports tab game is one in which players purchase a numbered tab (ticket) from a game card containing one hundred tabs with different number combinations. Bettors win money or prizes if their numbers match those associated with a sporting event—for example, digits in the winning team's final score. The cost of sports tabs is limited by law to less than $5 each. Operators of sports tab games (except charities) are allowed to take no more than 10% of the total amount wagered to cover their expenses (charities are allowed to take 50%). Sports tab sellers must obtain a license from the state and pay licensing fees and gaming taxes.

OTHER STATES. Other states offering limited sports gambling are Washington, which permits $1 bets on race cars, and New Mexico, where small bets on bicycle races are legal. Office pools on sporting events are legal in a few states as long as the operator does not take a commission. Despite these examples of sports betting in other parts of the United States, though, the big money in legal sports gambling in America is in Nevada.

Nevada Sports and Race Books

Sports books are establishments that accept and pay off bets on sporting events. They are legal only in Nevada and are mostly located in casinos, where they are often combined with the casino race books. Sports betting in Nevada is permitted only for people over age twenty-one who are physically present in the state.

According to the Nevada Gaming Control Board there were 172 locations in the state as of August 2004 licensed to operate sports books and/or race books. More than half of them are in Las Vegas. Most books are operated in casinos. The typical casino book is a large room with many television monitors showing races and games from around the world. Most casinos have a combined race/sports book, although the betting formats are usually different. Race book betting is mostly of the pari-mutuel type. Sports book betting is by bookmaking.

BOOKMAKING. Bookmaking is the common term for the act of determining odds and receiving and paying off bets. The person performing the service is called the bookmaker or bookie, for short. Bookmaking has its own lingo, which can be confusing to those who are not familiar with it. For example, a "dollar" bet is actually a $100 bet, a "nickel" bet is a $500 bet, and a "dime" bet is a $1,000 bet. In order to place a bet with a bookmaker, the bettor lays down (pays) a particular amount of money to win a particular payoff.

Bookmakers make money by charging a commission called "juice" or "vigorish." Although the exact origins of the word "vigorish" are not known, *Webster's Dictionary* suggests that it may be derived from the Ukrainian word *vygrash* or the Russian word *vyigrysh,* both of which mean "winnings" or "profit." In any event, vigorish is a very important and very misunderstood concept for most bettors.

Most gambling literature describes vigorish as a 4.55% commission that a bookie earns from losers' bets. A differing interpretation of vigorish comes from J. R. Martin, a sports handicapper (or person who studies and analyzes betting odds and gives advice to bettors) and writer who publishes a Web site on professional sports gambling. According to Martin, statistically, only bettors who win exactly half of their bets pay exactly 4.55% in vigorish. Other bettors pay different percentages. Therefore, a bettor must win 53% of all equally sized bets to break even. However, this bettor would wind up paying a vigorish of at least 4.82%.

Some sports bets are simple wagers based on yes/no logic. Examples include under and over bets, where a bettor wagers that a particular game's final score will be under or over a specific number of points.

Most sports bets are based on the "line" set by the bookmaker. For example, the line for an NFL football game between the Miami Dolphins and the Tennessee Titans might say that the Dolphins are picked by seven and one-half points. A bettor picking the Dolphins to win the game wins money only if the Dolphins win the game by more than seven and one-half points.

The line is a concept designed to even up betting. It does not reflect by how much a sports expert actually believes a team will win. It is designed so that the bookmaker will get bets on both sides. This reduces the bookie's financial risk. Bookmakers will change lines if one side receives more betting action than the other. The skill aspect of sports gambling comes in recognizing the accuracy of the line. Experienced bettors choose games in which they believe the posted lines do not accurately reflect the expected outcomes. This gives them an edge.

The odds for most licensed sports books in Nevada are set by the company Las Vegas Sports Consultants, Inc. Formerly owned by SportsLine.com, Inc., the company was purchased in November 2003 by a group of private investors in Las Vegas.

HOW SPORTS GAMBLING CAME TO BE LEGAL IN NEVADA. Nevada legalized gambling during the Great Depression of the 1930s as a means to raise revenue. The 1930s also saw the development of the handicapping system, in which bookmakers establish the betting line. Charles McNeil, a Chicago securities analyst, is credited with this development. Prior to that time, there was little incentive for gamblers to bet on the underdog in a contest.

During the 1940s the Nevada legislature legalized OTB on horses. The sports and race books were popular in the state's casinos until the early 1950s. A series of Senate hearings, led by Senator Estes Kefauver of Tennessee, was held in 1950 and 1951 to investigate the role of organized crime in the gambling industry. The hearings were televised and focused the nation's attention on gangsters, corrupt politicians, and legal and illegal gambling. One of the results was the passage of a 10% federal excise tax (FET) on "any wager with respect to a sports event or a contest." The tax was devastating to the casino sports books, which were making only a small profit anyway. They were forced to shut down.

In 1974 the FET was reduced to 2%, and the sports books slowly made a comeback. Frank "Lefty" Rosenthal, a renowned handicapper, is credited with popularizing the sports book in Las Vegas during the 1970s.

The 1980s were boom years for the sports and race books. In 1983 the FET was reduced to only 0.25%. Jimmy "the Greek" Snyder brought some legitimacy to sports gambling through his numerous television appearances on network sports shows. The amount of money

FIGURE 8.10

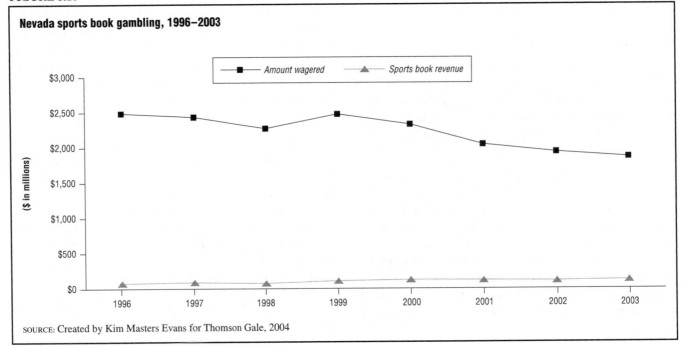

Nevada sports book gambling, 1996–2003

SOURCE: Created by Kim Masters Evans for Thomson Gale, 2004

wagered in the Nevada sports books increased by 230% between 1982 and 1987 alone. Betting volume continued to increase until the mid-1990s, when it began to level off.

MONEY AND GAMES. As shown in Figure 8.10 Nevada's sports books had a betting volume (or handle) of $1.86 billion during fiscal year 2002–03. This is down 4% from the previous fiscal year and down 25% from the $2.5 billion wagered in 1996.

Despite the decrease in betting volume the sports books actually took in more revenue over this time period, from $77 million in 1996 to $122.6 million in 2003. In 2003 this revenue represented 6.6% of the total amount wagered. This means that $1.74 billion was paid out to gamblers.

According to the Nevada Gaming Commission and Gaming Control Board, football wagers accounted for 44% of the state's sports book wagering during 2002, the latest year available. (See Figure 8.11.) Basketball and baseball accounted for 27% and 20%, respectively. Other sports and parlay bets were far less popular. A parlay bet is a combination bet in which the bettor selects the winners of two or more events. Every selection must be correct for the bettor to win the wager.

Football's share of sports betting was around 40% during every year from 1996 to 2002. The Super Bowl alone generated $81 million in wagers in 2004 as shown in Table 8.6. Sports book revenue (or win) was $12.4 million. However, the largest single wagering event for the Nevada sports books is believed to be the men's Division I college basketball tournament known as "March Madness." Betting volume for the 2004 tournament exceeded $85 million in Nevada.

Industry experts estimate that one-third of the bets placed in the Nevada sports books are on college sporting events. Wagering is not allowed on high school sporting events and Olympic events. Bets were prohibited on amateur sporting events either held in Nevada or involving Nevada teams prior to 2001. Nevada law restricts the sports books to wagering on events that are athletic contests. Betting is not allowed on related events, such as who will win most valuable player awards.

THE CONTROVERSY OVER COLLEGE SPORTS. In 2000 Senator John McCain of Arizona introduced the Amateur Sports Integrity Act to ban betting on college sports at the Nevada sports books. Although it was brought up again in 2001, 2002, and 2003, the act had not been passed by Congress as of mid-2004. The act is supported by the American Council on Education (ACE), the NCAA, and numerous other organizations representing colleges and universities.

During testimony before the U.S. Senate in April 2001, an ACE spokesperson gave the following reasons in support of the act:

- Gambling on college sports threatens the integrity of intercollegiate athletic competition.

- The state of Nevada has been arbitrary and selective in choosing which amateur sporting events are permissible for betting.

- Colleges cannot combat illegal campus gambling as long as legal gambling on intercollegiate sports is condoned by society.

Nevada politicians and the American Gaming Association (AGA) are opposed to a federal ban on legal wager-

FIGURE 8.11

Nevada sports book wagering by sport, 2002

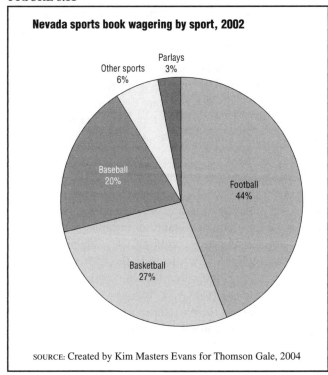

SOURCE: Created by Kim Masters Evans for Thomson Gale, 2004

TABLE 8.6

Nevada sports book wagering on Super Bowls, 1995–2004

Year	Wagers	Win/(loss)	Win%	Game results
2004	$81,242,191	$12,440,698	15.3%	New England 32, Carolina 29
2003	$71,693,032	$ 5,264,963	7.3%	Tampa Bay 48, Oakland 21
2002	$71,513,304	$ 2,331,607	3.3%	New England 20, St. Louis 17
2001	$67,661,425	$11,002,636	16.3%	Baltimore 34, N.Y. Giants 7
2000	$71,046,751	$ 4,237,978	6.0%	St. Louis 23, Tennessee 16
1999	$75,986,520	$ 2,906,601	3.8%	Denver 34, Atlanta 19
1998	$77,253,246	$ 472,033	0.6%	Denver 31, Green Bay 24
1997	$70,853,211	$ 2,265,701	3.2%	Green Bay 35, New England 21
1996	$70,907,801	$ 7,126,145	10.1%	Dallas 27, Pittsburgh 17
1995	$69,591,818	$ (396,674)	(0.6%)	San Francisco 49, San Diego 26

SOURCE: "Summary of Nevada Sports Book Performance for the Last Ten Super Bowls," in *Nevada Gambling Control Board Press Release: Super Bowl 2004,* State of Nevada Gaming Control Board, February 3, 2004, http://gaming.nv.gov/documents/pdf/pr_04superbowl.pdf (accessed September 28, 2004)

ing on college sporting events. The AGA advocates better enforcement of the existing laws against illegal sports gambling and stiffer penalties for those who engage in it. According to the AGA, the Nevada sports books have a direct computer link with the NCAA and share betting information with the NCAA. Further, the FBI credits this practice with bringing to light a gambling scandal at Arizona State University during the mid-1990s. The basketball team's coach was notified about a possible problem after Nevada sports books alerted the Pac-10 conference and the FBI about betting irregularities. The NCAA hopes that a ban on all college sports wagering will pressure newspapers to stop publishing the line on college games. The NCAA has repeatedly asked major media outlets not to post lines on college sports because it encourages gambling. However, the NCAA has been accused in the media of hypocrisy for its stance on legal gambling on college sports. The NCAA has a multiyear deal worth billions of dollars with television broadcaster CBS, even though CBS is part-owner of SportsLine.com, an Internet Web site that posts the line on college games.

THE INTERNET CHALLENGE. Following the advent of Internet gambling in the late 1990s, the Nevada sports books began to feel some serious competition. Internet gambling is technically illegal in the United States because it violates the federal Wire Act of 1961. However, online gambling is increasingly popular among Americans, particularly sports gamblers, who can place their bets from home or the office. The Internet provides gamblers with an easier way to monitor the many games of the tournament and to keep up with changing betting lines.

In response to this potential new gambling market, Nevada politicians began a drive to make Internet gambling legal in the state. In August 2002 the U.S. Department of Justice (DOJ) sent a letter to the Nevada Gaming Commission warning that any state legislation seeking to make Internet gambling legal would be in violation of federal law. The commission, on the other hand, has indicated that the state will continue to pursue legalization of online gambling for its residents, despite significant technical and legal obstacles.

A major problem in regulating any Internet gambling, including sports gambling, is the determination of jurisdiction. The Internet knows no state boundaries. Nevada officials hope that technology can be developed that will allow gambling Web sites to determine in what state a potential gambler lives. In this way, Internet gambling could potentially be allowed for the residents of Nevada only. Although several major casinos were working to take their games and sports books online, the political climate for legalized Internet gambling in the United States as of mid-2004 was not promising.

ILLEGAL SPORTS GAMBLING

The AGA estimates that the Nevada sports books account for only 1–3% of all sports gambling conducted in the country. The vast majority of sports bets, then, 97–99%, are illegal. This makes it difficult to assess exactly how much money is involved.

The 1999 final report of the NGISC estimated that $80 billion to $380 billion per year is wagered illegally on sports in the United States. In 1998 the FBI estimated that illegal sports gambling was a $100 billion industry.

Illegal sports gambling encompasses a wide variety of activities. Most illegal bets on sporting events are placed with bookies. Internet gambling and office pools are also popular methods. In addition, there are some "sporting" events, illegal in themselves, that are popularly associated with gambling—for example, cockfighting and dog fighting.

The Link to Organized Crime

Illegal sports gambling has long been associated with organized crime in the United States. During the 1920s and early 1930s, illegal sports gambling became big business for mobsters as they set up organized bookmaking systems around the country. Betting on horses, in particular, was popular during this time period.

In 1931 Nevada legalized casino gambling again, and organized crime soon controlled most of the casino business. During the 1940s Nevada legislation was expanded to include OTB on horses. At that time two illegal and nationwide wire services were operated by known mobsters: Continental Wire Service and Trans America Wire. The latter was under the direction of notorious gangster Al Capone. The mobsters set up the services because the legitimate wire service, Western Union, was prohibited by law from transmitting race results until races were officially declared over. Sometimes this declaration did not take place for several minutes after the race finish. To prevent bettors from taking advantage of these delays by posting winning bets before the official results were wired, the mobsters set up their own wire services. Trans America became widely used in Nevada thanks in large part to the efforts of famous Las Vegas gangster and casino owner Ben "Bugsy" Siegel.

During the 1950s the federal government cracked down on organized crime and eventually drove mobsters out of the Nevada casino industry. As the casinos were taken over by corporations, organized crime strengthened its hold on the illegal business of bookmaking. Although law enforcement officials acknowledge that there are now many "independent" bookies operating throughout the country, the big money in sports gambling is still controlled by organized crime figures.

The Link to the Nevada Sports Books

Most illegal books use the odds posted by the Nevada sports books because these are well publicized. They also provide illegal bookies with a means for spreading the risk on bets. Illegal bookies who get a lot of action on one side of a bet often bet the other side with the Nevada sports books to even out the betting.

Transmitting gambling information across state lines for the purpose of placing or taking bets is illegal. News items about point spreads (the predicted scoring difference between two opponents) can be reported for informational and entertainment purposes only, but betting lines are still published by many U.S. newspapers. The Newspaper Association of America, which represents nearly 90% of daily-circulation papers in the country, defends the practice as free speech protected under the First Amendment of the Constitution. The association claims that readers want to see the lines to learn which teams are favored to win, not necessarily for betting purposes.

The NCAA hopes that a ban on all college sports wagering will pressure newspapers to stop publishing point spreads. The AGA counters that betting lines would still be accessible through independent sports analysts, offshore Internet gambling sites, and other outlets.

The AGA conducted an informal poll during March 2001, around the time of March Madness, the men's collegiate Division I basketball tournament. The AGA asked the student newspapers at all sixty-five colleges that qualified for the tournament whether or not they would accept advertising for Internet gambling sites, despite the fact that Internet gambling is illegal in the United States. All of the newspapers indicated that they would do so. The AGA criticized the NCAA for blaming illegal collegiate sports gambling on the Nevada sports books while illegal Internet gambling is promoted on college campuses.

Animal Fighting

The practice of gambling on animal fights has a long history in the United States, despite its unsavory reputation. Most staged animal fights involve cocks (male chickens) or dogs specially bred and trained. Although such fighting is usually associated with rural areas of the country, urban police reports about cockfighting and dog fighting have increased in recent years, as the "sport" has become popular among street gangs. Animal fights are of particular concern to law enforcement authorities because typically large amounts of cash and weapons are present.

Although no national statistics are available on animal fighting, some animal welfare groups collect data on its prevalence. Pet-Abuse.com is a Web site devoted to collecting and documenting information about animal abuse cases. The Web site is operated by a nonprofit organization based in California. As of December 2004 the Web site database included 239 documented cases of animal fighting.

COCKFIGHTING. Cockfighting is performed by cocks, which are male chickens also known as roosters. In the wild, cocks fight and peck one another to establish a hierarchy within their social order. However, these altercations rarely lead to serious injury. Fighting cocks are specially bred and trained by humans to be as aggressive as possible. They are given stimulants, steroids, and other drugs to heighten their fighting nature. Sharp spikes called gaffs are attached to their legs. The cocks are thrown into a pit together where they cannot escape. They slash and peck at one another, often until death. Spectators wager on the outcome of these fights. Cockfighting was banned by most states during the 1800s. It is now illegal in forty-eight states.

TABLE 8.7

State laws on cockfighting, April 2004

State	Cockfighting: on the law books	Cockfighting: a felony or a misdemeanor	Loophole: possession of cocks for fighting	Loophole: being a spectator at a cockfight	Loophole: possession of Implements
Alabama	§ 13A-12-4	Misdemeanor	Legal	Legal	Legal
Alaska	§ 11.61.145	Felony	Felony	Misdemeanor [5]	Legal
Arizona	§ 13-2910.03 and § 13-2910.04	Felony	Felony	Misdemeanor	Legal
Arkansas	§ 5-62-101	Misdemeanor [3]	Legal	Legal	Legal
California	Cal Pen Code § 597b, 597c, 597i, 597j	Misdemeanor [6]	Misdemeanor	Misdemeanor	Misdemeanor
Colorado	§ 18-9-204	Felony	Felony	Felony	Felony
Connecticut	§ 53-247	Felony	Felony	Felony	Legal
Delaware	11 Del. C. § 1326	Felony	Felony	Misdemeanor	Legal
Florida	§ 828.122	Felony	Felony	Felony	Felony
Georgia	§ 16-12-4	Felony [3]	Legal	Legal	Legal
Hawaii	§ 711-1109	Misdemeanor	Legal	Legal	Legal
Idaho	§ 25-3506	Misdemeanor	Legal	Misdemeanor	Legal
Illinois	510 ILCS 70/4.01	Felony [2]	Felony [2]	Misdemeanor	Misdemeanor
Indiana	§ 35-46-3-8 to § 35-46-3-10	Felony	Misdemeanor	Misdemeanor	Misdemeanor
Iowa	§ 717D.2 and § 725.11	Felony	Felony	Misdemeanor	Felony
Kansas	§ 21-4319	Misdemeanor	Legal	Misdemeanor	Legal
Kentucky	§ 525.130	Misdemeanor	Legal	Misdemeanor	Legal
Louisiana		Legal	Legal	Legal	Legal
Maine[1]	17 M.R.S. § 1033	Felony	Felony	Misdemeanor	Legal
Maryland Md.	Crim . Law Code Ann. § 10-608	Felony	Felony	Misdemeanor	Felony
Massachusetts	ch. 272, § 94 and § 95	Felony	Felony	Misdemeanor	Legal
Michigan	§ 750.49	Felony	Felony	Felony	Felony
Minnesota	§ 343.31	Felony	Felony	Misdemeanor	Legal
Mississippi	§ 97-41-11	Misdemeanor	Legal	Legal	Legal
Missouri	§ 578.173	Felony	Legal[7]	Misdemeanor	Misdemeanor
Montana	§ 45-8-210	Felony	Felony	Legal	Legal
Nebraska	§ 28-1005	Felony	Felony	Felony	Legal
Nevada	§ 574.060	Felony[2]	Legal	Felony [2]	Legal
New Hampshire	§ 644:8-a	Felony	Felony	Felony	Legal
New Jersey[1]	§ 4:22-24	Felony	Felony	Felony	Legal
New Mexico		Legal[7]	Legal	Legal	Legal
New York NY	CLS A gr & M § 351	Felony	Misdemeanor	Misdemeanor	Legal
North Carolina	§ 14-362	Felony[2]	Legal	Misdemeanor	Legal
North Dakota	§ 36-21.1-07	Felony	Felony	Misdemeanor	Legal
Ohio	§ 959.15	Misdemeanor	Misdemeanor	Misdemeanor	Legal
Oklahoma	21 Okl. St. § 1692.2,§1692.5, § 1692.6	Felony	Felony	Misdemeanor	Legal
Oregon	§ 167.355	Felony	Felony	Misdemeanor	Misdemeanor
Pennsylvania	18 Pa.C.S. § 5511	Felony	Felony	Felony	Legal
Rhode Island	§ 4-1-9 to § 4-1-11	Felony	Felony	Felony	Legal
South Carolina	§ 16-17-650	Misdemeanor	Legal	Misdemeanor	Legal
South Dakota	§ 40-1-9	Misdemeanor	Legal	Misdemeanor	Legal
Tennessee	§ 39-14-203	Misdemeanor	Misdemeanor	Misdemeanor	Legal
Texas	Tex. Penal Code § 42.09	Felony	Legal	Legal	Legal
Utah	§ 76-9-301 and § 76-9-301.5	Misdemeanor	Legal	Misdemeanor	Legal
Vermont	13 V.S.A. § 352	Felony	Felony	Felony	Legal
Virginia	§ 3.1-796.125	Misdemeanor [4]	Legal	Misdemeanor [8]	Legal
Washington	§ 16.52.117	Misdemeanor	Misdemeanor	Misdemeanor	Legal
West Virginia	§ 61-8-19, §61-8-19a, §61-8-19b	Misdemeanor	Misdemeanor	Misdemeanor	Legal
Wisconsin	§ 951.08	Felony	Felony	Misdemeanor	Legal
Wyoming	§ 6-3-203	Misdemeanor	Misdemeanor	Misdemeanor	Legal
	48 Illegal	31 Felony	24 Felony	11 Felony	5 Felony
	2 Legal	17 Misdemeanor	8 Misdemeanor	30 Misdemeanor	5 Misdemeanor
		2 Legal	18 Legal	9 Legal	40 Legal

According to the HSUS, cockfighting was legal only in parts of Louisiana and New Mexico as of April 2004. (See Table 8.7.) It was a felony in seventeen states and a misdemeanor offense in thirty-one others. States differ in their treatment of cockfight spectators and those caught in possession of birds for fighting. The federal Animal Welfare Act prohibits the interstate transport of birds for cockfighting into states with laws against cockfighting.

Because cockfighting is still legal in some parts of the United States, in Mexico and the Caribbean, and in many Asian countries, there is a commercial breeding industry in America. The industry is represented by an organiza-tion called the United Gamefowl Breeders Association and similar groups operating at the state level. Although these groups claim to be agricultural organizations, the HSUS accuses them of promoting cockfighting.

In July 2004 South Carolina's agriculture commission-er, Charles Sharpe, was arrested and charged with taking payoffs from the South Carolina Gamefowl Management Association (SCGMA). According to media reports Sharpe lied to law enforcement officers investigating activities tak-ing place at a SCGMA facility in Aiken County (Jennifer Holland, "Sharpe Indicted," *The State*). Sharpe allegedly told the officers that the facility was a legal operation

TABLE 8.7

State laws on cockfighting, April 2004 [CONTINUED]

State	Cockfighting: on the law books	Cockfighting: a felony or a misdemeanor	Loophole: possession of cocks for fighting	Loophole: being a spectator at a cockfight	Loophole: possession of Implements
Washington DC	§ 22-1015	Felony	Felony	Misdemeanor	Legal
American Samoa	Legal	Legal	Legal	Legal	Legal
Guam	Legal	Legal	Legal	Legal	Legal
Puerto Rico	Legal	Legal	Legal	Legal	Legal
Virgin Islands	Legal	Legal	Legal	Legal	Legal

[1]These states do not use the terms "felony" or "misdemeanor," but rather have felony and misdemeanor equivalent penalties.
[2]A repeated offense can trigger a felony prosecution.
[3]While it is not specifically prohibited by state law, cockfighting can be prosecuted under the general anti-cruelty statute. On June 9, 2003, three people were indicted under felony charges for cockfighting under Georgia's new felony cruelty law.
[4]While it is not specifically prohibited by state law, cockfighting can be prosecuted under the general anti-cruelty statute as well as other statutes addressing cockfighting.
[5]In Alaska, a first offense is a violation, and a second offense becomes a misdemeanor.
[6]Felony charges may also be leveled against persons responsible for the mutilation of birds.
[7]In New Mexico, cockfighting has been prohibited in 13 counties and 28 municipalities
[8]In Virginia, being a spectator at an animal fight is only illegal if an admission fee is paid.

SOURCE: "Cockfighting: State Laws," in *Cockfighting: State Laws,* Humane Society of the United States, April 2004, http://files.hsus.org/web-files/PDF/cockfighting_statelaws.pdf (accessed September 13, 2004)

because it was conducting fighting only to test the bloodline and hardiness of cocks. In November 2003 the facility was shut down by authorities, and more than a hundred people were arrested for cockfighting. Sharpe was subsequently indicted for taking at least $20,000 in payoffs from the SCGMA during 2002 and 2003. It is also alleged that he used his position as agriculture commissioner to influence regulations that were beneficial to the SCGMA. Sharpe has proclaimed his innocence in the case.

The database maintained by Pet-Abuse.com lists dozens of documented cases of cockfighting reported in the United States during the early 2000s. One of the largest cases occurred in July 2004 in Sacramento County, California. A law enforcement raid busted a cockfighting ring involving approximately five hundred birds. Fights conducted at the facility were estimated to involve up to $90,000 in wagers per fight. Officials said it was common for dozens of birds to die during each fight. Two people were charged in the incident.

In June 2004 police in Wayne County, West Virginia, raided an ongoing cock fight and arrested 125 people on drug and animal fighting charges. Approximately $30,000 in cash and nearly eighty roosters were confiscated.

DOG FIGHTING. Dog fighting is conducted between two dogs placed in a pit or small boarded arena. Spectators place bets on the outcome of the fights. Fights can go on for hours, sometimes to the death. Dogs that show any cowardice or unwillingness to fight are killed on the spot by their owners. American pit bull terriers are the most commonly bred and trained for this purpose because of their powerful jaws. Fighting dogs are bred, trained, and drugged to enhance their aggressiveness. Authorities report that the dogs are often draped in heavy chains to build muscle mass and systematically deprived of food and water. Stolen and stray pet dogs and cats are commonly used as bait to train the fighters. The smaller animals are stabbed or sliced open and thrown to the fighting dogs to enhance their blood lust.

Dog fighting is illegal in all fifty states. (See Table 8.8.) According to the HSUS as of April 2004 dog fighting is a felony in forty-eight states and a misdemeanor in only two states, Idaho and Wyoming.

In January 2004 Georgia authorities busted the largest dog fighting ring ever reported in the state. Sheriff's deputies in Jones County arrested 123 people after raiding a vacant house in which a dog fight was taking place. Officers found one dog that had already died from its wounds and two that were mortally wounded. Ten surviving dogs were turned over to animal control agencies. The people arrested were charged with a variety of offenses, including animal cruelty, gambling, and weapons and drug charges. A number of guns and thousands of dollars in cash were seized along with dog fighting paraphernalia, including trophies and plaques that were to be awarded to the owners of winning dogs.

In December 2000 the Harvard Medical School's *Weekly Addiction Gambling Education Report* published its research findings on the cultural aspects of dog fighting in the southern United States. Researchers conducted interviews with thirty-one men involved in dog fighting in Louisiana and Mississippi. They found that dog fighting was closely associated with the men's need to assert their masculinity. An aggressive, brave dog reflected well on its owner, even if it lost. The perceived "macho qualities" of the dog brought the owner status and prestige within the group. A dog showing cowardice or a willingness to quit reflected poorly on its owner's masculinity. Such dogs are called curs and are killed by their owners. Research showed that favor among their peers was more important to the men than even gambling winnings.

TABLE 8.8

State laws on dogfighting, April 2004

State	Dogfighting: on the law books	Dogfighting: a felony or a misdemeanor	Loophole: possession of dogs for fighting	Loophole: being a spectator at a dogfight
Alabama	§ 13A-12-4	Misdemeanor	Legal	Legal
Alabama	§ 3-1-29	Felony	Felony	Felony
Alaska	§ 11.61.145	Felony	Felony	Misdemeanor
Arizona	§ 13-2910.01 to 02	Felony	Felony	Felony
Arkansas	§ 5-62-120	Felony	Felony	Misdemeanor
California	§ 597.5	Felony	Felony	Misdemeanor
Colorado	§ 18-9-204	Felony	Felony	Felony
Connecticut	§ 53-247	Felony	Felony	Felony
Delaware	§ 1326	Felony	Felony	Misdemeanor
Florida	§ 828.122	Felony	Felony	Felony
Georgia	§ 16-12-37	Felony	Legal	Legal
Hawaii	§ 711-1109.3	Felony	Felony	Legal
Idaho	§ 25-3507	Misdemeanor	Legal	Misdemeanor
Illinois	510 ILCS 5/26-5	Felony	Felony	Misdemeanor
Indiana	§ 35-46-3-4 to 9.5	Felony	Misdemeanor	Misdemeanor
Iowa	§ 717D.1 to 6	Felony	Felony	Misdemeanor
Kansas	§ 21-4315	Felony	Felony	Misdemeanor
Kentucky	§ 525.125 to130	Felony	Felony	Misdemeanor
Louisiana	14:102.5	Felony	Felony	Misdemeanor
Maine[1]	17 MRS §1033	Felony	Felony	Misdemeanor
Mary land	Art 27 § 59	Felony	Felony	Misdemeanor
Massachusetts	Ch. 272 § 94 to 95	Felony	Felony	Misdemeanor
Michigan	§ 28.244	Felony	Felony	Felony
Minnesota	§ 343.31	Felony	Felony	Misdemeanor
Mississippi	§ 97-41-19	Felony	Felony	Felony
Missouri	§ 578.025	Felony	Felony	Misdemeanor
Montana	§ 45-8-210	Felony	Felony	Felony
Nebraska	§ 28-1005	Felony	Felony	Felony
Nevada	§ 574.070	Felony	Legal	Felony[2]
New Hampshire	§ 644:8-a	Felony	Felony	Felony
New Jersey[1]	§ 4:22-24	Felony	Felony	Felony
New Mexico	§ 30-18-9	Felony	Felony	Felony
New York	Agr & M § 351	Felony	Misdemeanor	Misdemeanor
North Carolina	§ 14-362.2	Felony	Felony	Felony
North Dakota	§ 36-21.1-07	Felony	Felony	Misdemeanor
Ohio	§ 955.15 to 16	Felony	Felony	Felony
Oklahoma	21 § 1694 to 1699.1	Felony	Felony	Misdemeanor
Oregon	§ 167.365	Felony	Felony	Felony
Pennsylvania	18 Pa.C.S. § 5511	Felony	Felony	Felony
Rhode Island	§ 4-1-9 to 13	Felony	Felony	Felony
South Carolina	§ 16-27-10 to 80	Felony	Felony	Felony[2]
South Dakota	§ 40-1-9 to 10.1	Felony	Felony	Misdemeanor
Tennessee	§ 39-14-203	Felony	Felony	Misdemeanor
Texas	§ 42.10	Felony	Misdemeanor	Misdemeanor
Utah	§ 76-9-301.1	Felony	Felony	Misdemeanor
Vermont	13 VSA § 352	Felony	Felony	Felony
Virginia	§ 3.1-796.124	Felony	Felony	Misdemeanor
Washington	§ 16.52.117	Felony	Misdemeanor	Misdemeanor
West Virginia	§ 61-8-19 to 19a	Felony	Misdemeanor	Misdemeanor
Wisconsin	§ 951.08	Felony	Felony	Misdemeanor
Wyoming	§ 6-3-203	Misdemeanor	Misdemeanor	Misdemeanor
	50 I llegal	48 Felony	41 Felony	20 Felony
	0 Legal	2 Misdemeanor	6 Misdemeanor	28 Misdemeanor
			3 Legal	2 Legal
Washington, DC	Ch. 106	Felony	Felony	Misdemeanor
American Samoa	Legal	Legal	Legal	Legal
Guam	§ 34205	Violation	Legal	Legal
Puerto Rico	15 LPRA § 235	Felony	Legal	Misdemeanor
Virgin Islands	19 VIC § 2613a	Felony	Felony	Felony

[1]These states do not have felony or misdemeanor offenses per se, but rather have felony and misdemeanor equivalent penalties.
[2]A repeated offense can trigger a felony prosecution.

SOURCE: "Dogfighting: State Laws," in *Dog Fighting: State Laws,* Humane Society of the United States, April 2004, http://files.hsus.org/web-files/PDF/dogfighting_statelaws.pdf (accessed September 13, 2004)

Dog fighting is not limited to southern states and rural areas. In February 2004 a reporter for the *Buffalo News* reported on the growing problem of dog fighting in urban neighborhoods of Buffalo, New York (T. J. Pignataro, "Betting on Cruelty," February 8, 2004). The article describes drug and weapons raids by police that accidentally uncovered well-organized dogfighting operations around the city. One detective is quoted as saying "There is big money involved in this, and there are substantial bets." Authorities report that thousands of dollars in cash and other valuables, such as car titles, guns, and drugs, are commonly wagered at these dog fights. Gruesome scenes are described in which owners chop off the heads of dogs that disgrace them by losing or backing down during a fight. Trash bags full of mangled pit bulls have been found by city authorities in vacant fields or along city streets.

THE EFFECTS OF ILLEGAL SPORTS GAMBLING ON SOCIETY

Money and Crime

Because the vast majority of sports gambling that occurs in this country is illegal, it is difficult to determine its economic effects. However, the only people certainly benefiting from illegal sports gambling are the bookmakers. Large bookmaking operations overseen by organized crime groups take in billions of dollars each year. The betting stakes are high and the consequences for nonpayment can be violent. Small independent bookies typically operate as entrepreneurs, taking bets only from local people they know well. Illegal bookmaking cases reported in the media range from multi-million dollar enterprises to small operations run by one person.

In 2004 five people were arrested for running a massive bookmaking operation in Chicago. The illegal business made profits of $3 million between 1999 and 2002. Prosecutors allege that Joseph "The Pooch" Pascucci and his accomplices took bets on football, basketball, and baseball games. They were also charged with income tax evasion. In June 2004 Pascucci pleaded guilty in federal court and could be sentenced to up to fifty-one years in prison.

In late 2003 police in the small town of West Newport, California, arrested a bartender at a popular restaurant for operating a small illegal bookmaking operation. The man was allegedly taking bets on sporting events. Undercover agents reported making bets at the bar and receiving payouts of several thousand dollars. Authorities believe the bookie was acting alone without the knowledge of restaurant managers.

College Students

The extreme popularity of sports gambling has to do in large part with the perception that it is a skills-based risk-taking activity. This type of activity appeals to men in general and young men in particular. Because of the high concentration of young men on college campuses, sports gambling is believed to be very prevalent among college students. The issue first came to light in 1992 in a *New York Times* article titled "Newest Concern for Colleges: Increases in Sports Gambling." In this article the director of Harvard University's Center of Addiction predicted that "we will face in the next decade or so more problems with youth gambling than we'll face with drug use."

In April 1995 *Sports Illustrated* magazine published a three-part report on sports gambling on college campuses. The first installment, titled "Bettor Education," reported that collegiate gambling was rampant and estimated that nearly one-fourth of college students gamble at least once a week. Reporters visited campuses around the country and found sophisticated bookmaking operations with large numbers of students, mostly men, as clients. These young men shared some common traits: an obsession with sports, a social network in which gambling was acceptable and supported by peer pressure (such as a fraternity house), access to money, intelligence, and naive illusions about what they were actually doing.

The report found instances of athletes jeopardizing their athletic futures by betting on games, as well as students betting above their means and getting into serious debt. Some students ultimately went to the police or their parents when they got in too deep. However, parents tended to treat the problem lightly—much less seriously than other concerns, such as drug use.

Several academic studies examining illegal sports gambling by college students were published during the late 1990s and early 2000s. These included "Prevalence and Risk Factors of Problem Gambling among College Students," in *Psychology of Addictive Behaviors* (1998), "Sports Betting by College Students: Who Bets and How Often?" in *College Student Journal* (1998), "The Extent and Nature of Gambling among College Student Athletes" published by the University of Michigan Department of Athletics in 1999, and "Gambling, Its Effect and Prevalence on College Campuses: Implications for Student Affairs" by the NASPA Center of Student Studies and Demographics (2002). The studies noted that thriving sports books operated by college students had been discovered by authorities in Arkansas, Florida, Iowa, Maine, Michigan, Rhode Island, South Carolina, and Texas.

Sports Tampering

Sports tampering is officially defined by the U.S. Criminal Code as follows: "To unlawfully alter, meddle in, or otherwise interfere with a sporting contest or event for the purpose of gaining a gambling advantage." The most common form of sports tampering is called point shaving. Point shaving occurs when a player deliberately limits the number of points scored by his or her team in exchange for payment of some sort—for example, if a basketball player purposely misses a free throw shot in exchange for a fee.

There have been some famous sports scandals involving gambling, mostly in college basketball games. However, any link between an athlete and gambling gives rise to suspicions about the integrity of the games in which that athlete participates.

The professional baseball player Pete Rose is an excellent example. On September 11, 1985, at Riverfront

TABLE 8.9

Comparison of statistics on gambling by student athletes reported by the National Collegiate Athletic Association and the Harvard School of Public Health College Alcohol Study, 2004

Study	Student athletes who gamble on anything		Student athletes who gamble on any sport		Student athletes who gamble on college sprots		Student athletes who gamble on the Internet	
	Women	Men	Women	Men	Women	Men	Women	Men
NCAA	47%	69%	10%	35%	6%	21%	2%	6%
CAS[1]	33%	57%	10%	33%	6%	26%	2%	5%

[1]CAS student athletes self-reported that they played or practiced intercollegiate sports.

SOURCE: "Table 1. Comparison between NCAA and CAS Statistics on Student Athletes Who Gamble," in *Pushing the Limits: Gambling among NCAA Athletes,* in *The Wager,* vol. 9, no. 21, May 26, 2004. Data from Harvard School of Public Health College Alcohol Study (CAS), Harvard School of Public Health, Boston, MA, 2004 and Executive Summary for the National Study on Collegiate Sports Wagering and Associated Health Risks, National Collegiate Athletic Association, Indianapolis, IN, 2004.

TABLE 8.10

Summary of gambling risks and avoidance strategies noted by the National College Athletic Association

Potential risks of gambling
- Removal from team
- Expulsion from college
- Humiliation in the media
- Embarrassment to your family and team
- Banishment from professional sports
- Association with organized crime
- Financial or physical ruin
- Poor employment prospects
- Incarceration

Avoidance strategies
- Walk away from friends who bet
- Call Gamblers Anonymous
- Call the state council on problem and compulsive gambling
- Do not give out information on your team
- Do not talk about odds or point spreads
- Do not associate with bookies or gamblers
- Do not accept money or gifts from people associated with sports
- Keep up your guard
- Talk to your coach, athletic director, NCAA official, or law enforcement officer if you are being pressured
- Start on the road to legal financial independence

SOURCE: "Table 1: Summary of Gambling Risks and Avoidance Strategies Noted by the NCAA," in "Don't Bet on It: Curtailing Gambling among Student-Athletes," in *The Wager,* vol. 7, no. 18, Harvard Medical School, May 1, 2002. Data from "Don't Bet on It," National Endowment for Financial Education, Greenwood Village, CO, and the National Collegiate Athletic Association, Indianapolis, IN, 2004.

Stadium in Cincinnati, Ohio, Rose broke Ty Cobb's all-time hit record. Before the end of the decade, however, Rose was under investigation by the commissioner of Major League Baseball and by federal prosecutors for betting on sporting events and associating with known bookies. He agreed to leave baseball, and the case was dropped. At the time Rose denied ever betting on baseball games. However, in January 2004 he admitted that he had bet on baseball games while he managed the Cincinnati Reds team during the late 1980s. His misdeeds mean that he can not be eligible for induction into the National Baseball Hall of Fame.

THE INTEGRITY OF COLLEGE SPORTS. The widespread popularity of sports gambling among college students also leads to suspicions that athletes, coaches, and officials associated with collegiate sports could be wagering on the very games in which they are participating.

A study titled "Gambling with the Integrity of College Sports" was conducted at the University of Michigan in March 2000. Researchers found that 84% of college referees polled admitted they had gambled at some point during their careers. Nearly 40% had bet on sporting events, and 20% had bet on the NCAA basketball tournament. Two of the referees even admitted that the published point spread on games they were officiating affected the manner in which they officiated those games.

Several gambling-related scandals involving college athletes and coaches were publicized in the media during the early 2000s. These included University of Washington football coach Rich Neuheisel, University of Michigan basketball player Chris Webber, Florida State quarterback Adrian McPherson, and University of Florida basketball player Teddy Dupay.

In May 2004 the extent of gambling among college athletes was examined in "Pushing the Limits: Gambling among NCAA Athletes," in *The WAGER. The WAGER* is published by the Harvard Medical School and the Massachusetts Council on Compulsive Gambling. The article summarized the findings from two major studies: the NCAA's "Executive Summary for the National Study on Collegiate Sports Wagering and Associated Health Risks" and Harvard School of Public Health's "Correlates of College Student Gambling in the United States," published in the *Journal of American College Health* in 2003.

Table 8.9 compares the findings of the studies regarding gambling prevalence among student athletes. The NCAA study reports gambling activities reported by students during the previous twelve months. The other study asked students about gambling participation during the current school year. The results indicate that approximately one quarter of the male student athletes had gambled on college sporting events.

The NCAA opposes both legal and illegal sports gambling in the United States. Bylaw 10.3 of the NCAA prohibits staff members and student athletes from engaging in gambling activities related to college and professional sporting events. It also forbids them from providing any information about collegiate sports events to persons involved in organized gambling activities.

The NCAA opposes illegal sports gambling for the following reasons:

- It attracts organized crime.
- The profits fund other illegal activities, such as drug sales and loan-sharking.
- Student athletes who become involved can become indebted to bookies, leading to point shaving schemes.

Table 8.10 is an NCAA summary of the potential risks of illegal sports betting and ways for college athletes to avoid that temptation.

CHAPTER 9
INTERNET GAMBLING

Internet gambling is a relatively new phenomenon. The first gambling Web sites on the Internet launched in the mid-1990s. The new medium has since soared in popularity, particularly in the United States. Millions of Americans gamble online each year, even though the government considers the practice to be illegal. In April 2003 the U.S. Department of Justice estimated that there would be 1,800 Internet gambling sites operating around the world by the end of 2003 earning revenues around $4 billion.

Industry analyst Christiansen Capital Advisors, LLC, estimates that Internet gambling generated nearly $5.7 billion of revenue in 2003. Revenue is expected to double by 2006 and exceed $18 billion by 2010.

Exact figures on Internet gambling revenue are not known. Online gambling sites are not permitted to operate within the United States, and most of the countries that do allow them to operate do not collect or report revenue statistics. Bear Stearns & Co., Inc., reports that three-fourths of Internet gambling operations are located in small Caribbean countries that provide little or no government oversight of the industry.

It is believed that many Internet gambling sites do not pay taxes to their home countries, or pay lower taxes than land-based businesses. According to Mike Brunker in "Antigua Aims for Silicon Makeover" (MSNBC.com, November 19, 2003), the tiny island of Antigua in the Caribbean is home to about a hundred online gambling sites that pay $7 million in licensing fees to the government. Other popular locations include Central and South America, Australia, and the British Isles.

Unlike most land-based casinos, the vast majority of Internet gambling sites are operated by small, virtually unknown companies. Gambling Web sites are much cheaper to build and operate than traditional casinos. A land-based casino could cost hundreds of millions of dollars and require hundreds of employees. An online casino can be set up and operated by a handful of people for an initial investment of $1–2 million. The low setup and operating costs make the businesses very profitable and allow them to offer higher payoffs to winners than traditional casinos.

THE INTERNET

Online gambling would not exist without the Internet. The Internet is a vast computer network including hundreds of millions of computers in more than a hundred countries. It is not operated by any one business or government but is a cooperative venture in which many companies, organizations, and individuals choose to participate by making their computers part of the network. The Internet has been evolving since the 1960s, when researchers at the U.S. Department of Defense began trying to link computers located far from each other. Today, the Internet is a vast network that allows computer users at various locations to share information and data and communicate with one another.

Special computers called routers communicate with each other and calculate the best route for data packets to take as they travel the network. Each computer connected to the Internet has a unique Internet protocol (IP) address. This is a numerical address (such as 140.147.248.209) that other computers use to identify it. In 1984 domain names were introduced to make the network more user-friendly. A domain name (like uscongress.gov) is the word equivalent of an IP address. However, an IP address is not a geographical address. It does not tell one computer exactly where another computer is physically located.

Accessing the Internet from a personal computer requires a means for connection, plus software through which to communicate. Connection is via phone lines, cable, radio waves, or satellite to a special-purpose computer, called a server or host system. These powerful computers, which are usually operated by companies called

Internet service providers (ISPs), are in communication with each other throughout the network and provide the backbone of the Internet infrastructure.

The World Wide Web is an information system that makes the Internet easier to use. It is a special way to encode, retrieve, and navigate the many resources that are stored on Internet-linked computers. It is based on client-server interaction. A Web server is a computer that knows where to find resources (given their address) and how to extract them when someone asks. The company or individual that maintains a particular Web site is called its webmaster.

In order to access a particular Web site, a software program such as Netscape or Internet Explorer is required. Every Web address has a syntax—for example, http://www.webpage.com—in which "http" stands for a specific set of communication rules that are used to exchange data, and "www" identifies the data as being on the World Wide Web. The remainder of the Web address is the domain name of the computer on which those data are stored.

Computer Industry Almanac, Inc., estimated that 955 million people worldwide had Internet access in 2004. That number is expected to grow to nearly 1.5 billion by the year 2007.

INTERNET GAMBLING BECOMES BIG BUSINESS

As soon as the Internet was opened up to commercial enterprise, Web sites were developed to sell goods and services to the public. According to statistics available at the Pew Internet & American Life Project Web site (www.pewinternet.org), as of February 2004, 65% of American adults who access the Internet had purchased a product online.

There is no consensus on when the first Internet casino began operating and who started it. However, it is generally agreed that the first online casinos began operating sometime in 1995 or 1996. Among the first was Intercasino, based in Antigua. This small Caribbean island has positioned itself as one of the leaders in Internet gambling. In 1996 the country legalized and licensed online gambling sites. The companies that operate these Web sites are trade zone corporations, foreign-owned corporations operating in specific areas of the country as if they were on foreign soil. In Antigua, trade zone corporations cannot produce products for domestic consumption, so Antiguans are not allowed to participate in online gambling with any trade zone companies located there.

Because Internet gambling is not regulated by the federal government, various agencies and private entities have attempted to estimate the extent of the industry, including the National Gambling Impact Study Commission, the U.S. Department of Justice, and such industry researchers as Christiansen Capital Advisors and Bear

Stearns & Co., Inc. However their estimates differ, these analysts agree that the growth of online gambling has been phenomenal. In 1997 there were fifty to sixty Internet casinos in operation, most based in the Caribbean. In total the industry earned approximately $300–$350 million that year. By 2000 there were an estimated 600 to 700 sites, and revenues approached $2 billion. In 2003 the number of sites had grown to about 1,800, and revenues were estimated at $4–$6 billion.

ONLINE GAMES

In 2002 the General Accounting Office (GAO) conducted a comprehensive analysis of Internet gambling. The GAO is the investigative arm of the U.S. Congress. The findings were published in December 2002 in *Internet Gambling: An Overview of Issues*. The report notes that at that time there were 1,783 unique gambling Web sites listed by industry analyst River City Group, LLC of Christiansen Capital Advisors, LLC. The GAO selected a representative sample of 202 of these Web sites and reviewed them to determine the types of games and payment options available.

Table 9.1 shows the breakdown of Web sites by game type. Note that the values do not sum to 100%, because some Web sites offer more than one type of game. Nearly 80% of the Web sites offered casino type games. Almost half processed sportsbook wagers on sporting events, such as football games. Betting on horse and/or dog racing was offered on 23% of the Web sites. Only a small percentage of Web sites (7%) conducted lottery games. Many European countries operate Web sites for their lotteries where players can buy chances to win. Access is usually limited to citizens of each country.

Casino sites offer the same kind of games offered in actual casinos: poker, blackjack, roulette, slot machines, and so forth. Bet denominations range from pennies up to thousands of dollars. Some casino sites have card rooms where players compete against each other rather than against the house. This is an example of person-to-person or P2P betting. It also occurs at some sports betting sites.

Online casino games operate in much the same way as the electronic games found in actual casinos. Both depend on random number generators. Real slot machines have a computer chip built in. Online games have random number generators written into their programming. While slot machine payoff percentages are dictated by the state, online payoffs are not. However, online providers who never have winners would not have return customers. Therefore, their programs are designed to pay out a particular percentage. Online games are particularly appealing to people who enjoy card games because the betting limits are much lower than in actual casinos. For instance, an online gambler can play blackjack for $1 a hand, while many actual casinos require a $10 or $25 per hand minimum.

TABLE 9.1

Analysis of Internet gambling Web sites by type, 2002

Types of gambling on site	Percentage of sites	Number of sites
Casino	79.6%	129
Sportsbook	49.4%	80
Lottery	6.8%	11
Bets on horse/dog racing	22.8%	37
Internet gambling payment options		
Credit cards:		
Visa	85.8%	139
MasterCard[1]	85.1%	137
American Express	4.9%	8
Discover	1.2%	2
3rd-party payment transfer services:		
PayPal	66.7%	108
FirePay	21.0%	34
NETeller	32.7%	53
EZPay	1.2%	2
Equifax	0.0%	0
Direct wire transfer:		
Bank wires	59.3%	96
Western Union	46.9%	76
Money orders and various checks:		
Money orders	27.8%	45
Traveler's checks	8.0%	13
Bank drafts, cashier's checks, certified checks	40.1%	65
Personal checks	29.6%	48
Electronic banking systems or processors:		
Idollar [2]	5.6%	9
Electronic Financial Services [1]	15.5%	25
Other banking systems[1]	28.0%	45

[1](out of 161)
[2](out of 160)

SOURCE: Adapted from "Table 2. Results of Internet Gambling Web Site Survey," in *Internet Gambling: An Overview of the Issues*, U.S. General Accounting Office, December 2, 2002

Some sites require players to download software onto their personal computers in order to play. The software still runs through a program at the Web site, so the user must be online to play. Other games are played right at the Web site. Many Web sites use high-technology software that allows players to play gambling games in virtual reality. They can "look" around the table or around the casino room. Players can even "chat" with each other via online messaging during a game. Both of these effects make online gambling more interactive for the user.

Many sites offer free play to introduce visitors to the types of games offered and give them a chance to practice. Visitors who decide to play for money must register, open an account, and deposit money into that account. This requires input of personal information, including name and address. Typically, the user sets up a user name and password for future access. Money is transferred to the gambling site via credit or debit card, through an account with an online bank or payment service, or via electronic check or wire transfer.

Most online sites offer bonuses of 5–20% of the amount of the initial deposit. These bonuses usually

FIGURE 9.1

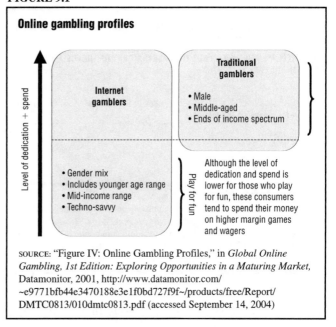

Online gambling profiles

SOURCE: "Figure IV: Online Gambling Profiles," in *Global Online Gambling, 1st Edition: Exploring Opportunities in a Maturing Market,* Datamonitor, 2001, http://www.datamonitor.com/ ~e9771bfb44e3470188e3e1f0bd727f9f~/products/free/Report/ DMTC0813/010dmtc0813.pdf (accessed September 14, 2004)

require that the gambler wager an amount two to three times the size of the bonus. Other sites offer prizes, such as trips, for repeat business. Winnings are typically deposited into the user's online account or paid via a certified check mailed to the winner.

ONLINE GAMBLERS

While traditional casino and sports gamblers tend to be middle-aged men, studies have found that Internet gambling appeals strongly to younger people, both men and women. In general, online gamblers are more knowledgeable about computers and technology than traditional gamblers and tend to be more middle-class in regards to income. (See Figure 9.1.)

Polls conducted by the Gallup Organization in 1996, 1999, and 2003 found that very few American adults had gambled for money on the Internet. As shown in Table 9.2 at most 1% of those asked had participated in Internet gambling.

Bear Stearns & Co., Inc., reported that there were approximately four million online gamblers worldwide in 2000 and that Americans accounted for about half of them. Most analysts estimate that Americans make up 50–65% of all Internet gamblers. The market is expected to attract more European and Asian gamblers in the next few years, and the U.S. market share is expected to drop.

In February 2002 the Internet research firm Jupiter Media Metrix began tracking Internet gambling as a distinct category in its syndicated monthly industry reports on Internet usage. At that time, the company estimated that 13.5 million people visited online casinos in December 2001 alone, spending approximately twenty minutes per visit. One-third of the online gambling visits occurred

TABLE 9.2

Poll results regarding Internet gambling within the previous year, selected years 1996–2003

PLEASE TELL ME WHETHER OR NOT YOU HAVE DONE ANY OF THE FOLLOWING THINGS IN THE PAST 12 MONTHS

Gambled for money on the Internet	Yes %	No %	No opinion %
2003 Dec 11–14	1	99	*
1999 Apr 30–May 23	*	100	—
1996 Jun 27–30	1	99	—

*Less than 0.5%

SOURCE: Jeffrey M. Jones, "Please tell me whether or not you have done any of the following things in the past 12 months. Gambled for money on the Internet?" in *Gambling a Common Activity for Americans,* The Gallup Organization, March 24, 2004, http://www.gallup.com/content/default.aspx?ci=11098 (accessed August 14, 2004). Copyright © 2004 by The Gallup Organization. Reproduced by permission of The Gallup Organization.

during typical work hours, suggesting that many online gamblers are playing at work. Most of the gamblers (73%) were aged twenty-five to fifty-four years. Only 8% of the gamblers were aged eighteen to twenty-four. The report noted that 11% of Internet users earn less than $25,000 per year. However, these people make up 13% of visitors to online gambling sites.

Greenfield Online, a market research firm, conducted a survey of one thousand people on Internet usage during 2001. The survey found that 35.6% of respondents had visited an online casino site. Only 13% of those visitors actually bet money on the site. The majority (59%) played free games, and 28% did not play any games at all. The survey revealed that 82% of the visitors were concerned about either credit-card security or receiving payoffs from Web-based casinos. About two-fifths (41%) of the visitors indicated that they would prefer to deal with online casinos run by well-known companies in the gambling industry.

A survey conducted in spring 2003 by the Pew Internet & American Life Project found that 4% of American adults who used the Internet had used it to play the lottery or to gamble online at some point. This was significantly lower than the number who had played any game online (39%) during the same period.

THE LEGAL ISSUES

This kind of activity is clearly illegal, and we're not going to put up with it in our state.

—Attorney General Jay Nixon of Missouri

Regulating any activity on the Internet has turned out to be a political and legal headache for authorities. Every country wants jurisdiction (the authority to enforce its own laws) over content that its citizens can access over the Internet. However, this has proved to be very difficult, because the Internet has no boundaries. A business based on a host computer might be legal in the country in which it is physically located but illegal in another country where it can be accessed over the Internet. This is the case for American online gamblers. Most countries are much less restrictive of gambling activity than is the United States.

In America, regulation of gambling falls under state jurisdiction. Although there are federal antigambling laws, they defer to the Tenth Amendment of the Constitution, which guarantees the rights of the states to govern their own affairs. Utah and Hawaii, for example, prohibit all types of gambling. Commercial casino gambling is legal in eleven states. Pari-mutuel wagering on horse and dog races is legal in more than forty states. Gambling on sporting events through a bookmaker is legal only in Nevada. Every state allows or disallows different forms of gambling, but the Internet has no borders. A user in any state can access online gambling sites operated from countries around the world where gambling is legal.

Determining jurisdiction is a major problem for authorities. Does online gambling occur at the location where the Web site is hosted or at the location where the gambler is located? The U.S. Department of Justice has said that gambling occurs in both places. The problem grows even more complicated when one or the other is not on U.S. soil. Although an international treaty with extradition rights could settle such matters, it is extremely unlikely to happen.

Various forms of gambling are legal in many parts of Europe, Central and South America, and the Caribbean, as well as Australia and New Zealand. In March 2001 Britain announced that it would legalize Internet sports gambling. In June 2001 the Australian Senate passed the Interactive Gambling Act, which prohibits online casinos in the country from taking bets from Australians. The law has provisions allowing interactive sports gambling and wagering services. Foreign residents can gamble at the Australia-based online casinos unless their governments sign up to be excluded from the program.

In September 2001 MGM Mirage started its own online casino, the first U.S. casino company to do so. The company set up its operations on the Isle of Man, a tiny island located in the center of the British Isles. Although it is a dependency of the British Crown, it is not part of the United Kingdom but institutes its own legislation and handles its own tax matters. The online casino did not accept bets from U.S. residents. The company closed down operations in 2003 citing concerns about legal and political issues affecting online gambling in the United States.

Federal Laws

Three federal laws on the books are directly applicable to online gambling: the Interstate Wire Act (18 U.S.C. § 1084 [a]), the Illegal Gambling Business Act (18 U.S.C.

§ 1955), and the Foreign Travel or Transportation in Aid of Racketeering Enterprising Act (18 U.S.C. § 1952). Only the Interstate Wire Act has been used in federal prosecutions of online gambling sites.

THE INTERSTATE WIRE ACT. In 1961 President John F. Kennedy signed the Federal Interstate Wire Act, which is widely known as the Wire Act. The Wire Act, § 1084(a) of Title 18 of the U.S. Code, makes it a crime to use telephone lines ("wire communication") in interstate or foreign commerce for the placement of sports bets or even to transmit information assisting in the placement of bets on sporting events. The act applies only to the gambling business, not to gamblers themselves.

In February 2001 the Harvard Medical School's *Weekly Addiction Gambling Education Report* examined the legal issues involved in Internet gambling, particularly criticisms of the Wire Act. Many legal experts say that it does not directly apply or is too ambiguous to apply to offshore online gambling sites for the following reasons:

- The Internet did not exist when the act was made law.

- Gambling Web sites maintained on offshore computers are not under U.S. jurisdiction.

- Internet service providers do not fall under the definition of wire communications facilities (particularly those associated with satellite and mobile phone transmissions).

- The law only specifically mentions sports betting, not casino games.

- Prosecutors cannot prove that online gambling sites "knowingly" transmit bets from U.S. citizens, because there is no way to know for sure the physical location of online gamblers.

The states have interpreted the Wire Act to mean that online wagering is illegal if it occurs to or from any state in which gambling is illegal. In 1999 the issue was addressed by the New York Supreme Court in *People v. World Interaction Gaming Corp.* (WL 591955 NY Sup. Ct. July 22, 1999).

The state of New York brought suit against World Interactive Gaming Corporation (WIGC) and Golden Chips Casino, Inc., for offering online gambling to residents of New York. Golden Chips Casino operated a legal land-based casino in Antigua. The company was wholly owned by WIGC, a Delaware-based corporation with corporate offices in New York. The suit alleged that the casino had installed interactive software on its computer servers in Antigua that allowed Internet users around the world to gamble. The online casino was advertised on various Internet sites and in U.S. gambling magazines, both of which were accessible to New York residents.

The New York attorney general's office actually downloaded the software and gambled at the Web site. Users had to wire money to a bank account in Antigua and type in their permanent address prior to play. Only users who entered addresses within states that permitted land-based gambling, such as Nevada, were allowed to play. A user who entered a New York address was not granted permission. However, the suit alleged that the barrier was easily overcome by typing in an out-of-state address, because the software had no way of checking the physical location of the user. The state did not consider this a "good faith effort" to keep New Yorkers from gambling as required by law.

WIGC argued that the federal and state laws in question did not apply to an offshore casino operated in full compliance with the law in the country in which it was located. The court ruled in favor of the state, saying that the act of entering the bet and transmitting the betting information originated in New York and constituted illegal gambling activity. The legality of gambling in Antigua was not an issue.

Furthermore, the court ruled that the gambling activity violated three federal laws: the Wire Act, the Foreign Travel or Transportation in Aid of Racketeering Enterprising Act (18 U.S.C. § 1952), and the Interstate Transportation of Wagering Paraphernalia Act (18 U.S.C. § 1953). The so-called Travel Act prohibits the use of "any facility in interstate or foreign commerce" with intent to promote any unlawful activity. The "Paraphernalia Act" is specific to gambling activity, prohibiting the interstate or foreign transmission of any item for use "in (a) bookmaking; or (b) wagering pools with respect to a sporting event or (c) in a numbers, policy, bolita, or similar game." WIGC violated this law because it had used the U.S. mail to send literature to potential investors and to send computers to the Antigua operations.

During the late 1990s federal prosecutors went after the operators of offshore sports books that had taken bets from Americans via the Internet and telephone. In March 1998 they charged twenty-two defendants with conspiring to violate the Wire Act. Ten defendants pled guilty to that charge, and three pled guilty to related misdemeanor charges. Seven of the defendants could not be apprehended and are considered fugitives. The last defendant, a U.S. citizen named Jay Cohen, decided to stand trial. Cohen and three of the fugitives operated a sports book called World Sports Exchange on Antigua.

The trial was held in Manhattan federal court for two weeks during February 2000. Prosecutors presented evidence that Cohen, as president of the company, solicited American customers through U.S. newspaper and magazine advertisements, encouraging them to contact World Sports Exchange via a toll-free telephone number and Internet site to place sports bets.

On February 28, 2000, Cohen was convicted of conspiracy to violate the Wire Act and seven substantive violations of the Wire Act. He was sentenced to twenty-one months in prison and assessed a fine of $5,000, the lightest sentence that the judge could assess under federal sentencing guidelines. Although Cohen's lawyers appealed the decision, a federal appeals court upheld his conviction in July 2001. His lawyers petitioned the U.S. Supreme Court to review the case, but the Court refused in June 2002.

Legal experts say that in this instance, the government's case under the Wire Act was strong because Cohen is an American and his company clearly accepted bets over the telephone on sporting events. The ramifications of the case to online gambling companies operated by non-Americans and those that offer only casino games are not clear.

THE INTERNET GAMBLING PROHIBITION ACT. Politicians have long recognized the shortcomings of the Wire Act to address modern gambling technologies. The NGISC recommended in 1999 that Congress enact federal legislation that would prohibit wire transfers from U.S. banks to online gambling sites or their banks.

Some form of the Internet Gambling Prohibition Act has been circulating around Congress since 1997. It was originally introduced by Senator Jon Kyl, a Republican from Arizona, to amend the Wire Act to specifically prohibit online gambling via the Internet and satellite technologies.

Senator Kyl has publicly called online gaming "the crack cocaine of gambling." The Kyl bill would have allowed individual states to permit online forms of gambling already allowed in their states (such as lotteries and casino games), while prohibiting forms that are not allowed (chiefly sports gambling). The Kyl bill never received popular support and was considered virtually impossible to enforce. It failed to pass in 1997 and 1999.

Between 2000 and 2002, other bills to combat online gambling were proposed by Republican representatives Jim Leach (Iowa), Bob Goodlatte (Virginia), and Michael Oxley (Ohio) and Democratic representative John LaFalce (New York). On October 1, 2002, the Unlawful Internet Gambling Funding Prohibition Act was passed by the House of Representatives. The so-called Leach bill would update the Wire Act to specifically outlaw the use of credit cards or electronic payment services for online gambling. However, the bill was not passed by the Senate.

In January 2003 Leach and Oxley introduced a new version of the bill as H.R. 21. It was modified and reintroduced in May 2003 as H.R. 2143. The new version gave enforcement power to the Federal Trade Commission. The bill was ultimately passed by the House of Representatives and was referred to the Senate. Meanwhile, in March 2003 Kyl and fellow-Senators Richard Shelby (R-Alabama) and

Dianne Feinstein (D-California) introduced a somewhat different bill (S. 627) with the same title. As of fall 2004 neither bill had been considered by the full senate.

Federal legislation against online gambling has been difficult to pass for a variety of reasons. There are special-interest groups and lobbyists on all sides of the issue. The horse- and dog-racing industries want to be exempted from any ban on online gambling, as do Native American tribes running casinos. Internet service providers and financial institutions do not want to be burdened with enforcement duties or threatened with penalties for their involvement.

All of the major casino companies that originally fought for legislation against online gambling are now changing their stance. Many operate free-game Web sites that they hope to convert to money-based gambling sites once the legal issues are settled. They feel their name recognition and existing client base might allow them a substantial profit from such enterprises.

State Laws

The attorneys general of many states have publicly stated their belief that Internet gambling is illegal based on their interpretation of existing gambling laws. According to the U.S. General Accounting Office (GAO), the investigative arm of the U.S. Congress, five states have enacted laws specifically prohibiting aspects of Internet gambling:

- In Illinois, Public Act 91-0257 became effective January 1, 2000. It amended the state's criminal code to prohibit anyone from establishing, maintaining, or operating an Internet gambling site and prohibits making a wager by means of the Internet.

- Louisiana's R.S. 14:90.3 was enacted July 15, 1997. It prohibits operating an Internet gambling business and providing computer services to Web sites primarily engaged in gambling businesses.

- Oregon's Senate Bill 755 was passed in 2001. It prohibits the collection of Internet gambling debts through credit-card payments, checks, or electronic fund transfers. Credit-card providers are not held liable for debts incurred by Internet gamblers.

- South Dakota's House Bill 1110 was passed in 2000. It prohibits anyone engaged in a gambling business from using the Internet to take bets and prohibits anyone from establishing an Internet gambling business in the state. The law does not apply to the state's licensed casinos.

- Nevada's Senate Bill 318 was passed in November 1997, making it illegal to make or take an Internet bet within the state.

NEVADA. Nevada was one of the first states to make online gambling illegal (in 1997). However, the statute excluded bets transmitted to licensed gambling establishments within the state as long as the wagering was conducted in compliance with all applicable laws and regulations. In June 2001 legislation was enacted that allows the Nevada Gaming Commission to adopt regulations for the licensing and operation of online gambling. The following conditions apply to any online gambling systems developed:

- They must be reliable and secure.

- They must provide reasonable assurances that minors cannot play.

- They must ensure that wagering occurs only in jurisdictions where it is lawful.

In August 2002 the U.S. Department of Justice sent the Nevada Gaming Commission an advisory letter outlining the federal government's stance on online gambling in Nevada. The letter said that "federal law prohibits gambling over the Internet, including casino-style gambling." The letter also clarified that the federal government considers online gambling to occur both at the location of the bettor and the location of the gambling business. Nevada still plans to continue investigating online gambling opportunities.

NEW JERSEY. New Jersey, another state heavily dependent on traditional gambling markets, has taken a different approach to online gambling. The state's Division of Gaming Enforcement filed civil lawsuits against eleven online gambling sites during 2001 and 2002 for taking bets from New Jersey residents. The companies had gotten very bold, even advertising on billboards along major highways. Most of the companies have refused to acknowledge U.S. jurisdiction and ignored papers that the state has tried to serve to them.

Credit-Card Issuers and Other Financial Institutions

In 1997 and 1998 a California woman named Cynthia Haines charged more than $70,000 in online gambling losses to her credit cards. Providian National Bank, which issued the cards, sued her for nonpayment. In June 1998 Haines countersued the bank, claiming that it had engaged in unfair business practices by making profits from illegal gambling activities. At that time, all casino gambling was illegal in California. Haines's lawyers argued that her debt was void because it arose from an illegal contract. Providian ultimately settled out of court, forgave her debt, and paid $225,000 of her attorney's fees. The company decided to no longer accept online gambling transactions.

The settlement caught the attention of other major credit-card issuers. Nonpayment of outstanding credit-card charges results in serious losses, called "charge-offs" in the industry. Faced with the potential for massive charge-offs and legal uncertainties, many card issuers decided to stop accepting financial transactions from online gambling sites. This includes such major companies as Bank of America, Chase Manhattan, Citibank, Direct Merchants,

Fleet, and MBNA. Issuers that do accept online gambling transactions generally delay payment of part or all of the money to the online sites for several months in case the user decides to dispute the charges.

In December 2002 the GAO issued *Internet Gambling: An Overview of the Issues*. The report discusses the payment systems, chiefly credit cards, used in Internet gambling. The four major credit cards issued in the United States are VISA, MasterCard, Discover, and American Express. The first two cards are issued by a large network of financial institutions that have credit-card associations. These associations set policies for the member institutions and provide the computer systems used to process financial transactions between the institutions and merchants. The Discover and American Express cards are issued and processed by their respective companies. Just over 500 million credit cards were in use in the United States at the end of 2001.

Experts estimate that 90–95% of all online gambling transactions are performed with credit cards. All of the major credit-card companies have enacted measures to restrict the use of their cards for Internet gambling. Discover and American Express primarily do so by preventing Internet gambling sites from becoming merchants in the first place. All potential merchants are screened, and existing merchants are spot-checked to make sure that they are not engaged in online gambling.

The credit-card associations allow their member institutions to decide whether or not to accept transactions from online gambling sites. The associations have a coding system that merchants must use to distinguish transaction types when the card is checked for authorization. This system was refined in 1998 so that Internet gambling transactions can be easily identified. Online gambling sites must enter a special two-part code that tells the issuer the nature of their business and gives the issuer a chance to deny authorization. Figure 9.2 shows how an online gambling transaction can be blocked at various points in the process. The GAO estimates that member institutions controlling more than 80% of the VISA and MasterCard credit cards issued in the United States deny payment authorization for online gambling transactions.

The coding system, however, has several problems. It does not distinguish between legal and illegal transactions. For example, Americans visiting countries in which online gambling is legal may find their credit cards rejected when they try to gamble over the Internet. The coding system can also be tricked by unscrupulous merchants who enter the wrong code for their businesses. The credit-card associations reported various instances in which Internet gambling merchants had been caught doing this.

The GAO states that four out of five credit-card transactions are now blocked at online gambling sites. Increas-

FIGURE 9.2

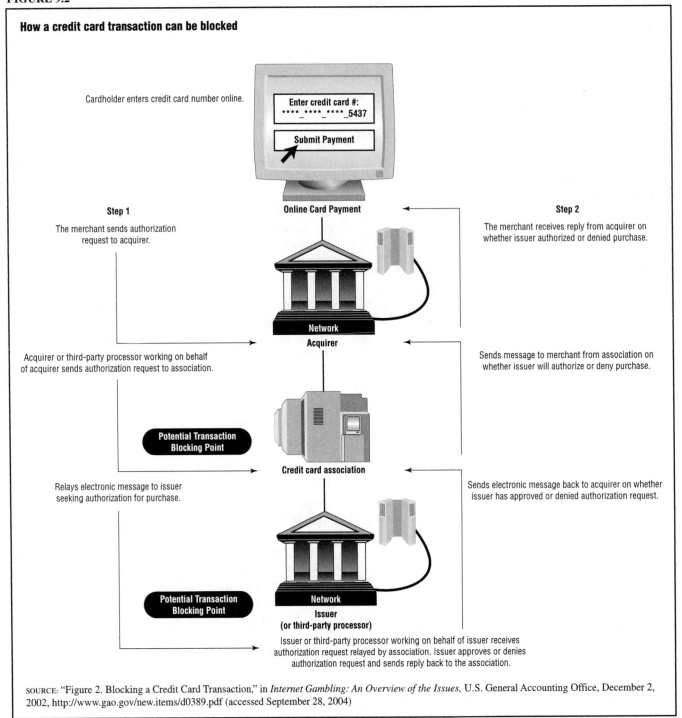

How a credit card transaction can be blocked

Cardholder enters credit card number online.

Enter credit card #:
**** _ **** _ **** _ 5437

Submit Payment

Online Card Payment

Step 1

The merchant sends authorization request to acquirer.

Step 2

The merchant receives reply from acquirer on whether issuer authorized or denied purchase.

Acquirer or third-party processor working on behalf of acquirer sends authorization request to association.

Network
Acquirer

Sends message to merchant from association on whether issuer will authorize or deny purchase.

Potential Transaction Blocking Point

Credit card association

Relays electronic message to issuer seeking authorization for purchase.

Sends electronic message back to acquirer on whether issuer has approved or denied authorization request.

Potential Transaction Blocking Point

Network
Issuer
(or third-party processor)

Issuer or third-party processor working on behalf of issuer receives authorization request relayed by association. Issuer approves or denies authorization request and sends reply back to the association.

SOURCE: "Figure 2. Blocking a Credit Card Transaction," in *Internet Gambling: An Overview of the Issues,* U.S. General Accounting Office, December 2, 2002, http://www.gao.gov/new.items/d0389.pdf (accessed September 28, 2004)

ingly, merchants and gamblers are turning to alternative payment systems, called online payment providers. These services allow customers to transfer money from their credit cards into accounts that can then be debited to pay for a variety of online goods and services, including gambling. Money going to and from these intermediary accounts is not easily traced. Online payment providers include PayPal, NETeller, FirePay, and ECash. Some credit-card associations are refusing to do business with online payment providers unless they receive assurances that money will not be transferred to Internet gambling sites.

In 2002 and 2003 the online payment network Pay-Pal, Inc., paid millions of dollars in fines to settle allegations that the company violated the Patriot Act during 2001 and early 2002 by processing online gambling transactions from American citizens. The Patriot Act (officially titled Uniting and Strengthening America by Providing Appropriate Tools Required to Intercept and Obstruct Terrorism Act of 2001) forbids the electronic transmission of funds known to be associated with criminal acts. PayPal stopped handling online gambling transactions in November 2002.

Federal Crackdown on Advertising

Web languages include a navigational tool called hypertext that allows immediate jumping from one Web site to another. An Internet user who clicks on a hypertext link will immediately access the Web site associated with that link. Many online businesses pay other Web sites to offer such links. Every so-called click-through earns a commission for the webmaster offering the link. Webmasters can also earn money by renting out advertising space on their Web pages.

According to the Newsbytes News Network, a technology news Web site operated by the Washington Post Company, online casinos were the fifth-largest Internet advertisers at the end of 2001, following companies offering books, investments, consumer credit, and travel. Jupiter Media Metrix reported that there were 170% more advertisements for online casinos during 2001 than the year before. Increasingly, these advertisements are on mainstream Web sites rather than just in niche markets. However, some Web sites have run into trouble with other advertisers for including Internet gambling advertisements. In 2000 Web portal Yahoo pulled Internet gambling advertisements from its football pages after the National Football League complained.

In April 2004 major Internet search engines, including Yahoo and Google, announced that they would no longer display ads for online gambling sites that targeted American citizens. The companies reportedly acted to head off plans by the U.S. Department of Justice to pursue legal action against them.

THE EFFECTS OF ONLINE GAMBLING

Just like any other form of gambling, online gambling has various social and economic effects on society. Because this gambling medium is rather new, there are a limited number of studies on its effects on people and their gambling habits. Likewise, economic factors are difficult to assess because most online gambling sites operate in foreign countries with little government oversight.

Economics

Unlike traditional casinos, online gambling sites are not licensed or taxed by state governments. Therefore, they provide no revenue for social and educational programs. The primary financial beneficiaries are the online gambling companies themselves, the foreign countries in which they are located, and the companies that process their financial transactions. For example, credit-card companies typically receive 2–5% of each transaction amount. In addition, they earn interest on the debt incurred by the card user. Because most companies consider money used for online gambling as a cash advance, the interest rates are very high—20% or more.

Other businesses that benefit directly or indirectly from online gambling include Internet service providers, phone and cable companies, nongambling Web sites that feature advertisements for online gambling sites, and software companies. Major software providers to online gambling sites include WagerLogic, Boss Media, Microgaming Systems, and World Gaming.

Mobile phone companies expect cellular gambling to become commonplace in the near future, particularly for phones with video streaming. Ladbrokes and William Hill are traditional British bookmakers that accept wagers via cellular phones using wireless application protocol (WAP). The company Eurobet launched wireless betting during the summer of 2000. In December 2003 industry analysts at Juniper Research released a report predicting that gambling via cellular phones would be a $6.7 billion business by 2006. In July 2004 the Philippines government decided to ban cell phones from the country's schools because students were using them to place online bets during school hours.

The economic effects of online gambling are discussed at length in an article by Ryan D. Hammer in the December 2001 issue of *Federal Communications Law Journal* of the Indiana University School of Law. The article "Does Internet Gambling Strengthen the U.S. Economy? Don't Bet on It" argues that people who do not gamble on the Internet suffer financially from online gambling. The high costs of litigation and unpaid bills are passed on from credit-card companies to other consumers in the form of higher interest rates and fees. Taxpayer money funds federal and state lawsuits against online gambling sites. State governments receive no licensing fees or tax revenues from online gambling sites but must fund treatment programs for pathological gamblers, a growing number of whom are online gamblers. The federal government collects income taxes from the big winners of lotteries and traditional casino games, but no taxes are collected from online gambling winners.

Crime

Besides the legality of the activity itself, other criminal issues are associated with online gambling. The 1999 report of the NGISC lists three of the major ones: operator abuses, computer hacking, and money laundering.

OPERATOR ABUSES. Operator abuses include stealing credit-card information and money from players, refusing to pay winnings, and manipulating the game software to increase profit. Because the industry is not regulated by any American government agencies, it is difficult to know how prevalent these problems are. Gambling Web sites can be extremely fluid, moving or closing down without notice. The NGISC report mentions an Internet gambler who was cheated out of $7,000 by an unscrupulous gambling Web site that refused to pay his winnings and immediately closed down. Studies have shown that lack of trust is a major factor keeping many traditional gamblers away from Internet sites. They worry that the games are "fixed" or that winnings will not be paid.

Internet gambling operators complain that most credit-card fraud is perpetrated against them rather than by them. There are many reports by industry insiders of stolen credit cards being used by online gamblers. These activities represent a financial loss to the operator, as well as the credit-card issuers. Because credit-card holders are not held liable for the fraudulent use of their credit cards, it is less of a financial burden for them, although it is still a matter of great concern.

COMPUTER HACKING. Computer hackers, savvy computer operators who illegally gain entry into others' computer systems, are also a problem in the online gambling industry (as in all Internet-based industries). Operators of gambling Web sites complain that hackers break into their financial databases and steal credit-card information or manipulate gaming software in their favor.

MONEY LAUNDERING. The biggest concern to law enforcement authorities is money laundering. Money laundering is the transfer of money gained via illegal means through third parties to purposely make its origins obscure. For example, a criminal could deposit large sums of cash with an Internet gambling site and later withdraw it via transfer to a legitimate bank account. This makes it very difficult for authorities to trace the path of money obtained illegally.

The GAO's *Internet Gambling: An Overview of the Issues* examined the vulnerability of Internet gambling to money laundering. In general, law enforcement agencies believe that Internet gambling could be a significant medium for money laundering, while banking and gambling regulatory officials do not. According to law enforcement officials, the factors that make online gambling susceptible to money laundering include the speed and anonymity with which financial transactions take place, as well as their offshore locations outside U.S. jurisdiction. However, many financial analysts believe the risk is low when credit cards are used because credit-card transactions are closely monitored and recorded. There is a fear that other, less traceable payment methods will become popular, as credit-card use is increasingly being blocked at online gambling sites.

Compulsive Gambling

Experts say that the fast pace and instant gratification associated with online gambling make it more addictive than other types of gambling. Online gambling is quite different from traditional casino gambling. Casino gambling is a social activity, usually conducted in the company of family or friends. Online gambling is a solitary and anonymous activity. The Council on Compulsive Gaming of New Jersey estimates that 90–95% of online gamblers gamble alone. Online gamblers who contact the organization for help are usually younger than traditional gamblers and have built up large amounts of debt in a shorter time than traditional gamblers.

In general, online gamblers are younger than traditional gamblers because younger people are more computer-savvy. Many younger people have grown up playing video games and are comfortable with online games. However, younger people are also more likely to take risks. This makes them particularly susceptible to serious gambling problems.

In March 2002 a study on Internet gamblers was published by the American Psychological Association in its journal *Psychology of Addictive Behaviors*. The study was performed by researchers at the University of Connecticut in Farmington. Patients seeking free or reduced-cost services at the university's health and dental clinics were questioned about their gambling habits. The respondents filled out surveys left at the clinics between August 1999 and September 2000.

In total, 389 patients completed the questionnaires in full. Every one of the respondents reported gambling at some point in their lives. Nearly all (90%) had gambled in the previous year, and 42% had gambled in the previous week. Only 8% of the respondents had gambled online during their lifetimes. However, 4% gambled online on a weekly basis.

The younger respondents were more likely to have Internet gambling experience than the older respondents. The median age of the online gamblers was 31.7 years, compared to 43.5 years for traditional gamblers. Ethnicity also made a difference. Non-Caucasians comprised only 16% of the total group surveyed but nearly 36% of the Internet gamblers.

All participants were given the South Oaks Gambling Screen (SOGS), a common series of questions used to determine the probability that a person has a gambling problem. Results showed that the mean SOGS score of online gamblers was 7.8, compared to 1.8 for those without online gambling experience. Researchers categorized all respondents into levels depending on their SOGS scores. Level 1 gamblers had a SOGS score of 0–2 and were considered not to have a gambling problem. Level 2 gamblers had a SOGS score of 3–4 and were considered probable problem gamblers. Level 3 gamblers had a SOGS score of 5 or greater and were considered probable pathological gamblers.

Internet gamblers were much more likely to have a gambling problem than non-Internet gamblers. Just over 74% of Internet gamblers were rated at Levels 2 or 3, compared to just under 22% of the traditional gamblers. Although this research was performed with a relatively small number of Internet gamblers, it does suggest that there may be a relationship between online gambling and serious gambling problems.

Psychologists George T. Ladd and Nancy M. Petry, authors of the University of Connecticut study, wrote that "the availability of Internet gambling may draw individuals who seek out isolated and anonymous contexts for their gambling behaviors." The Internet is also hard for problem gamblers to ignore in their daily lives. While they might be able to resist traveling to another state to casinos, the easy availability of online gambling is difficult to avoid. Internet gambling sites are always open and accessible.

Experts hope that online sites will use sophisticated software to identify problem players—for example, those who engage in incremental betting or gamble frequently—and either warn such gamblers or limit their play.

Underage Gambling

On January 16, 2001, the APA issued a public health advisory about Internet gambling. The advisory, from the Committee on Treatment Services for Addicted Patients, states that Internet gambling has undergone explosive growth in recent years. However, few safeguards are in place to ensure the fairness of the games or to establish exactly who has responsibility for operating them. Because there is no federal or state regulation of online gambling sites, no measures are taken to prevent underage gamblers from participating. Children and teenagers already play nongambling games on the Internet and are at significant risk of being lured to gambling sites.

In June 2002 the U.S. Federal Trade Commission (FTC) issued a Consumer Alert warning parents about children and online gambling. The FTC says that it is too easy for kids, particularly teenagers, to access online gambling sites. The agency complained that many nongambling game-playing sites popular with kids contain links to gambling sites. The FTC also conducted an informal survey of one hundred Internet gambling sites and found that 20% had no warnings at all to children. Many sites lacked measures to block minors from gambling.

THE FUTURE OF ONLINE GAMBLING

Economic Projections

Despite being illegal in the United States, online gambling is an extremely popular activity for many Americans. Market projections made in 1999 and 2000 predicted robust growth for the industry particularly if it became regulated. For example, Christiansen Capital Advisors, LLC, predicted in 2000 that a regulated industry could generate as much as $231 million in tax revenues between 2003 and 2005 and achieve an average 15% market share. However, the unfavorable political climate for online gambling caused many analysts to downplay their market projections during 2002. The lowered expectations are blamed on legal issues and the reluctance of credit-card companies and other cash-handling services to process online gambling transactions.

Determining Where Online Gamblers Are

Being able to determine the geographic location of online bettors is essential to the legalization of online gambling in the United States. State governments will not legalize the industry unless they can regulate it and tax it. Industry insiders believe that high-tech computer systems utilizing global positioning, prepaid "smart cards," and/or fingerprint recognition need to be developed to ensure the location and age of online gamblers.

IMPORTANT NAMES AND ADDRESSES

Alaska Department of Revenue
333 Willoughby Ave.
11th Floor
P.O. Box 110420
Juneau, AK 99811
(907) 465-2301
FAX: (907) 465-2389
E-mail: linda_wahto@revenue.state.ak.us
URL: http://www.revenue.state.ak.us/

American Gaming Association
555 13th St. NW
Suite 1010 East
Washington, DC 20004
(202) 637-6500
FAX: (202) 637-6507
E-mail: info@americangaming.org
URL: http://www.americangaming.org/

Arizona Department of Racing
1110 West Washington
Suite 260
Phoenix, AZ 85007
(602) 364-1700
FAX: (602) 364-1703
E-mail: ador@azracing.gov
URL: http://www.raccom.state.az.us/

Arizona Lottery
P.O. Box 2913
Phoenix, AZ 85062
(480) 921-4400
E-mail: feedback@lottery.state.az.us
URL: http://www.arizonalottery.com/

Arkansas Racing Commission
1515 West Seventh St.
Suite 505
P.O. Box 3076
Little Rock, AR 72203
(501) 682-1467
FAX: (501) 682-5273
E-mail: bob.cohee@dfa.state.ar.us
URL: http://www.accessarkansas.org/dfa/
racing/

Birmingham Racing Commission
Energen Plaza
2101 Sixth Ave. N
Suite 725
Birmingham, AL 35203
(205) 328-7223
E-mail: ledadimperio@bellsouth.net
URL: http://www.mindspring.com/~brc/

California Horse Racing Board
1010 Hurley Way
Suite 300
Sacramento, CA 95825
(916) 263-6000
FAX: (916) 263-6042
E-mail: Mike.Marten@Prodigy.net
URL: http://www.chrb.ca.gov/

California Lottery
600 North 10th St.
Sacramento, CA 95814
(916) 322-5136
Toll-free: 1-800-LOTTERY
URL: http://www.calottery.com/

Christiansen Capital Advisors, LLC
41 Campus Dr.
New Gloucester, ME 04260
(207) 688-4500
E-mail: jaypaw@maine.rr.com
URL: http://www.cca-i.com/

Colorado Division of Gaming
1881 Pierce St.
Suite 112
Lakewood, CO 80214
(303) 205-1355
FAX: (303) 205-1342
URL: http://www.revenue.state.co.us/
Gaming/home.asp

Colorado Division of Racing Events
1881 Pierce St.
Suite 108
Lakewood, CO 80214

(303) 205-2990
FAX: (303) 205-2950
E-mail: racing@spike.dor.state.co.us
URL: http://www.revenue.state.co.us/
racing_dir/coracing.html

Colorado Lottery
Wells Fargo Bldg.
201 West Eighth St.
Suite 600
Pueblo, CO 81003
(719) 546-2400
FAX: (719) 546-5208
URL: http://www.coloradolottery.com/
home.cfm

Connecticut Division of Special Revenue
P.O. Box 310424
Newington, CT 06131
(860) 594-0500
FAX: (860) 594-0696
E-mail: dosr@po.state.ct.us
URL: http://www.dosr.state.ct.us/

Connecticut Lottery Corporation
270 John Downey Dr.
New Britain, CT 06051
(860) 348-4000
FAX: (860) 348-4015
E-mail: clc@po.state.ct.us
URL: http://www.ctlottery.org/

**DC Lottery and Charitable Games
Control Board**
2101 Martin Luther King Jr. Ave. SE
Washington, DC 20020
(202) 645-8000
URL: http://lottery.dc.gov/main.shtm

**Delaware Department of Agriculture,
Delaware Thoroughbred
Racing Commission**
2320 South DuPont Hwy.
Dover, DE 19901
(302) 698-4500

FAX: (302) 697-6287
E-mail: john.wayne@state.de.us
URL: http://www.state.de.us/deptagri/
thoroughbred/index.htm

Delaware Lottery
1575 McKee Rd.
Suite 102
Dover, DE 19904
(302) 739-5291
FAX: (302) 739-6706
URL: http://lottery.state.de.us

**Florida Department of Business and
Professional Regulation, Division of
Pari-Mutuel Wagering**
1940 North Monroe St.
Tallahassee, FL 32399
(850) 922-8981
E-mail: Call.Center@dbpr.state.fl.us
URL: http://sun6.dms.state.fl.us/dbpr/pmw/
index.shtml

Florida Lottery
250 Marriott Dr.
Tallahassee, FL 32301
(850) 487-7777
E-mail: asklott@flalottery.com
URL: http://www.flalottery.com/

Gamblers Anonymous
P.O. Box 17173
Los Angeles, CA 90017
(213) 386-8789
FAX: (213) 386-0030
E-mail: isomain@gamblersanonymous.org
URL: http://www.gamblersanonymous.org/

Georgia Lottery Corporation
250 Williams St.
Suite 3000
Atlanta, GA 30303
(404) 215-5000
E-mail: media@galottery.org
URL: http://www.galottery.com/

Greyhound Protection League
P.O. Box 669
Penn Valley, CA 95946
Toll-free: 1-800-446-8637
URL: http://www.greyhounds.org/

Hoosier Lottery
Pan Am Plaza
201 South Capitol Ave.
Suite 1100
Indianapolis, IN 46225
(317) 264-4800
Toll-free: 1-800-955-6886
E-mail: playersupport@hoosierlottery.com
URL: http://www.in.gov/hoosierlottery/

Idaho Lottery
1199 Shoreline Ln.
Suite 100
Boise, ID 83702

(208) 334-2600
E-mail: info@idaholottery.com
URL: http://www.idaholottery.com/

Idaho State Police Racing Commission
P.O. Box 700
Meridian, ID 83680
(208) 884-7080
FAX: (208) 884-7098
E-mail: ardie.noyes@isp.idaho.gov
URL: http://www.isp.state.id.us/race/index.
html

Illinois Gaming Board
160 North LaSalle
Suite 300
Chicago, IL 60601
(312) 814-4700
FAX: (312) 814-4602
URL: http://www.igb.state.il.us/

Illinois Lottery
101 West Jefferson St.
Springfield, IL 62702
Toll-free: 1-800-252-1775
E-mail: lottery.info@isl.state.il.us
URL: http://www.illinoislottery.com/

Illinois Racing Board
100 West Randolph
Suite 7-701
Chicago, IL 60601
(312) 814-2600
E-mail: racing_board@irb.state.il.us
URL: http://www.state.il.us/agency/irb/

Indiana Gaming Commission
115 West Washington St.
South Tower
Suite 950
Indianapolis, IN 46204
(317) 233-0046
FAX: (317) 233-0047
URL: http://www.in.gov/gaming/

Indiana Horse Racing Commission
ISTA Center
150 West Market St.
Suite 530
Indianapolis, IN 46204
(317) 233-3119
FAX: (317) 233-4470
URL: http://www.in.gov/ihrc/

Institute for Problem Gambling
955 South Main St.
Middletown, CT 06457
(860) 343-5500
FAX: (860) 347-3183
E-mail: herb@theconnectioninc.org
URL: http://www.gamblingproblem.org/

**International Gaming Institute at
University of Nevada at Las Vegas**
4505 Maryland Pkwy.
P.O. Box 456037

Las Vegas, NV 89154
(702) 895-3903
FAX: (702) 895-1135
E-mail: hosinfo@unlvedu.org
URL: http://www.unlvedu.org

Iowa Lottery
2015 Grand Ave.
Des Moines, IA 50312
(515) 281-7900
E-mail: web.master@ilot.state.ia.us
URL: http://www.ialottery.com/

Iowa Racing and Gaming Commission
717 East Court
Suite B
Des Moines, IA 50309
(515) 281-7352
FAX: (515) 242-6560
E-mail: irgc@irgc.state.ia.us
URL: http://www3.state.ia.us/irgc/

Jockey Club
40 East 52nd St.
New York, NY 10022
(212) 371-5970
FAX: (212) 371-6123
URL: http://home.jockeyclub.com/

Kansas Lottery
128 North Kansas Ave.
Topeka, KS 66603
(785) 296-5700
E-mail: lotteryinfo@kslottery.net
URL: http://www.kslottery.com/index.html

Kansas Racing and Gaming Commission
3400 Southwest Van Buren
Topeka, KS 66611
(785) 296-5800
FAX: (785) 296-0900
E-mail: kracing@cjnetworks.com
URL: http://www.accesskansas.org/krc/

Kentucky Lottery
1011 West Main St.
Louisville, KY 40202
(502) 560-1500
E-mail: CUSTSRVS@KYLOTTERY.COM
URL: http://www.kylottery.com

Kentucky Horse Racing Authority
4063 Iron Works Pkwy.
Bldg. B
Lexington, KY 40511
(859) 246-2040
E-mail: krc.info@mail.state.ky.us
URL: http://www.state.ky.us/agencies/cppr/
krc/GeneralInformation.htm

Louisiana Gaming Control Board
9100 Bluebonnet Centre Blvd.
Suite 500
Baton Rouge, LA 70809
(225) 295-8450
FAX: (225) 295-8479

E-mail: tfuselie@dps.state.la.us
URL: http://www.dps.state.la.us/lgcb/

Louisiana Lottery Corporation
555 Laurel St.
Baton Rouge, LA 70801
(225) 297-2000
URL: http://www.louisianalottery.com

Maine Harness Racing Promotion Board
State House, Station 28
Augusta, ME 04333
(207) 287-3221
E-mail: info@maineharnessracing.com
URL: http://www.maineharnessracing.com/

Maine State Lottery
10-12 Water St.
Hallowell, ME 04347
(207) 287-3721
Toll-free: 1-800-452-8777
URL: http://www.mainelottery.com/

Maryland Racing Commission
500 North Calvert St.
Second Floor, Rm. 201
Baltimore, MD 21202
(410) 230-6330
FAX: (410) 333-8308
E-mail: racing@dllr.state.md.us
URL: http://www.dllr.state.md.us/racing/

Maryland State Lottery Agency
1800 Washington Blvd.
Suite 330
Baltimore, MD 21230
(410) 230-8800
E-mail: paffairs@msla.state.md.us
URL: http://www.msla.sailorsite.net/

Massachusetts State Lottery Commission
60 Columbian St.
Braintree, MA 02184
(781) 849-5555
E-mail: webmaster@masslottery.com
URL: http://www.masslottery.com/

Massachusetts State Racing Commission
1 Ashburton Place
Rm. 1313
Boston, MA 02108
(617) 727-2581
FAX: (617) 727-6062
E-mail: racing.commission@state.ma.us
URL: http://www.state.ma.us/src/

Michigan Gaming Control Board
1500 Abbott Rd.
Suite 400
East Lansing, MI 48823
(517) 241-0040
FAX: (517) 241-0510
E-mail: MGCBweb@michigan.gov
URL: http://www.michigan.gov/mgcb

Michigan Lottery
101 East Hillsdale
P.O. Box 30023

Lansing, MI 48909
(517) 335-5756
FAX: (517) 335-5644
E-mail: milottery@michigan.gov
URL: http://www.michigan.gov/lottery

Michigan Racing Commission
37650 Professional Center Dr.
Suite 105A
Livonia, MI 48154-1100
(734) 462-2400
URL: http://www.michigan.gov/mda

Minnesota Gambling Control Board
1711 West County Road B
Suite 300 South
Roseville, MN 55113
(651) 639-4000
URL: http://www.gcb.state.mn.us/index.html/

Minnesota Racing Commission
1100 Canterbury Rd.
P.O. Box 630
Shakopee, MN 55379
(952) 496-7950
FAX: (952) 496-7954
E-mail: richard.krueger@state.mn.us
URL: http://www.mnrace.commission.state.mn.us/

Minnesota State Lottery
2645 Long Lake Rd.
Roseville, MN 55113
(651) 297-7456
E-mail: lottery@winternet.com
URL: http://www.lottery.state.mn.us/index.html

Mississippi Gaming Commission
P.O. Box 23577
Jackson, MS 39225
(601) 576-3800
Toll-free: 1-800-504-7529
FAX: (601) 576-3843
E-mail: info@mgc.state.ms.us
URL: http://www.mgc.state.ms.us/

Missouri Gaming Commission
3417 Knipp Dr.
P.O. Box 1847
Jefferson City, MO 65102
(573) 526-4080
FAX: (573) 526-1999
E-mail: PublicRelation@mgc.dps.mo.gov
URL: http://www.mgc.state.mo.us/

Missouri Lottery
1823 Southridge Dr.
Jefferson City, MO 65109
(573) 751-4050
FAX: (573) 751-5188
URL: http://www.molottery.state.mo.us/

Montana Department of Livestock—Board of Horse Racing
P.O. Box 202001
Helena, MT 59620

(406) 444-4287
FAX: (406) 444-1929
E-mail: livemail@state.mt.us
URL: http://www.discoveringmontana.com/liv/HorseRacing/index.asp

Montana Gambling Control Division
2550 Prospect Ave.
P.O. Box 201424
Helena, MT 59620
(406) 444-1971
E-mail: gcd@state.mt.us
URL: http://www.doj.state.mt.us/department/gamblingcontroldivision.asp

Montana Lottery
2525 North Montana Ave.
Helena, MT 59601
(406) 444-5825
FAX: (406) 444-5830
E-mail: montanalottery@mail.com
URL: http://www.montanalottery.com/

Multi-State Lottery Association
4400 Northwest Urbandale Dr.
Urbandale, IA 50322
(515) 453-1400
URL: http://www.musl.com/

National Association of Fundraising Ticket Manufacturers
1360 Energy Park Dr.
St. Paul, MN 55108
(651) 644-4710
FAX: (651) 644-5904
E-mail: MaryMagnuson@naftm.org
URL: http://www.naftm.org/

National Coalition Against Legalized Gambling
100 Maryland Ave. NE
Rm. 311
Washington, DC 20002
(307) 587-8082
Toll-free: 1-800-664-2680
E-mail: ncalg@vcn.com
URL: http://www.ncalg.org/

National Council on Problem Gambling, Inc.
216 G Street NE
Suite 200
Washington, DC 20002
(202) 547-9204
Toll-free: 1-800-522-4700
FAX: (202) 547-9206
E-mail: ncpg@ncpgambling.org
URL: http://www.ncpgambling.org/

National Indian Gaming Association
224 Second St. SE
Washington, DC 20003
(202) 546-7711
FAX: (202) 546-1755
URL: http://www.indiangaming.org/

National Indian Gaming Commission
1441 L St. NW
Suite 9100
Washington, DC 20005
(202) 632-7003
FAX: (202) 632-7066
E-mail: info@nigc.gov
URL: http://www.nigc.gov/

Nebraska Lottery
301 Centennial Mall S
P.O. Box 98901
Lincoln, NE 68509
(402) 471-6100
E-mail: lottery@nelottery.com
URL: http://www.nelottery.com/

Nebraska Racing Commission
301 Centennial Mall S
Sixth Floor
P.O. Box 95014
Lincoln, NE 68509
(402) 471-4155
FAX: (402) 471-2339
E-mail: racing@nol.org
URL: http://www.horseracing.state.ne.us/

**Nevada Gaming Commission and State
Gaming Control Board**
1919 East College Pkwy.
Carson City, NV 89706
(775) 684-7750
FAX: (775) 687-5817
E-mail: liaison@gcb.nv.gov
URL: http://gaming.nv.gov

New Hampshire Lottery
P.O. Box 1208
Concord, NH 03302
(603) 271-3391
Toll-free: 1-800-852-3324
FAX: (603) 271-1160
E-mail: webmaster@lottery.state.nh.us
URL: http://www.nhlottery.org/

**New Hampshire Pari-Mutuel
Commission**
244 North Main St.
Concord, NH 03301
(603) 271-2158
FAX: (603) 271-3381
E-mail: pkelley@nhpmc.state.nh.us
URL: http://webster.state.nh.us/nhpmc/

New Jersey Casino Control Commission
Tennessee Ave. & Boardwalk
Atlantic City, NJ 08401
(609) 441-3799
E-mail: dheneghan@ccc.state.nj.us
URL: http://www.state.nj.us/casinos/

New Jersey Lottery
P.O. Box 041
Trenton, NJ 08625
(609) 599-5800
FAX: (609) 599-5935

E-mail: publicinfo@lottery.state.nj.us
URL: http://www.state.nj.us/lottery/

New Jersey Racing Commission
140 East Front St.
Fourth Floor
P.O. Box 088
Trenton, NJ 08625
(609) 292-0613
FAX: (609) 599-1785
URL: http://www.state.nj.us/lps/racing/

New Mexico Gaming Control Board
6400 Uptown Blvd. NE
Suite 100-E
Albuquerque, NM 87110
(505) 841-9700
E-mail: webmaster@gcb.state.nm.us
URL: http://www.nmgcb.org/

New Mexico Lottery
P.O. Box 93130
Albuquerque, NM 87199
(505) 342-7600
E-mail: custserv@nmlottery.com
URL: http://www.nmlottery.com/

New Mexico Racing Commission
300 San Mateo NE
Suite 110
Albuquerque, NM 87108
(505) 841-6400
FAX: (505) 841-6413
E-mail: nmrc@state.nm.us
URL: http://nmrc.state.nm.us/

New York State Lottery
P.O. Box 7500
Schenectady, NY 12301
(518) 388-3300
URL: http://www.nylottery.org/index.php

**New York State Racing and
Wagering Board**
1 Watervliet Ave. Ext.
Suite 2
Albany, NY 12206
(518) 453-8460
E-mail: info@racing.state.ny.us
URL: http://www.racing.state.ny.us/

**North American Association of State and
Provincial Lotteries**
2775 Bishop Rd.
Suite B
Willoughby Hills, OH 44092
(216) 241-2310
FAX: (216) 241-4350
E-mail: NASPLHQ@aol.com
URL: http://www.naspl.org/

**North Carolina Department of Crime
Control and Public Safety, Alcohol Law
Enforcement Division, Bingo
Licensing Section**
4701 Mail Service Ctr.
Raleigh, NC 27699

(919) 733-3029
URL: http://www.nccrimecontrol.org/
Index2.cfm?a=000003,000005,000077

North Dakota Lottery
600 East Boulevard Ave.
Dept. 125
Bismarck, ND 58505
(701) 328-1574
E-mail: ndlottery@state.nd.us
URL: http://www.ndlottery.org

**North Dakota Office of Attorney General,
Gaming Division**
600 East Boulevard Ave.
Dept. 125
Bismarck, ND 58505
(701) 328-4848
Toll-free: 1-800-326-9240
FAX: (701) 328-3535
URL: http://www.ag.state.nd.us/Gaming/
Gaming.htm

**Ohio Attorney General, Charitable
Law Section**
150 East Gay St.
23rd Floor
Columbus, OH 43215
(614) 466-3180
FAX: (614) 466-9788
URL: http://www.ag.state.oh.us/sections/
charitable_law/

Ohio Lottery Commission
615 West Superior Ave.
Cleveland, OH 44113
(216) 787-3200
URL: http://www.ohiolottery.com/index.
html

Ohio State Racing Commission
77 South High St.
18th Floor
Columbus, OH 43215
(614) 466-2757
FAX: (614) 466-1900
E-mail: SAM.ZONAK@RC.STATE.OH.US
URL: http://www.state.oh.us/rac/
commission.stm

Oklahoma Horse Racing Commission
Shepherd Mall
2401 Northwest 23rd St.
Suite 78
Oklahoma City, OK 73107
(405) 943-6472
FAX: (405) 943-6474
E-mail: ohrc@socket.net
URL: http://www.ohrc.org/

Oregon Lottery
500 Airport Rd. SE
Salem, OR 97301
(503) 540-1000
FAX: (503) 540-1001
E-mail: lottery.webcenter@state.or.us
URL: http://www.oregonlottery.org/

Oregon Racing Commission
800 Northeast Oregon St.
Suite 310
Portland, OR 97232
(503) 731-4052
FAX: (503) 731-4053
E-mail: jodi.hanson@state.or.us
URL: http://racing.oregon.gov

Pennsylvania Lottery
2850 Turnpike Industrial Dr.
Middletown, PA 17057
(717) 986-4699
FAX: (717) 986-4767
URL: http://www.palottery.com/

Pennsylvania State Horse Racing Commission
2301 North Cameron St.
Rm. 304
Harrisburg, PA 17110
(717) 787-1942
FAX: (717) 346-1546
URL: http://www.agriculture.state.pa.us/
agriculture/cwp/view.asp?a=3&q=128999

Public Gaming Research Institute, Inc.
218 Main St.
Suite 203
Kirkland, WA 98033
(425) 985-3159
Toll-free: 1-800-493-0527
E-mail: info@publicgaming.org
URL: http://www.publicgaming.org

Rhode Island Department of Business Regulation, Division of Racing and Athletics
233 Richmond St.
Providence, RI 02903
(401) 222-2246
FAX: (401) 222-6098
E-mail: RacingAthleticsInquiry@dbr.state.ri.us
URL: http://www.dbr.state.ri.us/race-athletics.html

Rhode Island Lottery
1425 Pontiac Ave.
Cranston, RI 02920
(401) 463-6500
URL: http://www.rilot.com/

South Carolina Education Lottery
P.O. Box 11949
Columbia, SC 29211
(803) 737-2002
FAX: (803) 737-2005
URL: http://www.sceducationlottery.com

South Dakota Commission on Gaming
425 East Capitol Ave.
Pierre, SD 57501
(605) 773-6050
FAX: (605) 773-6053
E-mail: gaminginfo@state.sd.us
URL: http://www.state.sd.us/dcr/gaming/

South Dakota Lottery
207 East Capitol
Suite 200
Pierre, SD 57501
(605) 773-5770
E-mail: lottery@state.sd.us
URL: http://www.sdlottery.org/

Tennessee Lottery
P.O. Box 23470
Nashville, TN 37202
(615) 324-6500
URL: http://www.tnlottery.gov

Texas Lottery Commission
P.O. Box 16630
Austin, TX 78761
(512) 344-5000
Toll-free: 1-800-375-6886
FAX: (512) 344-5080
E-mail: customer.service@lottery.state.tx.us
URL: http://www.txlottery.org/

Texas Racing Commission
P.O. Box 12080
Austin, TX 78711
(512) 833-6699
FAX: (512) 833-6907
E-mail: paula.flowerday@txrc.state.tx.us
URL: http://www.txrc.state.tx.us/

Vermont Lottery Commission
1311 U.S. Route 302—Berlin
Barre, VT 05641
(802) 479-5686
FAX: (802) 479-4294
E-mail: staff@vtlottery.com
URL: http://www.vtlottery.com/

Vermont Racing Commission
109 State St., Pavilion
Montpelier, VT 05609
(802) 828-3333
FAX: (802) 828-3339
URL: http://www.vermont.gov/tools/whats
new2/index.php?topic=BoardsAndCommis-
sions&id=151&v=Article

Virginia Department of Charitable Gaming
101 North 14th St.
17th Floor
Richmond, VA 23219
(804) 786-1681
FAX: (804) 786-1079
URL: http://www.dcg.state.va.us/

Virginia Lottery
900 East Main St.
Richmond, VA 23219
(804) 692-7000
FAX: (804) 692-7102
URL: http://www.valottery.com/

Virgin ia Racing Commission
10700 Horsemen's Rd.
New Kent, VA 23124
(804) 966-7400

FAX: (804) 966-7418
URL: http://www.vrc.state.va.us/

Washington Horse Racing Commission
6326 Martin Way E
Suite 209
Olympia, WA 98516
(360) 459-6462
FAX: (360) 459-6461
URL: http://www.whrc.wa.gov/

Washington Lottery
P.O. Box 43000
Olympia, WA 98504
(360) 664-4739
Toll-free: 1-800-732-5101
FAX: (360) 753-2602
E-mail: director's_office@lottery.wa.gov
URL: http://www.walottery.net/default.asp

Washington State Gambling Commission
P.O. Box 42400
Olympia, WA 98504
(360) 486-3440
Toll-free: 1-800-345-2529
FAX: (360) 486-3629
E-mail: cld@wsgc.wa.gov
URL: http://www.wsgc.wa.gov/

West Virginia Lottery
P.O. Box 2067
Charleston, WV 25327
(304) 558-0500
FAX: (304) 558-3321
E-mail: mail@wvlottery.com
URL: http://www.state.wv.us/lottery/

West Virginia Racing Commission
106 Dee Dr.
Charleston, WV 25134
(304) 558-2150
E-mail: oliver8@saintjoes.net
URL: http://www.wvf.state.wv.us/racing/

Wisconsin Division of Gaming
101 East Wilson St.
P.O. Box 8979
Madison, WI 53702
(608) 270-2555
FAX: (608) 270-2564
E-mail: RacingWeb@doa.state.wi.us
URL: http://www.doa.state.wi.us/gaming/
index.asp

Wisconsin Lottery
P.O. Box 8941
Madison, WI 53708
(608) 261-4916
E-mail: info@wilottery.com
URL: http://www.wilottery.com/index.asp

Wyoming Pari-Mutuel Commission
Hansen Bldg.
2515 Warren Ave.
Suite 301
Cheyenne, WY 82002

(307) 777-5928
FAX: (307) 777-3681
E-mail: flamb@state.wy.us
URL: http://parimutuel.state.wy.us/

RESOURCES

Several resources useful to this book were published by companies and organizations within the gambling industry. Most notable are *Harrah's Survey '04: Profile of the American Casino Gambler, The Vital Signs of Legalized Gaming in America, GTECH's 8th Annual National Gaming Survey (2000), 2004 State of the States: The AGA Survey of Casino Entertainment* from the American Gaming Association, *Lottery Insights* (the journal of the North American Association of State and Provincial Lotteries), and *Charity Gaming in North America, 2002 Annual Report* by the National Association of Fundraising Ticket Manufacturers. The National Indian Gaming Association (NIGA) published *Indian Gaming: Final Impact Analysis (2004)*. The NIGA's resource library also provided excellent information about tribal gambling.

Informative resources from industry analysts include *La Fleur's 2004 World Lottery Almanac* by TLF Publications, Inc., and publications from Christiansen Capital Advisors, LLC, including *E-gambling: The Economic Impact of a Burgeoning Industry* (2000) and *Internet Gambling: The State of a Developing Industry* (2000) by Sebastian Sinclair, and *The Gross Annual Wager of the United States, 2002* by Eugene Martin Christiansen and Sebastian Sinclair.

Information on particular gambling markets was obtained from *Indian Country Today*, the *Las Vegas Review Journal*, the *Las Vegas Sun*, the *Detroit News*, the *Biloxi Sun Herald*, and the *Norwich Bulletin* of Connecticut. The *New York Times, Washington Post*, and the *Wall Street Journal* were particularly useful in reporting on tribal gambling. The *Oregon Daily Emerald, USA Today, Sports Illustrated*, and ESPN provided historical information and recent stories on sports gambling and related scandals.

Many Internet sites were very helpful, particularly those of the state regulatory agencies overseeing gambling. Useful commercial sites include www.vegas.com, which describes the basics of sports betting. The Web site of the Las Vegas Convention and Visitors Authority, at www.lasvegas24hours.com, contains an excellent gaming guide, with instructions to many casino games. J. R. Martin publishes gambling advice at www.professionalgambler.com, including *A Crash Course in Vigorish, and It's Not 4.55%*. I. Nelson Rose, a professor of law at Whittier Law School, maintains a Web site (www.gamblingandthelaw.com) that is a valuable resource for historical and legal information on gambling. The National Council Against Legalized Gambling (www.ncalg.org) provides the latest news updates on gambling and politics around the United States.

The U.S. General Accounting Office (GAO) is the investigative arm of Congress. GAO publications used in this book include *Indian Issues: Improvements Needed in Tribal Recognition Process* (GAO-02-49, November 2, 2001) and *Internet Gambling: An Overview of the Issues* (GAO-03-89, December 2, 2002).

The FBI Law Enforcement Bulletin provided information on the effects of gambling on crime across the United States. Other government documents consulted for this book include *Occupational Outlook Quarterly,* a U.S. Department of Labor publication on career opportunities in many markets, including casinos. *Solutions* is a publication designed for policymakers in state governments that provided information about regulatory policies across the United States. Information on gambling policy and legislation is also available from the National Conference of State Legislatures. The Legislative Analyst's Office (LAO), which provides fiscal and policy advice to the California legislature, has published information papers on gambling on tribal lands.

The Greyhound Protection League and the Humane Society of the United States (HSUS) provided important information on the history and status of animal racing and fighting in this country. Additional statistics on animal fighting were obtained from the Web site www.pet-abuse.com. With regard to the horse-racing industry, the Jockey Club, the U.S. Trotting Association, and the *Daily Racing Form* issue informative materials.

The Gallup Organization provides valuable results from recent polls regarding gambling in the United States. Other valuable resources include *Illegal Sports Bookmakers* (2003) by Koleman S. Strumpf of the University of North Carolina at Chapel Hill; the PBS *Frontline* television special *Easy Money* (1997), which explains the odds against players in different casino games; and a TechTV special on the technical measures used by casinos to prevent crime. The Society for Human Resource Management (SHRM) provided valuable information about gambling in the workplace. Insights into the effects of tribal gambling were obtained from *Background to Dream: Impacts of Tribal Gaming in Washington State* (2002) by Cheryl King and Casey Kanzler, which was published in collaboration with the First American Education Project.

Scientific and educational publications devoted to problem gambling were invaluable to this book. They include the *Weekly Addiction Gambling Education Report*

(WAGER), which is published by Harvard Medical School and the Massachusetts Council on Compulsive Gambling, as well as the *Journal of Addiction and Mental Health* and *eGambling: The Electronic Journal of Gambling Issues*, both of which are published by the Centre for Addiction and Mental Health in Toronto, Ontario, Canada. Rachel A. Volberg, with Gemini Research, Ltd., wrote *Gambling and Problem Gambling in Nevada* (2002) and *Gambling and Problem Gambling among Adolescents in Nevada* (2002).

Organizations devoted to problem gambling that provided helpful data and information include Gamblers Anonymous (www.gamblersanonymous.org), the National Center for Responsible Gaming (www.ncrg.org), and the National Council on Problem Gambling (www.ncpgambling.org).

The Final Report of the National Gambling Impact Study Commission (1999) is a critical reference for information about the effects of gambling on society. The report is based on information submitted by various researchers, including the paper *State Lotteries at the Turn of the Century: Report to the National Gambling Impact Study Commission* (1999) written by Charles T. Clotfelter, Philip J. Cook, Julie A. Edell, and Marian Moore.

INDEX

sports gambling on college sports and, 115

"List of Excluded Persons" (Nevada Gaming Commission and State Gaming Control Board), 15

Loaded dice, 1

Loan-sharking, 15

Local governments
economic effects of casinos on, 67
involvement in gambling, 20

Local political influence, 77

Lodge, Edward, 98

Long, Earl, 45

Lotteries
administration of, 85–87
advertising themes identified in marketing plans of lottery agencies, 87t
characteristics of top 20% of lottery purchasers, 88 (t7.5)
college students' participation in, 21–22
effects of, 91, 93–97
future of U.S. lotteries, 97–98
gambling revenue, percentage of, 11
group play, 89–90
history of, 2, 4, 79–81
international lottery games, 85
legalization of, 5
lottery games, 81–85
lottery games, modern, 82t
lottery sales, 81f
lottery ticket sales in convenience stores, 13
in nineteenth century, 3
percentage of Americans who believe lotteries keep taxes lower, 89 (f7.5)
percentage of Americans who have purchased a lottery ticket within the previous 12 months, 87f
player demographics, 87–89
public opinion on states' use of lotteries to raise revenue, 88 (t7.4)
public opinion on whether lotteries are preferable to higher taxes, 89 (f7.6)
public opinion regarding state lotteries, 89 (f7.4)
reasons people play, 90–91
sports gambling lotteries, 112
state government run, 18
state lottery games, 84t
state lottery proceeds, cumulative distribution of, 92t–93t
states with lotteries, 80f
teenagers/college students and, 21
tickets sold by small businesses, 13
in twenty-first century, 6

Lottery commissions, 85–87

Lottery Gambling and Addiction: An Overview of European Research (Griffiths and Wood), 90

Lottery games
in general, 80
international, 85
modern, 82t
multistate games, 83–85
scratch games, 80–83
second-chance games, 83
state lottery games, 84t

video lottery games, 83

Lottery Insights (North American Association for State and Provincial Lotteries), 87–88

Lottery players
characteristics of top 20% of lottery purchasers, 88 (t7.5)
demographics of, 87–89
percentage of Americans who believe lotteries keep taxes lower, 89 (f7.5)
percentage of Americans who have purchased a lottery ticket within the previous 12 months, 87f
public opinion on states' use of lotteries to raise revenue, 88 (t7.4)
public opinion on whether lotteries are preferable to higher taxes, 89 (f7.6)
public opinion regarding state lotteries, 89 (f7.4)

Lotto
description of, 81
Powerball, 83–84

Lotto Captain program, 89–90

Louis IX, King of France, 2

Louisiana
casino revenue, 47f
casino statistics, 46t
cockfighting in, 117
commercial casinos in, 43, 45–46
gambling in nineteenth century, 3
Internet gambling law, 128
lottery history in, 79
lottery retailer program, 86
politics and casinos, 77

Louisiana Lottery Company, 79

Luntz Research Companies, 32, 65

Lure, 109

LVCVA (Las Vegas Convention and Visitors Authority), 41, 71

M

MADD (Mothers Against Drunk Driving), 62

Magna Entertainment
Advanced Deposit Wagering and, 105
in horse racing business, 13
racetracks/races and, 102, 103

Mahabarata, 1–2

Maine, rejection of tribal casinos in, 7, 32, 57

Mandalay Bay Resort Group, 12

"March Madness" basketball tournament, 114, 116

Mare reproductive loss syndrome (MRLS), 106

Martin, J.R., 113

Maryland
horse racing, economic effects of, 106
horse racing in, 101, 103
horse racing industry flow chart, 108f

Mashantucket Pequot Tribe, 62–63

Massachusetts, lottery sales in, 91

MasterCard, 129

Mazzetti, Mark, 18

McCain, John, 114

McCrary, Joseph, 95

McGill University (Montreal, Canada), 97

McNeil, Charles, 113

McPherson, Adrian, 121

Medieval period, gambling during, 2

Mega Millions
constitutional questions about, 85
description of, 84–85
group play in, 90

Men
casino acceptability and, 32
casino gambling preferences of, 34
dog fighting and, 118
illegal sports gambling and, 120
pathological gamblers, 26

Merriam-Webster's dictionary, 1, 31

MGC. *See* Missouri Gaming Commission

MGM Grand (Detroit, MI), 51–52

MGM Grand (Las Vegas, NV), 71

MGM Mirage
gambling operations of, 12
online casino of, 126

Michigan
commercial casino revenue, 52f
commercial casinos in, 51–52
crime and casinos, 73–74
minors and casinos in Detroit, Michigan, 77t
self-exclusion program in, 76
underage gambling in, 77

Michigan Gaming and Control Board Annual Report to the Governor: Calendar Year 2003 (Michigan Gaming Control Board), 52

Michigan Gaming Control & Revenue Act, 51, 77

Michigan Gaming Control Board, 51, 77

Michigan State University, 69

Military, U.S., 17–18

Miller, Donald, 93–94

Minner, Ruth Ann, 112

Minnesota
charitable gambling in, 17
state-owned casinos proposal in, 18

Minnesota Gambling Control Board, 17

Minors
minors and casinos in Detroit, Michigan, 77t
underage gambling, 76–77
underage Internet gambling, 133
underage lottery play, 94–95

Mississippi
bankruptcy rate in, 75
casino revenue, 45f
casinos, effect on tourism, 71
commercial casino statistics, 44t
commercial casinos of, 42–43
crime and casinos, 72, 73
domestic problems from casino gambling, 75
effects of casinos, 68
politics and casinos, 77

Mississippi Gaming Commission, 68

Mississippi Gaming Control Act, 43

Missouri
casino revenue, 51f
commercial casinos in, 50–51
crime and casinos, 72, 73
gambling hotline, 76
Lottery Captain program, 90
voluntary exclusion program of, 75–76

gambling participation among adolescents in New York, Georgia, Texas, Washington, Nevada, 23t
gambling participation in, 22–23
gambling revenue, 40f
government revenue from casinos, 67
illegal sports gambling, 116
Internet gambling law, 128–129
Nevada casinos, total win; win from games and tables; win from slot machines, percent change from previous year, 41t
Nevada race book gambling, 102 (f8.1)
organized crime and gambling, 15
problem gambling among adolescents in New York, Georgia, Texas, Washington, Nevada, 28 (t2.11)
problem gambling prevalence in, 26–27
sports book gambling, 114f
sports book wagering by sport, 115f
sports book wagering on Super Bowls, Nevada, 115t
sports gambling history in, 99
sports gambling in, 112, 113–115
suicide rate in, 74
underage gambling in, 77
Nevada Gaming Commission
establishment of, 4
Internet gambling law and, 129
"List of Excluded Persons," 15
underage gambling and, 77
New Hampshire
lottery in, 80
lottery relegalized in, 4
New Hampshire Sweepstakes, 4, 80
New Jersey
bankruptcy and casino gambling, 75
casino industry statistics, 42t
casinos, effect on tourism, 71–72
commercial casinos in, 41–42
horse racing gross purse of, 106
Internet gambling and, 129
lottery retailers, 86
lottery return in, 91
self-exclusion program in, 76
New Jersey Casino Control Commission, 42, 76
New Jersey Casino Control Commission 2003 Annual Report (New Jersey Casino Control Commission), 42
New Mexico
cockfighting in, 117
sports gambling in, 112
New Orleans (LA)
commercial casinos in, 43, 45–46
gambling in nineteenth century, 3
New Testament, 2
New York
adolescent gambling in, 22
dog fighting in, 119–120
gambling participation among adolescents in New York, Georgia, Texas, Washington, Nevada, 23t
horse fatalities/injuries in, 106
horse races in, 103
lottery established in, 4, 80
lottery, group play in, 90

lottery sales in, 91
lottery winnings withholding, 93
Mega Millions lawsuit in, 85
problem gambling among adolescents in New York, Georgia, Texas, Washington, Nevada, 28 (t2.11)
Thoroughbred horse racing in, 101
video lottery terminals in, 7, 83
New York City (NY), 20
New York City Off-Track Betting (NYCOTB) Corporation
founding of, 20
horse racing control of, 102
New York Racing Association (NYRA)
horse racing control of, 102–103
tax fraud case, 14
New York State Racing and Wagering Board, 106
New York Supreme Court, 127
New York Times (newspaper), 120
"Newest Concern for Colleges: Increases in Sports Gambling" (*New York Times*), 120
Newsbytes News Network, 131
Newspaper Association of America, 116
NFL (National Football League), 112
NGA (National Greyhound Association), 109, 110
NGISC. *See* National Gambling Impact Study Commission
NIGA. *See* National Indian Gaming Association
NIGC. *See* National Indian Gaming Commission
NIMBY ("not in my backyard") factor, 65
Nineteenth century, gambling in, 3
Ninth U.S. Circuit Court of Appeals, 98
Nixon, Jay, 126
Non-Thoroughbred horse racing, 103
Nonbanked game, 32
Nonproblem gamblers, 23
NORC. *See* National Opinion Research Center
North American Association for State and Provincial Lotteries (NASPL)
lottery administration information, 86
lottery claims by, 95
lottery demographics study, 87–88
lottery economics, 93
U.S. lottery sales, 85
North American Industry Classification System (NAICS) code, 31
North Carolina, 97–98
North Carolina House of Representatives, 97
North Dakota, 6
Numbers games, 15
NYCOTB (New York City Off-Track Betting) Corporation
founding of, 20
horse racing control of, 102
NYRA (New York Racing Association)
horse racing control of, 102–103
tax fraud case, 14

O

Occupational Outlook Quarterly (Bureau of Labor Statistics), 70

Occupational Safety and Health Administration (OSHA), 69
Occupations, casino, 69–70, 70t
Off-track betting (OTB) facilities
illegal sports gambling, 116
in Nevada, 113
pari-mutuel gambling at, 101
percentage of betting at, 102
"Office Betting Can Be Costly" (Hurwit), 16
Office pools
legal, 112
survey on, 15–16
Ogle, Samuel, 101
Ohio, Mega Millions lawsuit in, 85
Oklahoma
lottery in, 97, 98
racino legislation, 7
The Oklahoman (newspaper), 97
Oliver, Annie and Louie, 77
Oller, Pierre, 100
Oneida Tribe of Indians v. Wisconsin, 57
ONLAE (Organismo Nacional de Loterìas y Apuestas del Estado), 85
Online gambling. *See* Internet gambling
Online lottery games, 81
Operator abuses, 131–132
Oregon
Internet gambling law, 128
sports gambling in, 112
Organismo Nacional de Loterìas y Apuestas del Estado (ONLAE), 85
Organized crime
casino regulations and, 5
gambling enterprises of, 4
in gambling industry, 15
gambling linked with, 9
illegal sports gambling linked to, 116
involvement in casinos, 72
in Las Vegas casinos, 40
sports gambling and, 113
tribal casinos and, 66
OSHA (Occupational Safety and Health Administration), 69
OTB. *See* Off-track betting (OTB) facilities
Oxley, Michael, 128

P

Paragon Gaming, 62
Pari-mutuel gambling
age limit for, 21
California horse racing handle, 106f
decline of, 99
description of, 100–101
Florida pari-mutuel handle by industry, 109f
future of, 111–112
greyhound racing, 108–111
horse racing, 101–107
horse racing takeout dollar in California, distribution of, 105f
in Iowa, 52
jai alai, 111
Maryland horse racing industry flow chart, 108f
New York City Off-Track Betting Corporation, 20